Publications of Russell Sage Foundation

Kinship
and Casework

HOPE JENSEN LEICHTER
Teachers College, Columbia University

AND WILLIAM E. MITCHELL
University of Vermont College of Medicine

With the collaboration of
CANDACE ROGERS and JUDITH LIEB

Russell Sage Foundation
New York, 1967

Printed in the
United States of America

*Library of Congress
Catalog Card Number: 66–24898*

CONNECTICUT PRINTERS, INC.
HARTFORD, CONN.

Designer: Ernst Reichl

CONTENTS

Contents ix

TABLES

AND FIGURES

FIGURES

FOREWORD

In 1879 members of the American Social Science Association who were primarily concerned with the solution of practical problems of social welfare organized themselves into a separate and independent body then called The National Conference of Charities and Correction. Up to that time persons interested in social science, as well as those interested in its practical applications, participated in a common professional organization and in a common intellectual tradition.

Seen from today's perspective, this separation had both positive and negative values. On the one hand, it permitted scientist and practical worker to cultivate their own professional interests unhindered by fruitless controversies stemming from basic differences in orientation. Moreover, it made possible the benefits of specialization and the consolidation of a professional identity for social work. With these positive gains, however, came a progressive attenuation of contact and communication that has been costly both to social science and to social work. This is not the place to attempt a detailed analysis of the costs. For our present purpose it will suffice to note that with this failure to maintain a close liaison between the two fields the social sciences have tended to become insulated from important practical problems that deserve more attention as scientific problems than they are wont to get. The field of social work has suffered a severe impoverishment of the theoretical foundations for its practice and has failed to make adequate utilization of social science research findings and procedures that have very substantial potentialities for practical application.

It is encouraging that on both sides of this chasm there has developed a deeper recognition of the problem and a growing effort to effect a rapprochement. But recognition of the problem must lead to positive action; and here no magical formulas or easy short-cuts will be found. The road to effective communication and collaboration between social science and social work practice is steep, rugged, and, at times, well-nigh impassable. Certainly no one will affirm this more emphatically than the participants in the project from which the present volume emerged.

Claims as to the benefits to be derived from a closer liaison between social work and social science, of course, will remain unconvincing unless it can be shown that the use of social science theory and empirical knowledge results in an increase in professional capabilities for dealing with social work problems. But beyond this, it seems reasonable to expect that an increased grasp of social science can broaden the range of problems with which the profession will be competent to deal. The extensive revisions of curricula with special emphasis on enrichment of social science content now taking place at many leading schools will test the validity of these claims.

Another significant test is the degree to which social science research on problems in practice settings provides results that can strengthen the theory and techniques of practice. The present volume reports one such test. The project discussed was jointly sponsored by Russell Sage Foundation and the Jewish Family Service of New York at the request of the latter. It was hoped that research on the social relationships of clients outside the nuclear family would broaden the conceptual frameworks and the perceptions of social processes held by social workers and thereby increase their diagnostic and therapeutic capabilities. The Jewish Family Service is well known for the superior standards of training it demands of its staff, but it was becoming aware that the very excellence of the training it demanded could serve to restrict perspectives and skills to those processes emphasized in psychiatric theory and its applications to social work. The task, therefore, was to develop research that would show the influence of more extended interpersonal environments. After a long period of exploration the research staff responsible for this study elected to focus its attention on the kinship group as a significant feature of the social context in which to understand and treat problems of clients. The selection of this target is of special interest and significance, because it challenged theoretical positions that had become almost axiomatic not only in social work but in sociology as well.

Predominant doctrine in social casework for a generation has been founded on the assumption that the dynamics of the nuclear family and its impact on the intrapsychic structure of the person are of such central and exclusive importance that diagnostic and therapeutic effort need give little or no attention to any other aspect of social reality except as settings in which the intrapsychic system is expressed. This report shows that, at least for the particular client population studied, so narrow a position is hazardous indeed. Of more than passing interest, moreover, is the finding that the classical doctrinal position in casework supports and/or is supported by the personal value positions held by the caseworkers who participated in this investigation, contrasting sharply with the values of the clients that are much more positively oriented to the larger kin group.

From a somewhat different perspective many sociologists have also argued that the extended kinship group is of negligible significance in urban industrial societies. In these social systems, it is held, the large family has lost its functions and even the nuclear family has been markedly attenuated in significance as a social institution. Again, the findings of this study provide empirical evidence that the traditional theoretical position requires substantial modification.

It is appropriate, of course, to question the claim here made for the significance of the findings of this report on the grounds that the research was confined to a single ethnic subculture (Eastern European Jewish). However, this objection is adequately answered by the work of such able investigators as Marvin B. Sussman and Lee Burchinal, and Eugene Litwak, who have provided more general theoretical and empirical grounds for challenging accepted theory concerning the functional significance of familial and quasi-familial groups in modern industrial systems. Reports of their studies are included in the Bibliography to this volume.

But this book is more than a report of interesting research that challenges favored ideologies and theories. To refer to an earlier remark, the test of the value of social science to social work is the degree to which research findings make a difference in practice. The present work does more than merely report findings; it points the way to significant utilization of these findings in the diagnosis and treatment of the human problems confronting social work. Nor is the value of this work limited to its documentation of the significance of the kinship group. Rather, it indicates the need for a new and broader conceptual base for casework and for a correspondingly appropriate extension of casework technology and skill that will render professional practice more adequate in its analysis and management of relevant interactional contexts.

This careful and convincing documentation of its essential thesis points the way to significant topics for research and deserves high praise from both social workers and social scientists.

LEONARD S. COTTRELL, Jr.

Russell Sage Foundation
November, 1966

PREFACE

The Jewish Family Service has been engaged in some research activity continuously for over eighteen years, varying in size of effort, in the type of professional personnel, and in aim from "pure" to operational research; but whatever the variants, the agency has sustained an unflagging interest in utilizing scientific methods of study.

By now, the agency has lived so long with researchers as part of its staff that some of the feedbacks to the thinking and practice of the agency as a whole may simply be taken for granted and become an implicit part of agency life.

As Dr. Leichter reports elsewhere in this volume, the findings and conclusions of a study are only a small part, and perhaps the least part, of the enrichment to the agency that derives from its research activity. This study of kinship is exemplary of how in the process of developing an area of practice for study, of discovering the right questions to ask and of collecting the data, there is a built-in, continuous self-critical examination of the assumptions and lacunae of agency practice.

We believe this is enhanced to the degree that the research team is brought into contact with the professional practitioners and administration, rather than being sequestered and out of touch with the agency proper. Ideas are shared and mutually influenced; impediments to study methods which inhere in a naturally parochial view (for example, the "privacy" of casework interviews barring observers or interviews by researchers, and so on) are dissolved and the different approach of one discipline is in part integrated by the other.

We would summarize that the influence of this study was felt in the agency practice not alone on the critical reexamination of the boundaries of the family as empirical unit and not alone with respect to the importance of kinship ties or their lack in family functioning and reintegration. The ripple effects are to be seen in the deepened understanding of family role organization and the profoundly complicated question of the relations of the individual family (not families, generically) to subcultures and to social systems and other social institutions. These are results discussed in this volume by the authors and by Dr. Cottrell. More generally, but of equal significance, was the deepening of understanding by the casework staff and administration of the relevance of the social science conceptual framework, and also of the difficult process of its integration into clinical thinking. On another level and as a side dividend, the opening of clinical practice to research investigation has led to increased analysis of the interview and related casework procedures.

We hope that readers of this volume, especially those engaged in some form of clinical practice, will experience some of the nudging into different views of their practice toward a larger, gestaltian comprehension that we and the agency staff experienced throughout the study process.

We are especially grateful to Russell Sage Foundation for generous financial support and consultative assistance; to the Jewish Family Service Board of Directors for their deep faith in the importance of a research function in an operational agency; to the staff of the Jewish Family Service for its openness to learn and its easy surrender of any inhibiting defensiveness; and to the Rosenthal Foundation for its financial contribution.

FRANCES L. BEATMAN

SANFORD N. SHERMAN

Jewish Family Service
November, 1966

ACKNOWLEDGMENTS

It is a pleasure to express our thanks to the many persons and organizations that contributed valuable assistance in the conception and execution of this volume. We are especially indebted to Russell Sage Foundation and the Jewish Family Service of New York, cosponsors of the project, for their generous financial support and continued interest in the research.

We owe a special debt of gratitude to Dr. Leonard S. Cottrell, Jr., of Russell Sage Foundation for his personal encouragement and staunch support of the research from its inception to the completion of the present volume. Our debt to Dr. Orville G. Brim, Jr., president of Russell Sage Foundation, for wise counsel throughout the project is very deep indeed. Dr. Eleanor B. Sheldon and Dr. Stanton Wheeler, also of Russell Sage Foundation, contributed generously of their time and offered many helpful suggestions in the preparation of the manuscript.

We are indebted to the late Dr. M. Robert Gomberg, former executive director of the Jewish Family Service, for providing the initial impetus for a joint research venture with social scientists. To his successor, Frances L. Beatman, and to Sanford N. Sherman, associate executive director of the agency, we are grateful for their dedication to the principles of research, for having the administrative flexibility necessary to facilitate research, and for their helpful participation during every phase of the work. We are also fortunate to have had the participation of Arthur Leader on many occasions. To the agency's Board of Directors we are indebted for their interest in the research and their support of the importance of having research within a practice setting. As the present volume demonstrates, we are also deeply indebted to the many members of the agency staff who contributed to the project through participation in meetings in which the ongoing research was discussed.

As a member of the research staff, Joanne Burnett handled the many tasks of coordinating the diverse project activities with infinite skill and perseverance. Dr. Fred Davis was a stimulating colleague, as were Alice Liu Szema and Dianna Tendler, all of whom participated in the formulation of the research questions, the collection of research data and early analysis. Others who made special contributions at various points during the research were Constance Harris, who assisted in the analysis of data, and Sheila Okin and Judith Rowe, who gave assistance in collecting data. Helpful secretarial assistance was given by Harriet Gench early in the research and later by Charlotte Florer and Janice Guy. The contribution of Dr. Stephen Kempster and Dr. Alfred Messer in carrying out psychiatric interviews with the research families is acknowledged with gratitude.

We were fortunate in having Dr. Theodore Mills and Dr. Ezra Vogel as consultants in the early stages of the project. At a later stage Dr. Alfred Kahn offered important consultation. We are grateful to Dr. Morton Fried and Dr. David M. Schneider for incisive comments on parts of the analysis. We are also grateful to Dr. Herbert Spiegel for invaluable consultation. During the study we were fortunate in having stimulating and helpful discussions of the research with a number of individuals. These include: Dr. Millicent Ayoub, Dr. Donald A. Bloch, Dr. Marvin Bressler, Dr. Elaine Cumming, Dr. May Ebihara, Dr. Erving Goffman, Dr. Rhoda Métraux, Dr. Roger Peranio, Dr. Marvin B. Sussman, Dr. John W. M. Whiting, and Dr. Robert F. Winch.

We are indebted to Dr. Margaret Mead for giving us access to the research documents on Eastern European Jewish culture collected by the Columbia University Research in Contemporary Cultures and for discussing some of these findings with us. Dr. Conrad Arensberg and Dr. Natalie Joffee, participants in this research, were also helpful in orienting us to the cultural background of our research families.

Dominique Kolin contributed immeasurably to the task of revising an early draft of the manuscript. Her skillful assistance and interest in the project were a source of great help. We are also grateful to Marjorie Behrens for reading and commenting upon a draft of the manuscript.

The contribution of Margaret R. Dunne, editor for Russell Sage Foundation, is acknowledged with deep gratitude. The final version also owes much to the editorial help of Carol Levine.

Finally, this research could not have proceeded without the cooperation of the clients, social workers, executives, and board members of the Jewish Family Service who allowed us access to their activities with kin. They gave generously of their time and effort in the spirit of contributing to research knowledge.

Material from several papers read at annual meetings of the American Anthropological Association, Eastern Sociological Society, Groves Conference, National Conference on Social Welfare, and the Society for the Study of Social Problems during the course of this study and from previously published articles in periodicals is included in this volume. This material is listed in Section E of the Selected Bibliography.

H. J. L.
W. E. M.

November, 1966

The Family's

Kinship Environment

Two current concerns in the casework field are the attempts to develop methods of family diagnosis and treatment and to find social science knowledge relevant to social work practice. This volume reports the highlights of a study that grew out of both these interests.

The study focused on the kin relationships of Jewish families, mainly of Eastern European origin or descent, who live in a large city in an industrial society. The research was conducted primarily by social scientists—sociologists, an anthropologist, and a social worker with research training. But it was formulated and carried out in a family casework agency, Jewish Family Service of New York City. The families studied were clients of the agency; agency personnel cooperated in the research; and the research itself was conducted in light of questions arising from actual casework practice.

This volume is designed primarily for practitioners: those directly involved in treating individuals and families. Although the research was carried out with specific reference to family casework, it has relevance for other therapeutic practitioners, including psychiatrists, clinical psychologists, and marriage counselors. The analysis should also be useful for administrators in social agencies,

1

teachers, and researchers. The major findings of the research are discussed as theoretical issues of relevance to casework. Indeed, it is the ideas that emerged in the course of the research, rather than specific findings or methods, that are the prime focus of the present volume. A more complete presentation of certain research findings and a discussion of the changes these imply in anthropological and sociological theories of kinship are presented in separate papers.[1]

To provide the framework of concepts essential to an understanding of the significance of kinship for the family, Part One presents a discussion of the main characteristics of kinship systems in general and a description of the agency and its client families in terms of their socioeconomic status and Jewish cultural heritage. Part Two examines the kin relationships of the client families: their kinship values, kin networks, kin groups and assemblages, and kin conflicts. Casework intervention in kin relationships and the contrasting values and experiences of caseworkers and clients are treated in Part Three. The concluding chapter discusses the implications of this study for casework practice. An Epilogue describes the unique features of carrying out research in an agency setting; and discusses the task of applying research to practice; the Appendix treats the research methods in somewhat more detail than the text. One of the purposes of this volume is to stimulate interest in kinship and its relevance to casework; for this reason, a selected Bibliography has been included for those who wish to read further.

Family Diagnosis

In recent years family diagnosis and treatment has come to have ever-increasing importance in casework practice. Although social casework growing out of the general social welfare movement in America originally emphasized a social approach to problems, this approach was eclipsed in the 1930's by a greater emphasis on psychological, psychiatric, and psychoanalytic concepts. Ideas guiding the casework field came increasingly from psychiatry and focused more on the personal and emotional needs of clients than on their material and social handicaps. The individual was the main "treatment unit."

Recently it has become clear that the client cannot be understood in isolation; that it is essential to examine the nature of his relationships with others as well as his own individual needs and emotions. For this reason the family rather than the individual is often the unit of diagnosis and treatment and efforts are made to utilize concepts of the family as a system of interpersonal relationships.[2]

The present study extends the concern with the family to include the relationships of family members with those outside the nuclear family, that is, the husband, wife, and children. In order to understand and appraise the family it is necessary not only to know about relationships within it, but also about the impact of the relationships of family members with those outside the family. The present volume examines the involvement of client families with their kin, thereby demonstrating the importance of interchanges between the family and its environment.

A basic assumption of this analysis which can be derived by extension of some of the early arguments for family diagnosis is that for purposes of diagnosis the family can most usefully be considered an "open" system. Although recognition has been given in family diagnosis to the interplay between the family and its environment,[3] the family has been implicitly defined as a bounded unit, a homeostatic system, which is at least in part "closed." The main emphasis has been on processes within the family; no comparable emphasis has been given to systematic analysis of the interchanges between the family and its environment. Even where the environment has been examined as it impinges on the family, the organization of the family's environment as a system in its own right has seldom been considered.

Environmental Diagnosis of the Family

The reasons for "environmental diagnosis" of the family are logically similar to those for "family diagnosis" as distinct from individual diagnosis. Just as the individual cannot be understood or effectively treated apart from knowledge of the family's influence on his behavior, so the family must be viewed in the context of its environment. The environment in this sense is that outside the family, and it is not just social and cultural but is interpersonal and emotional also. The marital relations of a couple cannot be understood without knowledge of the ways in which the husband's job impinges on their married life. The husband's occupational role, in turn, is part of a broader occupational system and is influenced by that system.

One reason that has been given for treating the family as a unit is the frequent clinical observation that a change in the behavior in any individual in a family is likely to have consequences for others, and that as one individual "improves" another member of the family may develop new "symptoms" or aggravate existing ones. Such interrelations within the family have a counterpart in the interchange between the family and its environment. A man who changes his friendship patterns in order to spend more time with his family will alter the friendship ties of others as well. The friends and their families will have altered reactions toward the man who initiated the change. Thus the environment must be understood or the consequences of a change may be unanticipated.[4]

When, as is often the case, a central reason for diagnosing and treating the family unit is that this appears to be the best approach to understanding the problems of a particular individual, the need to examine the contribution of factors in the family's environment is particularly evident. Clearly the family is not the only influence on the behavior of its members. The study of delinquency, for example, indicates the importance of considering the influence of those outside the family, especially peer groups. Attempting to understand individual behavior only in terms of family relationships results in a single factor explanation that is clearly an oversimplification.[5]

Although for some purposes the family may be the most useful unit of diagnosis and treatment, it may not always be the most important system for understanding the behavior of its members. Thus the first question for the caseworker may be what is the most significant unit for understanding the problem at hand, not how can this family be diagnosed. The appropriateness of selecting the family as the unit should be constantly subject to question and revision in relation to a particular purpose.[6] For many purposes the family and a portion of its environment (peer group, occupational world, friends, and so on) may be a more meaningful unit than the family alone.

On a general level the analysis of human behavior has also pointed to the importance of examining one system in the context of those that surround it.[7] Even in the study of small communities it has proved impossible to have adequate understanding without reference to the influences of the world outside the community.[8] This logic applies to the family as well.

Interchanges Between the Family and Its Environment

The boundaries of a family are not the same at all times or for all members. In our society a child at birth is clearly considered a member of the family, but the definition of his membership is less clear when he leaves home to attend college or to marry. From his perspective his membership may have changed, but from the perspective of his parents, the definition of the family unit may remain the same. Family composition also varies with the society and with social and cultural definitions. In our society we tend to think of the nuclear family as *the* family, but this definition reflects a particular cultural view, one that is not even necessarily held by all those within our society. Comparative studies clearly show that the definition of who is included within a family or kinship group varies considerably. Even within our society household composition is not the same in all cultural groups. Separation, divorce, remarriage, and adoption all mean that the social and biological definitions of the family do not coincide.

Even when the family's boundaries are clearly defined from a given perspective, at a given moment, these boundaries are permeable. That is, exchanges, or inputs and outputs, occur between the family and its environment in a number of spheres. In our society family members are together physically only intermittently; much of their time each day is spent outside the family. The interchanges between the family and the economy include the time family members spend at their jobs and the motivation that the family helps to maintain for occupational performance. The family receives income from the economy, and it contributes its financial assets to the economy for goods and services. The family is constantly engaged in similar exchanges with the political system, with the community, and with its friends.

The family's boundaries are themselves a result of interchanges with its environment. They are not physical but definitional, although physical boundaries may play a part in such definitions. To understand the family as a unit, one should know how the family maintains its distinction from that which is outside it, and know the history of changes in the family's boundaries throughout its developmental cycle, as well as the part others play in defining it as a unit. Here the actions of family members as its representatives to the outside world, and the extent to which they define themselves in family terms when outside it, are important.

In therapeutic practice, as well as in social research, the external environment is frequently considered in relation to the family. In fact, performance in outside situations rather than the family relationship as such is often evaluated. The family caseworker is frequently concerned, for example, with children's school behavior or the husband's occupational performance. Often the treatment rationale for altering family relationships is not so much that they are of concern in themselves, but rather that family relationships are presumed to affect the way in which family members play their roles in external systems. Definitive norms for family relationships are often lacking.

In one sense the quest for family diagnosis depends on making norms for family relationships more explicit in order to evaluate them more readily. Implicit norms for family relationships do exist, of course, but they are often less clear than those for performance in roles outside the family. In occupational pursuits there are many clear standards not related to the personality of the individual; for example, how much he produces on his job or how much income he derives from it. In this sense casework is constantly attuned to one type of interchange between the family and its environment, although systematic concepts for analyzing such interchanges may be lacking and the reliance placed upon the external environment may not be explicitly recognized.

In our urban industrial society the nuclear family is generally highly differentiated from other social systems in both structure and function. It is not the primary center of formal education or religious activity or the typical unit of production as in some agrarian societies. This loss of function may be regarded as greater specialization rather than breakdown.[9] But in a society where the family is highly specialized it becomes *structurally dependent* on external systems, making it impossible for the family to exist as an entirely self-sufficient unit. This structural dependence makes it all the more important to understand the interchanges between the family and its environment.

The Research Focus on Kinship

This research focuses specifically on one dimension of the family's environment: its relationships with kin. Kin is a dimension of the family's environment that is of particular emotional and social importance for the family. Relationships with kin outside the present nuclear family are universal in all human societies, despite enormous variation under different conditions. These relationships have a profound emotional significance because they have a lifelong history for the individual and for others in the family.

Kin relationships are also important for a diagnostic understanding of the family because a marked shift in these roles occurs during the developmental process and as a result of cultural change. Just as the individual may be evaluated in terms of relative movement in the developmental process, many areas of a family's health may be evaluated in terms of its ability to make developmental transitions, for example, at marriage or with the birth of a baby. The transition in kinship roles is therefore the very essence of the family's development as a system, of its boundary processes, and of its identity. Both life-cycle transitions and cultural differences between generations may give rise to problems in relationships with kin, making this an area of casework concern.

In addition to these theoretical reasons, kinship became the focus in this research because early interviews with clients, as well as with caseworkers, pointed to extensive and emotionally intense involvement with kin in many client families. Radical cultural differences exist between the client group and the older generation, the parents of most clients. Cultural change and acculturation contribute to conflict-making kin relationships of special concern within the group.

Another reason for the central concern with kin was that preliminary data on clients in this study presented a picture contrary to certain hypotheses about kinship and society. Despite the universality of some form of kinship, in the past it had been assumed that extensive and elaborate relationships with kin outside the nuclear family, which typify many societies, were incompatible with an industrial economy and an urban setting. Because recent research findings indicate that relationships with kin are sometimes more extensive than had been presumed even under these conditions, and because it is probable that subgroups of varying cultural and social heritage differ in their kinship organization, client kinship presented a picture of critical theoretical interest.

Choices of Research Strategy

In any investigation the researcher has a relatively wide range of choices and available alternatives, even within the limits established by the principal substantive concerns of the research. In this study, within the general orbit of concern for kinship and casework, three choices were made, either at the outset or during the course of the research, that are relevant to an understanding of what follows.

First, this research emphasized current relationships with kin, rather than past histories. Developmental concepts and changes in kinship roles over time are certainly important, but the major focus in data collection was on present kinship roles. The kinship dimension of the family's present situation is often not given systematic attention, even where early relationships in the family of childhood are examined.

Standard casework practice, using models of personality and individual development, finds out about the experience of an individual in his family of childhood, that is, the family into which the person was born and reared. For example, "family of orientation" has been cited as one category on which data should be collected,[10] even in an individual history. Although the significance of current kin relationships rests in part precisely on their lifelong history and on their emotional impact in early childhood, this early history is only part of the picture. Relationships with kin continue in adult life even in societies where the marriage transition entails a shift of residence and a major reorientation of the individual's emotional ties. It is familiar in casework thinking that what may be termed "internalized kin," such as parent images, continue to have a significant impact even when the kin are deceased. But actual interaction with kin living at present is crucial for any family.

Second, the emphasis is on the interchange between the family and its kin rather than on one-way cause-and-effect relations. An initial focus examined kinship in terms of its impact upon the nuclear family. This initial focus proved inadequate because it gave too much emphasis to the impact on one system and underemphasized the process of interchange as such, as well as the organization of relationships within the kinship environment.

The relationships that a particular family has with its kin stem not only from its own organization, the personalities of its members, and those of its kin, but also from the relationships that these kin have with others. Thus understanding how kin impinge upon the nuclear family requires an examination of the processes of interchange with kin and also the organization of relationships among kin outside the family. For this reason, how kin define each other, geographic proximity and communication among kin, gatherings of kin for special occasions, and formal kinship organizations (family-kin businesses, and family circles and cousins clubs) were all examined.

Third, our emphasis is on kinship as it influences the social relationships of client families and not on the effects of kin relationships upon the personalities of family members. Thus we consider the implications of kinship for family functioning, particularly in terms of the ways in which kinship structure tends to predispose toward certain kinds of conflicts among and about kin, but we do not proceed to examine the further effects of kin relationships upon the personalities of family members. This emphasis was chosen because part of the purpose of this book is to contribute to casework those concepts from a social science perspective that represent the newest addition to the usual framework. Even when a caseworker is interested primarily in the consequences of family organization for the personalities of its members, it is essential to examine what might be considered intermediate steps in the process of interchange.

It is hoped that the discussion based on these choices will demonstrate the significance of kinship for the family in the most meaningful way. This level of analysis is by no means intended to replace other levels that are being used in the casework field but to broaden and supplement them, so that those dealing with family diagnosis and treatment will carry out their work with the most complete understanding possible.

NOTES TO INTRODUCTION

1. See the Bibliography to this volume.
2. Sherman, Sanford N., "The Concept of the Family in Casework Theory" in *Exploring the Base for Family Therapy,* edited by Nathan W. Ackerman, Frances L. Beatman, and Sanford N. Sherman. Family Service Association of America, New York, 1961, pp. 14–28.
3. Gomberg, M. Robert, "Family Di-

agnosis: Trends in Theory and Practice," *Social Casework,* vol. 39, February–March, 1958, p. 73; Ackerman, Nathan W., "A Dynamic Frame for the Clinical Approach to Family Conflict" in Ackerman, Beatman, and Sherman, editors, *op. cit.,* p. 55; Weiss, Viola W., and Russell R. Monroe, "A Framework for Understanding Family Dynamics: Parts I and II," *Social Casework,* vol. 40, February–March, 1959, pp. 3–9, 80–87.

4. Merton, Robert K., "The Unanticipated Consequences of Purposive Social Action," *American Sociological Review,* vol. 1, December, 1936, pp. 894–904.

5. Leichter, Hope J., "Boundaries of the Family as an Empirical and Theoretical Unit" in Ackerman, Beatman, and Sherman, editors, *op. cit.,* pp. 140–145.

6. Goode, William J., "The Sociology of the Family" in *Sociology Today: Problems and Prospects,* edited by Robert K. Merton, Leonard Broom, and Leonard S. Cottrell, Jr. Basic Books, New York, 1959, p. 185.

7. Cottrell, Leonard S., Jr., "The Analysis of Situational Fields in Social Psychology," *American Sociological Review,* vol. 7, June, 1942, pp. 370–382; Spiegel, John P., "A Model for Relationships Among Systems" in *Toward a United Theory of Human Behavior,* edited by Roy R. Grinker, Basic Books, New York, 1956, pp. 16–26.

8. Redfield, Robert, "A Community Within Communities" in *The Little Community.* Phoenix Books, University of Chicago Press, Chicago, 1961, pp. 113–131.

9. Parsons, Talcott, "The American Family: Its Relation to Personality and to the Social Structure" in Parsons, Talcott, and Robert F. Bales, *Family Socialization and Interaction Process.* The Free Press, Glencoe, Ill., 1955, pp. 3–33.

10. Voiland, Alice L., and associates, *Family Casework Diagnosis.* Columbia University Press, New York, 1962, p. 293.

PART ONE

The Problem and Setting

CHAPTER 1

Kinship Concepts

Those who are concerned with family problems ultimately deal with specific individuals and families who are the product of complex psychological, physiological, and environmental factors. Each individual is unique in so many respects that the more general features of human life everywhere can easily be taken for granted or overlooked, precisely because they are so universal.

Each individual is born into a family; that family is bound to other families in a complex structure of interlocking ties that shifts in composition through birth, marriage, and death. Kinship is an involuntary relationship; every individual has kin and is a kin. Some of a child's earliest experiences are with kin. The forms of this interlocking structure of kinship may vary; but everywhere some such structure exists. The forms may have become so familiar that a specific effort is required to see them as forms of a universal, not as the universal itself.

The family is founded on biological facts of sex and reproduction common to all men. The nuclear family of husband, wife, and children may be distinguished from, or integrated with, other groupings in a variety of ways. The purpose of this chapter, then, is to point out some of the ways all kinship systems are structured and some of the ways in which they may differ significantly.

13

KINSHIP SYSTEMS

In all societies an individual typically marries someone other than his father, mother, brother, or sister; that is, someone outside his family of origin. Thus every individual who marries is a member of two nuclear families. After he marries and establishes a new family, the ties to his family of childhood do not disappear but are altered. Each individual in the family has "boundary roles" with his other family, of which he remains in some sense a member. As a result each person links the members of his family of childhood with those of his family of marriage; each individual in a nuclear family has ties to those in another nuclear family; and these individuals, in turn, have similar ties to others. Thus the basic links of kinship rest on common membership in a nuclear family.

Two basic types of kinship links are by blood and marriage. These ties create two types of kin: *cognatic relatives,* or those linked by blood or common ancestry; and *affinal relatives,* or those linked by marriage.

The links of kinship extend outward in geometrically increasing numbers. Therefore, a distinctive pattern of behavior cannot be associated with each possible category of relationship. Instead, all societies solve the problem of the infinite number of biological links of kinship by grouping them. Many of the principal differences among kinship systems stem from the varying ways in which kin are grouped.

Marriage

Marriage is fundamental to all systems of kinship. Every group has definitions of who may marry. The definitions may be phrased in terms of broad social groupings. For example, it may be considered preferable to marry someone who is "educated" or someone of a given ethnic group. They may be phrased in terms of specific genealogical relationships; for example, the belief that one should marry a particular cousin. Certain categories of individuals are always prohibited as marriage partners, since all societies have some form of incest taboo. In the broad sense, incest means sexual relations between participants who are related by a bond of kinship, which is culturally regarded as a bar. Marriage within the nuclear family, between parents and children or between siblings, is almost universally prohibited. Beyond this, the kin who are defined as eligible to marry vary radically from one society to another.

Social definitions of marriage also cover the number of spouses permissible at a given time, and the procedures for selecting a marriage partner, ranging from "romantic love" and individual choice to arranged marriages.

Cultural expectations defining who may have a legitimate concern with the success of a marriage also vary. In our society marriage is considered to concern primarily a man and woman and the state, which legalizes the union, and in some cases, a religious institution which sanctions it. But in many societies marriage is a compact between the kin of the man and the kin of the woman who share common interests, often economic, in the marriage and in its continuance.

Forms of the Family

Two basic questions have been asked about forms of the family: First, is the nuclear family universally recognized as a social unit? Second, is marriage a socially recognized relationship in all societies? While conclusions have hinged to a large degree on issues of definition, cross-cultural data, for example, on the Israeli kibbutz[1] and the Nayar of India,[2] have revealed exceptions to the universality of both marriage and the nuclear family. Neither marriage nor the nuclear family is universally the basis of a household unit. If a socially recognized unit is defined broadly, both may be universal; but the variations are great. Marriage in some form may be socially recognized in all societies, but the nuclear family is by no means a universal unit of residence, or even of long-term cooperation of spouses, or a universal unit of child rearing.

A related question concerns what groupings form a recognized household unit. In many societies various composite forms of the family, that is, *extended families*, made up of two, three, or more nuclear families, living together as an economic unit, are standard. This form is related both to the marriage system and to the physical characteristics of the household and the environment. A number of kinds of extended or composite families have been observed in different societies. Several brothers and their wives may establish a common household. Another type may include a man, his married sons, his sons' sons, and their wives. Similarly, a family may consist of a woman, her daughters, her daughters' daughters, and their husbands. Another variation includes a married couple, some of their married sons and daughters, and some of their grandchildren. Further variations are possible, giving rise to a great many types of household composition, which vary greatly under different circumstances.[3]

Not only are the biological nuclear family and the household often different, but in many societies the nuclear family is not the most common household unit. A sample of societies on which anthropologists have made ethnographic reports indicates that in the majority some form of extended household exists.[4] Extended families have been the most important household unit not only in primitive societies but also in highly civilized societies.

Determining the boundaries of the household is complex. Eating a regular meal in another household may not make a person a member of that household. But it is also misleading to assume that the household is necessarily bounded by four walls. The physical characteristics of households vary greatly in different societies, depending on the climate, the ecological characteristics of the terrain, building materials, and the type of house structure. It is therefore difficult to find comparable household boundaries—even physical boundaries—under different conditions. Internal divisions of the household may have highly distinct quarters for some purposes such as sleeping, but common quarters for other purposes such as cooking. Within a household, space may be divided in terms of religious and ritual functions rather than in terms of physical partitions. Definitions of households in terms of functions—whether a family has a common budget, common cooking facilities, or common property—are therefore often more useful than those related to the physical boundaries of the household.

In all societies household composition varies with the life cycle of the individual and the domestic group. But the kinds of change made by an individual from one point in his life cycle to another are not always the same.

Residence

The idea that place of residence is systematically patterned and related to social values and expectations is one of the most basic concepts about kinship systems. In connection with kinship, *resi-*

dence refers to the place where individuals live in relation to kin at different stages of the life cycle. Anthropological classifications of types of residence have frequently been based on postmarital residence, or where the newly married couple goes to live. The major types are: *virilocal* residence, when the new couple lives in or near the husband's parental home; *uxorilocal* residence, when the couple lives in or near the parental home of the wife; and *neolocal* residence, when choice of residence is not based on proximity to kin.

Residence patterns vary greatly from one society to another. But definitions of residence exist in all societies, even when it is expected that the newly married couple will not reside near any kin.

Residence is related to the incest taboo. Generally, although not always, married couples live together. Since individuals cannot marry within their family of orientation, in founding a new family husband and wife both cannot remain with their own families of origin. There must be a dislocation of residence for one or both.

The problem of defining the boundaries of the place of residence is comparable to the problem of defining the boundaries of a household. In attempting to define place of residence, anthropologists have, for example, spoken of moving "*to* or *near* the parental home,"[5] but the meaning of living near the parental home of either spouse may vary greatly with the ecological conditions of the society, just as the boundaries of the household vary. However complex it may be to describe residence patterns, it is seldom a neutral issue; great emotional investment attaches to where one lives in relation to kin.

Extended Kin Groups

In some societies extended kin groups—that is, kin groups more extensive than the nuclear family—are the basis of organization for many of the society's activities. Extended kin groups may own land and other strategic resources. Although social groups may be based on a number of criteria other than kinship, such as age, sex, social status, and locality, in some cases almost all the groups of a society are based on kinship. In some groups membership and rights are transmitted through the female line (matrilineal), in others through the male line (patrilineal). Extended kin groups vary with marriage systems and the ways in which rights are reckoned for other purposes.

Kin Networks

The term "kin network" or kindred refers to the kin of a nuclear family or individual.[6] Regardless of other features of kinship organization, the individual and nuclear family always has a kin network although its structure and function may vary.[7]

One basic feature of a network as distinct from a group is that the boundaries are different from the perspective of each individual; the individuals that are considered kin by one person are not necessarily the same as those considered kin by a close relative of this person, even though they have certain kin in common. Kin within a network do not necessarily have any significant relationship to each other except that they are both related to the specific individual who is the reference point. No two individuals in the society, except unmarried siblings, have the same network of kin. Husbands and wives may come to be incorporated in each other's kin network but they bring to the family different perspectives on the issue of who is kin.

The boundaries of the network also shift with the criteria employed, and are different for different activities: the network may include all those the individual is able to name as kin or all those living within a given geographic area, but these may be different from the kin with whom the family exchanges economic services. For every kinship event the boundaries of kinship may be redefined; decisions must constantly be made about who is and who is not to be included as a kin for particular occasions.

In almost all societies more individuals are related by blood and marriage than are actually recognized as kin. The definition of an individual as a kin is social, not purely biological. Paternity, for example, is often a social rather than a biological fact, as in adoption within our own society.

Because of the multitude of biological ties to kin, all societies have developed procedures for defining who the individual's kin are for specific social purposes, such as mutual assistance, the regulation of marriage, and membership in kin groups. The ways in which an individual's kin are defined vary greatly.[8]

Kinship Bonds

In all societies kinship statuses are used as criteria for social interaction. Three characteristics of social statuses that are basic for kinship are generation, sex, and laterality, or the side of the family to which a kin status belongs.

Kinship *bonds* are ties of obligation and sentiment between those in specific reciprocal statuses. The concept of bond implies that certain relationships within a network are accorded a *priority*, and that this patterns the organization of the network; that is, stronger bonds serve as links for other relationships. Even among genealogically close kin, real choices exist in the allocation of time and resources; for certain purposes some kinship ties are given priority.

Examination of regularities in relationships among kin may be observed and analyzed from a variety of types of data, among them kinship values, legal norms, and legal sanctions. Regularities in relationships with kin may also be analyzed through examining the frequency with which interaction occurs with kin in particular kinship statuses. From observations of the frequency of interaction, it is possible to impute rights and obligations that probably underlie the interaction. This behavioral information can be compared with perceptions of norms. An analysis of actual behavioral choices made in relationships among kin in a given area of activity thus reveals the relative priority accorded to various bonds among kin.[9] In examining kinship bonds we are dealing with the *relative* strength of a tie between one set of reciprocal statuses as compared with another. In some societies, for example, the marital bond is accorded greater importance for most social purposes than the tie between an adult son and his mother, but in other societies the reverse is true.

The notion of bond specifically implies relative priority. On the other hand, the concept of *role* covers the general content of the rights, obligations, and expectations of the individual in a particular position and is broader than the concept of bond. Each role, moreover, has a number of reciprocal statuses related to it; the role of mother may include mother-son, mother-daughter relationships. Thus a bond is the relationship between a person in a role and one in a reciprocal status with respect to that role.

Both the role expectations that are characteristic of particular kinship statuses and the specific kinship bonds that are accorded priority vary greatly in the kinship systems of different societies.

We have considered some of the most important dimensions of a kinship system as it has been studied in anthropology and sociology. Other areas, such as kinship terminology, or the terms individuals use to address and refer to each other, have also been studied and are patterned differently from one society to another.

Relationships Among Features of the Kinship System

The wide variety found in kinship systems is not completely random and unlimited. Pressures toward consistency exist within kinship systems so that, for example, certain types of marriage systems tend to go with particular types of residence. But such regularities are not uniform; the dimensions of the kinship system are not so tightly associated that they can be combined in only one way. Yet observations indicate that a closer relationship exists within dimensions of the kinship system than between the kinship system and other features of the society.[10]

Many observations and hypotheses have been made of how the various dimensions of kinship systems tend to cluster. They are important here only to illustrate the general proposition that kinship systems are sufficiently connected so that the existence of one feature places certain limitations on the range within which other dimensions may vary.

The procedure of mate selection depends on how kin groups are incorporated into the nuclear family. If the new couple will reside with or near kin, members of the kin group have a stake in the marriage; since they will live in the same household with the new spouse, they have a reason for a voice in the selection.

Strict hierarchical distinctions based on age and birth order and a continuing authority of elder kin are frequently associated with incorporation of the nuclear family in extended kin households and a high degree of social involvement with kin, and also kinship as a major organizing principle for the society.[11]

The system of reckoning descent tends to be associated with the kinship bonds that are strongest, as well as with residence patterns. Among the North-Lapp nomads it was found that rigid generational differentiation went together with solidarity among siblings as the fundamental kinship bond.[12] It has also been noted that sibling solidarity is a characteristic of American kinship, which, too, is "bilateral."[13] It has been argued that matrilineal reckoning of descent tends to go with matrilocal residence, although the correlation is not absolute.[14]

Differences in the quality of the marital bond, particularly the stability of marriage, have been noted when matrilineal rather than patrilineal descent groups are present. It has been found that men hold the primary authority roles in both matrilineal and patrilineal descent groups. In a matrilineal system the husband is incorporated into his wife's kin group for certain purposes but exercises his primary authority within his own maternal kin group and therefore must maintain ties with it. Thus the husband is caught between competing ties, those to his wife's kin and those to his maternal kin.

In a patrilineal system the wife is incorporated into her husband's kin group, but because she does not have a significant authority role within her own paternal kin group she does not have comparable obligations to maintain strong ties with it, and is thus not confronted with the same degree of conflicting loyalties. A related phenomenon is the difference in the position of the husband and wife with respect to the authority of the household into which they marry in matrilineal and patrilineal systems. The degree of authority of a father-in-law over a son-in-law in a matrilineal system is not as great as that of a mother-in-law over a daughter-in-law in patrilineal descent groups.[15]

The focal points of conflict and strain in various kinship systems show certain associations with other features of the system. In either a virilocal or a uxorilocal residence system, the spouse who must move away from his or her home and enter the home of strangers is often placed in a position of stress, stemming in part from subjugation to the authority of elder kin in contrast to the problems that typify systems where the nuclear family resides as an independent unit. Here transitions to a new household exist for both spouses, and typical problems include "parental possessiveness," "childish overdependence," and the loss of status of the aged, since the authority of elder kin is diminished by separate residence.

Interrelationships among the dimensions of kinship systems are complex and all the possible combinations are unknown. But it is clear that elements of the kinship system do not combine at random.

Rather, certain clusterings tend to occur; roles within the family are associated with the organization of relationships among kin. Because of these connections, a change in one area may have implications that extend to other areas. A change in relations with kin may, for example, have consequences for the quality of the marital relationship.

KINSHIP AND SOCIETY

Kinship systems are interesting because of their enormous complexity and variety. In our society concern with the intricacies of reckoning descent is likely to appear either hollow and meaningless or a form of social snobbery. However, anthropologists and sociologists have studied kinship not because of an interest in complexity for its own sake, but rather because in many societies kinship ties are basic for the entire social organization.

Although we have only touched on the extensive variety of kinship systems, we have reviewed many of the major dimensions along which kinship may vary and the types of associations that have been found among these dimensions. We will now consider some of the functions that kinship may have for social organization, and the kinds of societies in which varying kinship systems have been found.

The Functions of Kinship for Social Organization

The organization of some entire societies is built on extended kin groupings; in other societies kinship plays a limited role. Where most of the social relations of the society are carried out through kin ties, kinship regulates behavior and allows individuals to know what to expect of each other in many activities.

Kinship and Economy. In our society kinship plays a relatively small part in structuring most work groups. In other societies kinship is a major, if not the exclusive, basis on which economic production is organized. Authority and decision-making within work groups, for example, may be assigned on the basis of kinship status, those in senior kinship statuses having authority over the work group. Distribution and exchange may also be organized on the basis of kinship. Exchange of basic economic resources may often be part of the ritual during ceremonies such as marriage. In all societies some kinds of property are held and transmitted on the basis of kinship; for example, fields, houses, and personal possessions. In some cases strategic resources, that is, the means of production, are held primarily by kin groups and are transmitted on the basis of kinship.

Kinship and Assistance. Societies organize in varying ways to assist their members in times of crisis or special need. In some societies many highly specialized institutions exist for assisting the individual, such as welfare institutions and social agencies, medical institutions, insurance organizations, and banks. But in societies where few specialized institutions exist, kin may constitute the most important source of assistance for the individual. Where kinship is an important basis for economic activity, assistance among kin is often tied up with their joint economic endeavors. In traditional Chinese society, for example, the family and the extended kin group were expected to care for ill members, and hospital care was suspect. Assistance in educational pursuits was also provided by kin; schools and special tutoring facilities were often provided by a clan to enable the brightest members of an extended kin group to pass the imperial examinations.

In a society where the only mode of obtaining assistance is through kin, a person without kin may be unable to manage. Kinship ties may be so essential that those lacking real kin may resort to fictitious kinship ties.

Kinship and Social Control. In all societies the household group plays a significant part in social control through socializing children and motivating the individual to conform to society's norms. Elaborate institutions of legal and political control may also exist apart from the family. In other cases, legal and political control is exercised mainly through the family and extended kin groups. The political and legal controls of kinship may be very powerful, particularly when the individual's social placement in many spheres is bound up with the same groups; for example, when the kin group is also the economic and religious group. Where the individual's social network is closely interlocked, gossip, public opinion, and other forms of primary group social control have particular importance.

Kinship and Social Status. All societies have procedures for the assignment of social positions. Some social statuses are always assigned on the basis of kinship criteria such as birth order and sex. In traditional Chinese society the eldest son of the eldest son occupied a special position of power and authority within the extended kin group. In societies where most economic activities are carried out by kin groups, the individual's position in these activities will depend on his kinship status. For example, occupations are sometimes inherited. Political positions such as those of chieftain may also be transmitted on the basis of kinship.

The process of social mobility may also be related to kinship. In our society we tend to think of mobility primarily in terms of an individual, although a man who raises his social status carries his wife and children with him. In other societies mobility is regarded more as collective than as individual; by achievement the individual raises not only himself and his immediate family, but many of his kin as well.

Kinship and Religious Activity. In many societies kinship is an important basis for organizing religious activities. The selection of individuals who participate in a religious ceremonial and their ceremonial duties are often defined in terms of kinship ties. Funerals, for example, are almost always organized, at least in part, on the basis of kinship with the expression of grief being related to kinship connections with the deceased.

Associations Between
Kinship Systems and Societal Conditions

A number of studies have tried to establish relationships between certain societal conditions and different forms of kinship. One type of analysis takes a particular kinship form and traces the range of societal conditions under which it is found. Studies have been made of the kinds of societies in which the independent nuclear family is found. Another approach examines specific kinds of societies and determines the kinship systems that occur in them. For example, urban industrial societies have been studied to determine what kinds of family organization and kin groups exist in them.

An analysis of the relation between societal conditions and kinship systems must cope with a fundamental logical problem: the conditions that cause or *give rise* to a particular form of kinship may not be the same as those that *perpetuate* it. For example, it has been noted that matriliny "survives under conditions other than those which gave rise to it, that we cannot outlaw the possibility that it can spread to groups where it would not originate, and that we cannot deduce theoretically the conditions likely to terminate it."[16] From an observed correlation between kinship and society it is not possible to conclude whether kinship is the determinant of the particular societal condition or the reverse. Nor is it possible to predict that kinship and societal conditions will necessarily change together.

Moreover, relating dimensions of a kinship system to those of the society is complicated because a great many societal conditions may be related to the many dimensions of kinship. Even in examining one aspect of societal conditions, such as the economy, complex classifications have been used. Economic variables that have been related to forms of the family include: (1) size of food supply; (2) degree of spatial mobility required in subsistence activities; and (3) kind and amount of family property. Some theorists have referred to urban industrial society, or western urban industrial society, as a category in which special types of kinship are likely to arise. But within this category many dimensions of relevance for kinship have been distinguished, including the difference between early and late stages of industrialization,[17] between those societies with indigenous industrialization and those with borrowed industrial patterns, between preindustrial and industrial cities,[18] between various types of labor and market economy,[19] and between different types of political ideology and political control.[20]

As yet no general theory of the association between kinship and society that covers all of these numerous dimensions has been substantiated. Nevertheless, a number of partial theories, observations, and hypotheses are worth examining.

Kinship in Urban Industrialized Society. Efforts to trace the types of societies in which the independent nuclear family exists reveal no simple correlation. An independent nuclear family is found under very different economic conditions, in modern industrial societies and also in simpler hunting and gathering societies. However, a similar factor exists in both types of society, namely, the need for physical mobility. "The hunter is mobile because he pursues the game: the industrial worker, the job."[21] By contrast, in a sedentary agricultural economy where the place of work is geographically fixed by the location of land, larger kin groups can remain in the same location and yet be available for their economic tasks.

A number of hypotheses have been developed about the kinds of kinship systems that are compatible with urban industrial societies. Some theorists have assumed that the existence of corporate kin groups and an extended family will interfere with the requirements of an urban society with an industrial economy.[22] This assumption is based on several features that are presumed to characterize an urban industrial society. Industry requires geographic mobility so that workers will be available at different times and places. Thus ties of kinship should not be so extensive that individuals would be unwilling to live geographically separated from their kin. An industrial economy also requires the assignment of occupations on the basis of objective criteria of technical competence. Extensive obligations of kinship would presumably interfere with the application of these objective criteria. It has also been assumed that the activities of an industrial economy require larger, more centralized units of production than can be organized on a relatively small family or kin group basis. It should be noted that these hypotheses pertain specifically to the urban segments of industrial societies. They do not apply to preindustrial urban centers. In the past it has been assumed that these hypotheses were supported by the prevalence of an independent nuclear family in urban industrial societies.

These hypotheses have also received support from the observed breakdown of corporate kin groups in societies undergoing industrialization.[23] In societies coming in contact with previously industrialized nations through their markets, the economic power of descent groups is often undermined.[24] In a study of kinship and industrialization in Lagos, Nigeria, it was noted that the opportunities for individual profit that accompanied industrialization undermined the economic base of kinship ties. Then social differences between the more and less successful reduced the feelings of obligations among kin, which otherwise ensured that wealth was redistributed within the kin network. In turn, differences in income and status among kin were further widened and ties of kinship were further reduced.[25]

Despite the evidence that traditional kinship systems tend, under some circumstances, to be disrupted and radically changed by industrialization, there are indications that urbanization as such, and industrialization under some conditions, do not necessarily break down all kinds of kinship ties. Although the claims of the family group may exert an outworn authority and inhibit ambition, "they also represent a system of social welfare," a challenge to self-seeking and class interest, a widespreading and secure emotional attachment. To abandon them would destroy the informal social justice and emotional security which maintain the balance of a rapidly changing society.[26] Thus a conflict may exist between the development of a modern economy and traditional loyalties of kinship, but the ties of kinship by no means disappear in the process of change.

There is evidence that kin groups may sometimes remain significant as units of economic production even in industrialized nations. After reviewing instances in which kinship serves as a basis of organizing industrial activities, it was concluded that, depending on the nature and size of the industrial organization, as well as the size of the family, kinship is not necessarily incompatible with efficient organization of industrial activities. This position is supported by a study of economic activity among French-Canadians in New England,[27] and also by studies of industrial organization among overseas Chinese[28] and familistic type of industrial organization in Japan.[29]

A number of recent studies of kinship in western industrial urban societies have contributed additional data on the conditions under which various types of kinship may exist.[30] Several of these have analyzed the relationship between the nuclear family and its kin, and the extent and forms of interaction with kin outside the nuclear family. One study claims that a modified, as compared with a classical, extended family can, and does, exist in an urban industrial society, and may foster rather than inhibit both occupational and geographic mobility.[31] On the basis of a general review of a number of studies of kinship in urban industrial societies, it was concluded that kinship remains an important basis for social contact, performing many important functions for the family.[32] Thus involvement with kin, as distinct from corporate kin groups, does not disappear or become insignificant with industrialization. Moreover, even the most general theories have noted the possible variation of kinship structures with a large-scale society from one ethnic or class subgroup to another.

We have not attempted a complete review of studies in kinship and society, or even of studies of urban industrial kinship. Our purpose has been to illustrate the complexity of the connections between kinship and society and the consequent need for caution in making assumptions about the forms of kinship possible in a particular kind of society. While the data in this book imply certain modifications and refinements in hypotheses about kinship in urban industrial society, these theoretical modifications will not be spelled out in detail here.

Where extensive ties with kin exist, they have implications for the family and for the personalities of family members. Since, as will be seen, we have found ties with kin to be more extensive than might have been presumed on the basis of some previous hypotheses, we will now review some of the functions that kinship has been found to have for family and personality in societies where involvement with kin is extensive.

KINSHIP, FAMILY, AND PERSONALITY

Because the family is in itself part of the kinship system, a special distinction must be made when speaking of the influence of the kinship system upon the family. But dimensions of kinship such as the modes of residence and marriage have a profound effect upon the family as they determine household composition, activities that are carried out by various kin units, and relationships within the family.

Social Identity

The degree of interconnection within the family's network of kin relationship has important consequences for relationships among kin, as well as those within the family. If an individual's various memberships overlap and similar behavior is expected in various situations, he is likely to have a more coherent self-image than if radically different behavior is expected of him in a series of relationships with others who have little in common. Similarly, if many social relationships are common to the entire family, and there is considerable overlap of the groups in which different activities are carried out, such as occupation and recreation, the family's identity is likely to be more unified than that of a family whose members participate relatively little in the same social relationships. The selection of marriage partners and the role of kin in the selection help to define the marital pair as a social unit, that is, their social identity. When marriage is considered a tie not merely between two individuals but also between two extended kin groups, many kin in addition to the husband and wife are involved in the marriage economically and ceremonially; all have a stake in its success.

Patterns of residence affect the composition of the household and thus exert an influence on the family. The social position of a newly married husband and wife is particularly influenced by the system of residence.

The sharp break in the life of one spouse that is likely when residence is with the kin of the other spouse has been noted. Since the spouse who shifts residence must move into a new set of social ties, the relative position of the spouses in their most immediate social groupings is affected by residence. Moreover, the conflicts that are likely to inhere in the position of each spouse are affected by whether a sharp transition to a new kin group is necessary.

The individual may be incorporated into a nuclear family and kin group in a variety of ways. Also, the lines that distinguish the individual, the nuclear family, and the other kin units may be drawn very differently; neither the individual nor the family is conceived in the same way in all societies. In some cases the family rather than the individual is defined as the unit for most purposes. In traditional Japanese society, for example, the peasant family was the unit of most social activity and the individual was not defined as independent for most purposes; he had little sense of private identity and few private choices.[33]

Thus kinship organization exerts a significant effect upon the position of the marital pair in their new household, as well as upon the family boundaries and the units of social action. This, in turn, influences other relationships within the family.

Authority and Control

In many societies extended kin exert control over members of the nuclear family. Although this authority is not solely the product of the family's incorporation in its network of kin, it is clearly influenced by the kinship structure. Residence patterns and household composition are significant for family authority in several respects: (1) some residence patterns introduce an asymmetrical element in authority relations between husbands and wives by placing one spouse in a position of continuing membership in his family of childhood, while the other spouse must go to live with comparative strangers; (2) when one spouse remains with his own group, that spouse may have authority through control over property and economic resources of the larger kin group; (3) an individual who remains within his own kin group after marriage may have limitations placed on his authority to his own kin in senior positions; (4) kin outside the nuclear family may be defined as having direct authority over family members in some spheres; (5) activities in the larger kin group that are based on kinship organization may support authority within the household.

Economic Relations

Kinship organization also influences the role of the nuclear family or household unit in economic activities. In our own society, although the family is generally not a major unit of economic production, it is a unit of consumption; as such, ties with kin affect its consumption activities. For instance, a Jewish family may keep a kosher household for the sake of parents. Kinship may also be the basic source of available welfare and assistance, thus affecting how the family seeks and obtains aid. Sometimes ceremonial activities among kin constitute a significant economic contribution to the family. Some basic economic activities of the family, such as house building, may be carried out through the help of kin.

Socialization

Composition of the household and the proximity of kin help to determine the adults who are significant in child rearing, which, in turn, has consequences for personality development.

When many kin live in or near the same household, they can easily exchange child-rearing tasks. Individuals other than the parents may feed the child, play with him, and discipline him. As suggested by a study of Truk culture in the South Pacific, the capacity for "deep" emotional attachment to one individual may be reduced by socialization in a kinship system that has many parental surrogates. On the other hand, the personality characteristics fostered under such circumstances may be compatible with that kind of society, for example, with the marriage system and the necessity of coping with complex role organization within the family.[34]

When the nuclear family is incorporated into a larger household group, or lives close to kin, the child must learn a complex set of role relationships: he must learn to relate to grandparents, to uncles, to aunts, to cousins, as well as to members of the nuclear family. In addition, the child can observe the multiple relationships among others; for instance, his own parents are children to his grandparents as well as parents to him. In many societies the child is confronted with this extended network almost at birth, not at a later stage.

Kinship structure also influences the form and resolution of the Oedipus complex. The universality of the Oedipus complex is controversial. But whether some special attachment to the parent of the opposite sex is universal, evidence indicates that its form varies with the kinship structure. For instance, in a society with matrilocal residence, the mother's brother is in some respects in a position similar to that of the father in other systems. Then, is the resentment of the son toward the father directed instead toward the mother's brother, who in this case is in a position of authority? Evidence from the Hopi Indians in southwestern United States indicates that the role of the mother's brother is not quite comparable to that of the father in other societies in terms of the Oedipus complex, because the mother's brother does not combine his authority position with being the sexual partner of the child's mother. Moreover, the relationship of the child to the mother's brother is tempered when the mother has more than one brother. However, the Oedipal conflict between father and child is reduced by diffusion of some of the father's authority to the mother's brother.[35]

Kinship structure also affects the kinds of intimacy that the child observes. Sleeping arrangements have been considered particularly important in some psychological theory. Sleeping arrangements vary greatly from one culture to another in relation to household composition, as well as to general definitions of space and concepts of privacy. Among the Hopi, the child sleeps close to many of the kin in his matrilocal extended family, has a chance to observe sexual relations from an early age, and to develop a sense of intimacy with the group that sleeps close together.

From an examination of relationships between kinship structure and child-rearing practices and personality development, it was hypothesized that insofar as kinship determines who acts as parents and parental surrogates it influences superego development. This hypothesis, based in part on psychoanalytic theory, was that "where the parents play a less important role in the socialization of their children, the children will tend to develop weaker superegos than where the parents play a more important role."[36] However, since parents play the dominant socializing role in most societies, the effects of secondary agents of socialization on superego formation were studied. It was assumed that relatives resemble parents more closely than nonrelatives, so that if relatives rather than nonrelatives are the more important secondary agents of socialization, a stronger superego formation should result. This hypothesis was supported by a significant correlation between residence patterns, the index of the importance of relatives as secondary socializers, and beliefs about the patients' responsibility for being ill—the index of guilt and superego formation. Here a specific relationship has been posited between one aspect of kinship structure and a dimension of personality.

Thus not only broad cultural patterns but social structure and, in particular, kinship structure affect socialization and personality. The relationships are complex, but kinship structure is clearly important.

Socialization occurs not only in early childhood but throughout life; entry into each new role entails socialization. Since kinship often is a basis for organizing religious and ceremonial activities, kin play an important part in rites accompanying life-cycle transitions. The ceremonial support of kin may assist those involved in accepting the idea of status transitions, for example, at marriage. Similarly the participation of kin in funeral ceremonies helps family members accept the alteration in their social status created by the loss.

Kinship structure therefore influences the way in which the family carries out its socialization functions in a variety of ways. Kin may be involved both in early training of children and in later socialization of adults, especially in connection with life-cycle transitions. Kinship structure exerts its major influence upon socialization as a determinant of who become the socializers. In some situations parental surrogates may play an active role in child rearing. The exact consequences for personality development of multiple parent figures and various ways of dividing aspects of the parental role are difficult to determine because so many factors enter into the socialization process. But it is clear that the socialization process proceeds in varied ways in different types of kinship systems.

Roles and Emotions

The composition of the household and definitions of bonds of kinship help to define the rights and duties of roles; for instance, whether the father will be the ultimate authority or merely a subordinate of his own father. In addition, the emotions that are likely to be felt by those in particular family positions are affected by the way in which the family's roles are organized with respect to kin.

The quality of the emotional relationship that is most typical between husbands and wives depends in part on how their roles fit into the kinship structure. "Romantic love as it occurs in our civilization, inextricably bound up with ideas of monogamy, exclusiveness, jealousy and undeviating fidelity," is unknown in many cultures. "The Samoans," for example, "laugh at stories of romantic love, scoff at fidelity to a long-absent wife or mistress, believe explicitly that one love will quickly cure another."[37] The notion of romantic love has a long history in western civilization, but it is also undoubtedly connected with certain features of present-day western urban kinship. In our culture romantic love serves as a basis for mate choice. However, in societies where marriages are arranged, this rationale is unnecessary. Thus the emotion of love is conditioned by the marriage system.

In any kinship system a large number of role relationships exist between different pairs of individuals, that is, between different paired statuses such as mother-son, grandson-grandmother, brother-sister. The definition of the quality of emotional relationships between those within the nuclear family is related to the definition of relationships between nuclear family members and kin. The relationship that is regarded as the individual's main source of emotional support varies from one kinship system to another. In our society the marital tie is normally considered to be the primary bond of an adult. In other systems, however, parent-child or sibling bonds may be more important and even take precedence over the marital tie as a source of emotional support.

In the traditional, and to some extent present-day, Japanese society, the kinship system is one in which the primary bond of obligation and emotional attachment is to someone other than the spouse. Even today the eldest son in the family frequently resides with his parents and his obligations to his parents are considered to be greater than those to his wife. In one recent study, respondents were asked whether an eldest son should divorce his wife if she does not get along with his mother.[38] Most of them said that the husband should not divorce his wife, but those who held "traditionalist views" felt emphatically that he should divorce her. In this point of view the parent-child bond is far stronger than the husband-wife bond.

In some instances elaborate cultural definitions prescribe the emotions that may be expressed between particular kin. This applies even to what might be considered "deeper" emotions of love and attachment. Anthropologists have used specific terms, "avoidance relationships" and "joking relationships," to refer to certain kinds of expressive behavior.[39] Such relationships have been considered to form a continuum from complete avoidance of speech and physical contact to extreme license or obligatory joking and horseplay. Joking and avoidance relationships, which are institutionalized between specific kin in many societies, exemplify one way in which an individual's emotional expression is conditioned by the definitions of kinship roles. Norms of this sort generally apply more directly to expressing an emotion than to feeling it, but the etiquette of expression undoubtedly tempers which emotions are felt.

The emotional expressions regarded as appropriate within the household are also conditioned by its composition. The traditional Chinese family, for instance, followed elaborate expressive etiquette for particular situations. Feelings were expressed by covert and indirect means to avoid embarrassment from acting openly toward a person in a way that might not be appropriate in front of someone of another status who was present within the house-hold.[40] The young wife, for instance, was not only constrained by expressive etiquette; she had especially limited possibilities of emo-tional expression because she was under the authority of her mother-in-law and was not even supposed to express her feelings to her husband. The composition of the household and the relation-ships within it vary greatly with other features of the kinship system such as residence patterns. The social organization of the family in relation to kin therefore has significant consequences for the defini-tion of roles and appropriate emotions of those within it.

The research, then, was guided by the concepts that have been outlined briefly in this chapter—that different kinship systems can exist under different social conditions, and that the dimensions of a kinship system are related to each other. The kin relationships of client families have both common and distinguishing features com-pared with other structures of kinship ties. Thus it was important to investigate kinship values and experiences for both clients and caseworkers to find similarities and divergent patterns to under-stand the ways in which kinship is dealt with in casework treat-ment. Moreover, the kinship environment of a client family has significant functions both for social organization outside the fam-ily and for relationships within the family. To diagnose and treat families most effectively it is essential, therefore, to have some knowledge about this aspect of its environment.

Some of the questions that these guiding concepts pose are: How are the boundaries of the kin network defined? What are the experiences concerning proximity to kin? Are extended kin groups present in an urban industrial setting? What are the consistent pat-terns of interaction and conflict? What is the strength of the mari-tal as compared with the parent-child bond? How do kinship ties influence economic relations among kin? What kinds of emotional support and assistance do kin offer the family? In what ways do kin exert a controlling influence on the behavior of family members?

These questions and others are of theoretical interest when ap-plied to any kinship system but they become particularly mean-ingful when applied to this group because it has the special char-acteristic of also being a group of casework clients. For it is the purpose of this book to describe kin relationships in order to assess their significance for casework.

NOTES TO CHAPTER 1

1. Spiro, Melford E., "Is the Family Universal?—The Israeli Case" in *A Modern Introduction to the Family*, edited by Norman W. Bell and Ezra F. Vogel. The Free Press, Glencoe, Ill., 1960, p. 74.
2. Gough, Kathleen, "Is the Family Universal?—The Nayar Case," *ibid.*, p. 80.
3. Murdock, George Peter, *Social Structure*. Macmillan Co., New York, 1949, p. 33.
4. *Ibid.*, pp. 34–35.
5. *Ibid.*, p. 16.
6. Bott, Elizabeth, *Family and Social Network*. Tavistock Publications, Ltd., London, 1957.
7. Mitchell, William E., "Theoretical Problems in the Concept of Kindred," *American Anthropologist*, vol. 65, April, 1963, pp. 343–354.
8. Parsons, Talcott, "The Kinship System of the Contemporary United States" in *Essays in Sociological Theory*, edited by Talcott Parsons. Rev. ed. The Free Press, Glencoe, Ill., 1954, p. 178.
9. For discussions of this point, see *Two Studies of Kinship in London*, edited by Raymond W. Firth, The Athlone Press, London, 1956; and Leach, E. R., "The Sinhalese of the Dry Zone of Northern Ceylon" in *Social Structure in Southeast Asia*, edited by George Peter Murdock, Quadrangle Books, Chicago, 1960.
10. Aberle, David, "Matrilineal Descent in Cross-Cultural Perspective" in *Matrilineal Kinship*, edited by David M. Schneider and Kathleen Gough. University of California Press, Berkeley and Los Angeles, 1961, pp. 655–727.
11. Williams, Robin M., Jr., *American Society: A Sociological Interpretation*. Alfred A. Knopf, Inc., New York, 1951, pp. 492–510.
12. Pehrson, Robert N., "Bilateral Kin Groupings as a Structural Type: A Preliminary Statement," University of Manila *Journal of East Asiatic Studies*, vol. 3, January, 1954, pp. 199–202.
13. Cumming, Elaine, and David M. Schneider, "Sibling Solidarity: A Property of American Kinship," *American Anthropologist*, vol. 63, June, 1961, pp. 498–507.
14. Gough, Kathleen, "The Modern Disintegration of Matrilineal Descent Groups" in Schneider and Gough, editors, *op. cit.*, pp. 631–652.
15. Schneider, David M., "The Distinctive Features of Matrilineal Descent Groups," *ibid.*, p. 16.
16. Aberle, David F., "Matrilineal Descent in Cross-Cultural Perspective," *op. cit.*, p. 659.
17. Litwak, Eugene, "Occupational Mobility and Extended Family Cohesion," *American Sociological Review*, vol. 25, February, 1960, pp. 9–21; and "Geographic Mobility and Family Cohesion," *American Sociological Review*, vol. 25, June, 1960, pp. 385–394.
18. Sjoberg, Gideon, "Familial Organization in the Preindustrial City," *Marriage and Family Living*, vol. 18, February, 1956, p. 32.
19. Gough, Kathleen, "The Modern Disintegration of Matrilineal Descent Groups" in Schneider and Gough, editors, *op. cit.*, pp. 631–652.
20. Yang, C. K., *The Chinese Family in the Communist Revolution*. The Technology Press, Massachusetts Institute of Technology, Cambridge, Mass., 1959.
21. Nimkoff, M. F., and Russell Middleton, "Types of Family and Types of Economy," *American Journal of Sociology*, vol. 66, November, 1960, pp. 215–225.

22. Parsons, Talcott, "The Social Structure of the Family in *The Family: Its Function and Destiny*, edited by Ruth N. Anshen, Harper and Bros., New York, 1949, pp. 173–201; and "Revised Analytical Approach to the Theory of Social Stratification" in *Class, Status and Power: A Reader in Social Stratification*, edited by Reinhard Bendix and Seymour M. Lipset, The Free Press, Glencoe, Ill., 1953, pp. 92–128. Also see Williams, Robin M., Jr., *op. cit.* For another classic statement of the hypothesis that kinship ties tend to break down in urban industrial societies, see Wirth, Louis, "Urbanism as a Way of Life," *American Journal of Sociology*, vol. 44, July, 1938, pp. 1–24.

23. Goode, William J., *World Revolution and Family Patterns*. The Free Press of Glencoe, New York, 1963, p. 369.

24. Gough, Kathleen, "The Modern Disintegration of Matrilineal Descent Groups" in Schneider and Gough, editors, *op. cit.*, p. 640.

25. Marris, Peter, *Family and Social Change in an African City: A Study of Rehousing in Lagos*. Routledge and Kegan Paul, London, 1961, pp. 136–137.

26. *Ibid.*, p. 141.

27. Bennett, John W., and Leo A. Despres, "Kinship and Instrumental Activities: A Theoretical Inquiry," *American Anthropologist*, vol. 62, April, 1960, p. 254; Despres, Leo A., "A Function of Bilateral Kinship Patterns in a New England Industry," *Human Organization*, vol. 17, Summer, 1958, pp. 15–22.

28. Barnett, Milton L., "Kinship as a Factor Affecting Cantonese Economic Adaptation in the United States, "*Human Organization*, vol. 19, Spring, 1960, p. 41.

29. Wilkinson, Thomas O., "Family Structure and Industrialization in Japan," *American Sociological Review*, vol. 27, October, 1962, pp. 678–682.

30. See Bibliography to this volume for listing of relevant books and articles.

31. Litwak, Eugene, "Occupational Mobility and Extended Family Cohesion," and "Geographic Mobility and Family Cohesion," *op. cit.*

32. Sussman, Marvin B., and Lee Burchinal, "Kin Family Network: Unheralded Structure in Current Conceptualizations of Family Functioning," *Marriage and Family Living*, vol. 24, August, 1962, pp. 231–240. Another review of studies of kinship in industrial society can be found in Wilensky, Harold L., and Charles N. Lebeaux, *Industrial Society and Social Welfare*, Russell Sage Foundation, New York, 1958.

33. Dore, Ronald P., *City Life in Japan: A Study of a Tokyo Ward*. University of California Press, Berkeley and Los Angeles, 1958, p. 376.

34. Gladwin, Thomas, and Seymour B. Sarason, "Culture and Individual Personality Integration on Truk" in *Culture and Mental Health: Cross Cultural Studies*, edited by Marvin K. Opler. Macmillan Co., New York, 1959, pp. 173–210.

35. Eggan, Dorothy, "The General Problem of Hopi Adjustment" in *Personality in Nature, Society, and Culture*, edited by Clyde Kluckhohn and Henry A. Murray. 2d ed. Alfred A. Knopf, Inc., New York, 1953, pp. 280–281.

36. Whiting, John W. M., and Irvin L. Child, "Origins of Guilt" in *Child Training and Personality: A Cross-Cultural Study*. Yale University Press, New Haven, 1953, p. 246. For another discussion that relates kinship structure and personality, see Winch, Robert F., *Identification and Its Familial Determinants*, Bobbs-Merrill

Co., Indianapolis, Ind., 1962.

37. Mead, Margaret, *Coming of Age in Samoa*. William Morrow and Co., New York, 1928, pp. 104–105.

38. Dore, Ronald P., *op. cit.*, p. 126.

39. Murdock, George Peter, *op cit.*, pp. 260–283.

40. Hsu, Francis L. K., *Americans and Chinese: Two Ways of Life*, Abelard-Schuman, Ltd., New York, 1953; and "Suppression versus Repression: A Limited Psychological Interpretation of Four Cultures," *Psychiatry*, vol. 12, August, 1949, pp. 223–242.

CHAPTER 2

The Agency
and the Clients

THE AGENCY SETTING

The Jewish Family Service of New York is a family counseling agency, primarily serving the Jewish community of New York City, although not entirely restricted to Jewish families. It receives most of its funds from the Federation of Jewish Philanthropies, of which it is a constituent agency. There are four district offices—two in Brooklyn, one in the Bronx, one in Manhattan—and a central office housing administrative office and special services.

A staff of professionally trained caseworkers provides individual and family counseling; a variety of other services are also available. Clients are referred to the agency from many sources, including relatives, friends and neighbors, other social agencies, rabbis, children's schools and camps, advertisements and telephone book listings, newspaper and magazine articles, medical doctors and psychiatrists. Virtually no one is referred through the courts. Fees based on income and responsibilities are charged for services. Although in most cases the family is formally considered to be the client, wives are seen somewhat more frequently than husbands. Problems of marriage and of parent-child relationships constitute the bulk of the agency caseload.

The clients studied came from the regular casework offices of the agency. For life-cycle contrast, certain clients in the special Service to the Aged of the agency were also studied.

PRESENTING PROBLEMS OF CLIENT FAMILIES

A sample of clients was asked in the research questionnaire (see Appendix: Research Methods) to indicate which of a list of problems was foremost in their decision to apply to the agency for help. Marital, parent-child, and child's behavior problems were indicated as the most important factors in the decision to seek help in 88 per cent of the cases. Although problems of relationships with kin frequently come up in the course of casework treatment, there were fewer than 1 per cent of the cases in which this was the most important part of the presenting problem (Table 1).

Table 1.   Major Presenting Problems as Seen by Clients[a]

	Per Cent
Marital problem	37
Parent-child problem	22
Child's behavior problem	29
Individual personality problem	5
Medical problem	1
Financial problem	2
Conflicts with relatives	[b]
Other	4
Total	100
	(377)

[a]In this and all following tables unless otherwise indicated, the figures in parentheses indicate the number of cases on which the percentages are based. This will sometimes be fewer than the total number who were asked the questions, for nonrespondents are not included in the total.

[b]Less than 1 per cent.

The data on presenting problems as perceived by clients are strikingly similar to those found in the routine agency statistics.

The clients studied constitute a random sample of the agency

caseload at a given time; the length of time they had been in treatment ranged from less than one month to several years.

SOCIOCULTURAL BACKGROUND
OF CLIENT FAMILIES

Stage of Life Cycle

The client families were married couples, mainly with children
still living at home. For 87 per cent the current marriage was their
only one. Relatively few were young couples; only 3 per cent of the
husbands and wives were twenty-five years old or younger. Relatively few were elderly; only 8 per cent of the husbands and wives
were fifty-six or older. The largest group, 45 per cent, were between
thirty-six and forty-five; 19 per cent were between twenty-six and
thirty-five; 25 per cent were between forty-six and fifty-five. All but
4 per cent of the families had children. Of those having children,
86 per cent had one, two, or three children at home. All the children
were under six in only 13 per cent of the families with children, and
in only 8 per cent all were over eighteen. Thus in most families the
children ranged from early school age through high school age.
Eighty-two per cent of the parents of husbands and wives were
living.

For comparison, data were also obtained from clients in the
agency Service to the Aged. Ninety-six per cent of the Service to
the Aged clients studied were over sixty, whereas only 3 per cent
of the clients in the district offices were as old; 51 per cent of the
Aged were seventy-one or more, while none of the regular clients
was as old. All the Aged who were studied had intact marriages. It
was assumed that the Aged were in many respects similar to the
parents of clients, although if anything they were probably less
traditional than many of the clients' parents. For example, they
were less frequently Orthodox in religion than the clients say is
true of their parents. Nevertheless, the data on the Aged made possible comparisons with those in a stage of the life cycle which almost
no clients had themselves reached. Since comparisons will be made
only at certain points, the background of the clients in the Service
to the Aged need not be described in detail.

Origins and Cultural Traditions

Birthplace. The Jews of New York City, who account for approximately 40 per cent of the nation's five million Jews, make up roughly a quarter of the city's inhabitants.[1]

The bulk of these two million Jews represent immigrants or descendants of immigrants from Poland and Russia, who came to this country around the turn of the century.[2]

Some of the clients were themselves immigrants, and their recollections of the experience are vivid. One man reported that he was shocked to see "how young people moved away from their parents and they knew darn well that they would never see them again. Like burying them alive."

As Table 2 indicates, however, the majority of the client sample is drawn from the children of immigrants.

Table 2.   Birthplace of Clients and Their Parents

	Husbands	Wives	Clients' Fathers	Clients' Mothers
	PERCENTAGES			
United States	76	80	8	13
Europe	22	18	91	85
Elsewhere	2	2	1	2
Total	100	100	100	100
	(186)	(209)	(378)	(388)

Immigration Experience. The distinction between first- and second-generation Americans may be less meaningful than age at immigration, and the historical period of immigration, as others have pointed out.[3] Clients whose parents came to the United States from Europe may be relatively far from the immigration experience or very close to it. Some in the second generation had siblings born in Europe and they themselves were born only a year or two after their parents arrived. Others are the children of immigrants who had lived many years in this country before the children were born. Two second-generation individuals of different ages may differ greatly in the extent to which their parents retained European ways, and the degree to which they grew up in an insulated ethnic enclave.

Most of the European-born were from Eastern Europe. Although it is extremely difficult to draw geographic boundaries that accurately define the area of "Eastern" Europe, particularly since national boundaries changed frequently, an earlier questionnaire administered as a routine agency procedure indicated that most parents of clients came from areas that could be considered Eastern Europe.[4]

Even among clients who were not themselves immigrants, there is scarcely any family wholly untouched by the experience. And even third-generation children may still be given vivid pictures of the immigration process and the terrifying social upheavals that surrounded it.

Recollections of crises in Europe are still vivid for many. In an interview one woman described how her family managed to survive in the wartorn Ukraine during the period of the Russian Revolution:

> I remember, in the section where we lived, there was a civil war . . . there was always the threat of a pogrom. . . . I had seen people die of hunger . . . my mother would think that she would have to hide [it] if we had too much meat on the table. She would hide it because if people were starving and they saw you eating, they resented it. And the reason we weren't starving was that money wasn't worth anything and my father had a store where he sold drygoods and clothing and material. . . . The peasant who used to bring into the market food would take [home] his material. You give them a tablecloth and they would [give] ten pounds of butter—regular trade, barter.

Eastern European Tradition. The culture of Eastern Europe from which the parents of most clients came was by no means unified. Many, but not all, came from *shtetl*, or small rural Jewish communities. Others came from cities. Moreover, cultural differences existed between different regions within Eastern Europe. Although acculturation was occurring in Europe, even in the *shtetl* community and particularly among those who had gone to the city, the *shtetl* community was a base for Eastern European Jewish culture. Despite the fact that these cultural traditions may be meaningful to different clients in varying degrees, it is useful, particularly for those unfamiliar with these traditions, to examine them briefly.

No analysis of *shtetl* life would be complete without noting the tremendous importance accorded to learning, particularly the study of the Jewish religious books.[5] The learned held the highest prestige in the community. Learning was a lifelong pursuit that did not necessarily correspond with a man's occupation, although a very gifted scholar might be supported by his family and the community to enable him to devote himself entirely to study. The extent of learning of a boy's or girl's family was a primary criterion in evaluating a prospective marriage partner.

Family and Kinship. The emphasis on learning was paralleled by a strict division of sex roles. Learning was for men only; women were considered inferior. Scholarship was given so much more importance than practical occupations that it was considered "correct for the wife of a gifted scholar to earn a livelihood for the family while he remains with his books."[6]

This sharp sex role division separated the mother from her son, who joined the male world of scholarship between the ages of three and five, when he entered the *kheder,* or first school. The ties of mother and son were disrupted, since the mother was in no way involved in the education of the child and the long hours of study required extensive separation. This sharp break in the mother-son relationship has been considered an important factor contributing to "a fixation of the mother on the earliest phase of the child's life,"[7] since this was the only period when the child was completely within her province.

Traditionally, marriages were arranged. Prestige derived from learning was a prime consideration in making matches. A matchmaker often had a notebook that included an "enumeration of learned men"[8] in the families of each of the boys and girls for whom matches were being considered. It was also considered appropriate for siblings to marry in their age sequence, presumably to minimize envy and quarreling and to stress the authority of age.

Arranged marriages de-emphasized romantic love as a basis for mate selection so that the marital bond was not supported by romantic attachments. A *shtetl* saying offered this advice: "First marry, then love."[9] In the system of arranged marriages the father rather than the daughter examined the prospective bridegroom and assessed his potential qualities and abilities. If the son-in-law was a sufficiently talented scholar, the institution of *kest* was employed to further his studies. As part of the marriage arrangement, he was brought to live in the home of his bride's parents, who supported his studies for a given period.

The lack of emphasis on romantic love, the importance of education, and monetary considerations in matchmaking are clear in the description given by the father of one client concerning his own arranged marriage in a small Russian town:

> FATHER: That was the time I was ready to go to marry my wife . . . the . . . *shadkhen,* what they call?
>
> MARRIED SON: Matchmaker.
>
> FATHER: Yes, matchmaker . . . they used to bring them together, somewhere in my house or her house. If we are satisfied, then all right. So, she was a dressmaker in Russia. . . . And I was a soldier. I didn't even have a penny in my pants . . . my parents [were not] rich, and I didn't want to go to fight. . . . Her parents wasn't rich too, but they are all working. . . . They saved a few dollars, so they make a few dollars. Over there, when a girl has a few dollars she could get a better husband . . . more educated . . . the matchmaker used to pick out the ones. Every matchmaker knows which . . . the groom or the bride should be. . . . She shouldn't be so dumb or not educated. . . . I was married through a matchmaker because I tell you, she wasn't in my country . . . over there it was twenty or thirty miles. . . . I didn't know her, I didn't know nobody from there . . . if I didn't like her I'll tell the matchmaker that it's not for me, I don't like her. But I saw her. She was very nice, and she was young. Now she's an old lady but she was very nice, and she had a few dollars, and I was very willing to take a few dollars to go, I should go to the United States, because I had to hide myself so the Russian army couldn't catch me.

The uxorilocal residence of the traditional marriage patterns encouraged greater involvement with the wife's than with the husband's family. A close relationship between a father and his son-in-law was expected, particularly if the son-in-law came into the home of his bride and was supported in *kest.* But it was apparently also a general expectation: "It is a commonplace that a man prefers his son-in-law to his son." And a proverb says, "Every son-in-law has in him something of his father-in-law."[10] A father's closeness with his son-in-law was a conflict with his own son, since the son-in-law was taking the place of the son and might actually receive the son's inheritance. The closer ties with the wife's than with the husband's family also extended to other kin. "It often happens that the mother's relatives are the ones best known to her children, even, in cases, to the entire ignorance of the father's kin."[11]

The *kest* was considered ideal, since it meant that the son-in-law was a promising scholar. Thus both the father-in-law and mother-in-law readily accepted a son-in-law as a member of their family. This residence pattern meant a sharper break at marriage for the son than for the daughter. Relationships after marriage with the son's family were fraught with conflict. The ties with his father may have been broken by the intrusion of his brother-in-law, and marriage was seen as a further break in his ties with his mother. A traditional saying exemplifies the break in the son's ties at marriage. "When the son marries, he gives the wife a contract and the mother a divorce."[12] Even when the marriage was arranged, the mother presumably felt that the son had committed a form of treason and it was expected that she would be extremely jealous and resentful of her daughter-in-law.[13] A young woman could face her mother-in-law only after she had had a child; then the mother-in-law would have to admit that the marriage was justified since then she was a grandmother. "Nevertheless, she is ever alert to the comment that her daughter-in-law does not cook or indulge or otherwise take care of the son as adequately as she did; and an angry husband will rebuke his wife as though in his mother's behalf saying, 'you can't cook as well as she did.'"[14] But the mother-in-law was also "highly critical of her daughter-in-law's methods of rearing the grandchild, her son's child, the more so as the harassed daughter-in-law turns to her own mother for help."[15]

Relationships between adult siblings and siblings-in-law were also a product of these marriage arrangements and uxorilocal residence. A young girl was expected to take on some of her mother's negative attitudes toward her sister-in-law: "It appears to us that in the relations between the sisters-in-law, it is the unmarried girl who originates the hostilities. She complains in idioms taken from her mother that her sister-in-law does not feed her brother properly, and that she acts as though she were more important than the sister."[16] But relationships between sisters-in-law became less strong over time as each became involved in her own maternal family.

Avoidance appears to have occurred in cross-sex sibling relationships, which meant that if these ties were to be maintained, parents often had to serve as intermediaries. However, obligations of assistance among cross-sex siblings were definite.

Relationships among adult brothers, however, were not close, perhaps in part because each became involved with his wife's kin. Presumably relationships among adult sisters might be fraught with jealousy since both were tied to the same maternal family. However, age differences, the tradition of marriage in age sequence, which was explicitly considered to be a way of forestalling jealousy, and the relatively short duration of the *kest* may have served to minimize jealousy.

Ties beyond the nuclear family, however, did not appear to have been greatly emphasized. In some respects the entire *shtetl* community in Eastern Europe was regarded as a kinship unit; ties could be traced either through blood or marriage to practically all members of the community.

However accurate or representative existing descriptions of Eastern European traditions may be, some variation of these basic patterns was undoubtedly important for many of those who emigrated to this country.

Neighborhoods

Not only did the parents of most clients have direct experience living in Eastern Europe, but the patterns of early settlement within this country helped to keep alive European traditions and a sense of ethnic identity.

The extent of ethnic segregation was reflected in the descriptions many clients gave of their childhood neighborhoods. One man, now in his midforties, told of street fights in his childhood, clearly indicating sharp ethnic distinctions:

It was on 19th Street, it was a locality where you have Jews on one side, and a block or two away were a mixed locality like Irish and Italians. . . . As Jewish boys [if] we happened to go over to their neighborhoods . . . if we had to go shopping or something . . . [we

would] get into a fight. . . . Or they came to our neighborhood. It
worked both ways, in other words. They used to call us names. . . .
And we resented that, and naturally we went into a fight. . . . You had
to show your courage or else you would never be able to walk over
there again.

Common language, observance of dietary laws, religious and
cultural traditions, and a general sense of familiarity bound many
to Jewish neighborhoods. Living in Jewish neighborhoods rein-
forced traditions even in families that were more assimilated. One
woman, for example, explained that she did not learn "Jewish"
[Yiddish] from her parents, who spoke only English, but from
friends in her childhood neighborhoods.

From the areas of original settlement, pulled by the lure of
more prosperous neighborhoods befitting their rise in living standard and pushed by the influx of less privileged immigrants, the
more successful members of the Jewish community began to move:
in Brooklyn, from Brownsville to Flatbush or the Bronx; from
Manhattan's Lower East Side to the Upper West Side; from the
East Bronx to the West.[17] Many of the areas of second settlement
are themselves beginning to deteriorate or to be threatened with
deterioration as the more prosperous again move out and new, less
privileged immigrants move in; others maintain a precarious stability on the edge of more prosperous sections such as those bor-
dering the Grand Concourse in the Bronx.

In addition to areas of second settlement, middle-income housing projects are another new kind of residential area. Some of these
approximate suburbia in their standardization and their lack of
ethnic flavor.

Parents often move to follow their married children. Moves
of this sort, together with the changing character of many neighborhoods, mean that even members of the older generation have
experienced changes in their surroundings and the extent of their
ethnic segregation. Cultural gaps between immigrant parents and
their children are reflected in the different neighborhoods in which
they have spent a good part of their lives, but the process of change
of neighborhoods and assimilation affects both generations.

At present the client families studied live in scattered sections
throughout the metropolitan area. They do not represent a real
social group that has contacts with each other. Only a small pro-

portion, 2 per cent, live in the suburban areas of Long Island and New Jersey, and some of these had moved to these areas during their contact with the agency. Very few have lived outside the New York City area for any significant period. The largest number, 50 per cent, are from Brooklyn; the next largest group, 30 per cent, from the Bronx; and the remaining 18 per cent, from Manhattan.

The diversity of neighborhoods is great. The extent of ethnic segregation varies widely, particularly in view of the rapid changes occurring in many areas, and the moves of clients from one area to another. Differences between childhood immigrant neighborhoods and those of present residence were often reported, even when the present neighborhoods were considered to be largely Jewish.

Religion

Like the neighborhood in which clients live, their religious beliefs and practices, particularly those pertaining to the many rituals of daily life, are extremely diverse. However, because the variations are so many, it is difficult to trace definite lines of acculturation and change. It has been pointed out that rabbinical thinking is itself geared to making an "appropriate interpretation of eternal law in the light of ephemeral conditions. If the interpretation is clever enough, it can eliminate hardship for all concerned. Such cleverness can go to great lengths without imposing any sense of disrespect to the Law, for to help humanity is an absolute good."[18] Despite variations two points are clear. Almost all clients express some degree of identification either with the Jewish religion or with the Jewish community; and most feel that modifications of religious practice result in differences between generations.

The degree of observance is so complex that it is difficult to compare families; one that considers itself Orthodox and observes dietary laws at home does not necessarily attend religious services regularly.[19] The ceremony of bar mitzvah or confirmation performed when a boy reaches the age of thirteen is another ritual that varies enormously in observance and significance. According to Hebrew law, it is the attainment of religious duty and responsibility, but in practice it may be more of a family celebration than a religious event. Even the distinctions among the various modes of observance—Orthodox, Conservative, and Reform—are not always very clear and may refer to the degree of observance of ritual rather than to denominational affiliation, as was indicated in interviews.

Individuals within the same family often vary in their beliefs and practices. One woman told the interviewer that her husband might be considered Orthodox because he goes to an Orthodox synagogue for the High Holidays, but she herself does not go. "My beliefs are very moderate, I don't really believe . . . in it . . . and I feel like a good Jew." Her father never went to synagogue either, though her mother was very devout.

Many in the client group feel identified with the Jewish community but are not particularly religious. One man, for example, explained that although he himself was not particularly religious, his sons were given a religious education and a bar mitzvah primarily so that they would know something of the religion and know they were Jews.

In the questionnaire one question on religious identification was phrased: "*Would you say you are: Hassidic, Orthodox, Conservative, Reform, 'just Jewish,' other?*" Thus clients could express their Jewish identification without necessarily committing themselves to a particular degree of religious observance. Slightly more than half the clients considered themselves "just Jewish," whereas the rest mainly defined themselves as either Orthodox or Conservative. Relatively few saw themselves as Reform. There were even fewer Hassidim, or members of an ultrareligious group with traditions that date back to eighteenth-century Poland. The "others" included Zionists, non-Jewish clients married to Jewish spouses, and clients who were the product of mixed marriages (Table 3).

Table 3.   Religious Identification of Clients and Their Parents

	Per Cent of Clients	Per Cent of Clients' Parents
Hassidic	1	5
Orthodox	13	45
Conservative	26	19
Reform	5	2
"Just Jewish"	53	26
Other	2	3
Total	100	100
	(390)	(390)

Clients were also asked to describe the religious identification of their parents. The parents of husbands and wives were almost the same. Practically no difference exists between clients and their parents in the proportion described as Reform, but clearly there is a trend away from orthodoxy between generations, or so the clients perceive: only 13 per cent of the clients described themselves as Orthodox, although they described their parents as Orthodox in 45 per cent of the cases; they described themselves as Conservative somewhat more frequently than they did their parents, and as "just Jewish" twice as often as they identified their parents this way.

Differences between generations in religious belief and observance are sometimes reduced by the fact that, as clients frequently reported, their parents also changed their religious practices as they became more Americanized. Moreover, it is clear that some of the older generation were emphatically secular in their orientations. Sometimes the direction of differences between generations is reversed, with the younger generation being more religious than the older.

Often the religious ceremonials of the parental generation, particularly weddings and bar mitzvahs, were less elaborate and lavish than they are today because economic conditions were poorer. In contrast, more recent weddings and bar mitzvahs were often described as highly elaborate and expensive, including catered "sit-down" dinners and bands. However, the trend toward more elaborate ceremonials does not necessarily mean greater religious observance.

In fact, the younger generation may serve as a guide to the older in matters of ceremonial style and appropriate behavior even when the members of the older generation are more religious in traditional terms. One young woman whose parents could not afford an expensive wedding for her sister reported advising her mother about appropriate behavior at the catered wedding which was given by the son-in-law's relatives:

> They had a caterer come in . . . and my mother said, "Should I make something?" And I said, "Look, mama, either you make the wedding or you do nothing. You just don't belittle yourself by coming in with your tray of gefilte fish. It doesn't look right. They planned this wedding without consulting you, and you just come as a guest then. It just isn't right for you to drag your gefilte fish across Long Island. It just isn't right. A little dignity, let's have.

However, the trend toward more lavish ceremonials does reflect changes, particularly in economic conditions, that affect both generations rather than a move of the younger generation away from the way of life of the older.

Because the religious rituals cover so many details of daily life, they may have concrete consequences for relationships among relatives. For example, parents who keep a kosher home may feel that they cannot eat in the homes of their less observant children. The very religious do not travel on the Sabbath or holidays, and this may influence visiting and family celebrations. Conflict may arise between generations if those in the younger generation do not follow the tradition of naming children in memory of deceased relatives or do not name them after the expected kin.

The complexities of keeping a kosher home are so great, and the variations so many, that it is particularly difficult to say that one family, or one generation, is more observant than another. Those who are fairly strict about keeping kosher within their home do not necessarily do so outside it.

The innumerable variations in ways of keeping kosher, which result from the intricacies of ritual detail, are sometimes a matter of uncertainty and concern for those who wish to be observant:

> When we first got married I observed as much as I could. But it always bothered me. I felt that if you *bentch licht* [light candles] then you shouldn't do anything on *Shabbos* [Sabbath] but he [my husband] did and so I just let it go. I keep a kosher home, but I assure you my grandmother couldn't eat in my house. I buy kosher meat, I wouldn't use ham, I have two sets of dishes, but if the kids make a big to-do about having shrimp, I let them have it. But I don't eat it. I can't take to it. It's a habit . . . I kosher all my meat. . . . I will not serve milk and butter at the table with meat. . . . But my sister . . . for instance, is very observing. She has different [dish] rags for *milkhedikh* [dairy] and *fleyshikh* [meat], with different colors; she has two [drain] boards at her sink. And yet, she rides on Saturday if she has to. Somehow, it's to me like whatever level you want to go to. It bothers me sometimes, because, we . . . , do you or don't you? It bothers me. . . . If you do this, why don't you do that? Sometimes it is just difficult.

Despite the enormous complexity and variation, most clients revealed some degree of Jewish identification in their style of cooking. Only 18 per cent indicated that their cooking was not either Jewish style or kosher. Forty-three per cent of the clients indicated that they were either strictly kosher or kept many of the dietary laws. Those who say their cooking is "somewhat Jewish style but not kosher" are likely to mean that they have lox and bagels and use lots of dairy products such as sour cream; that they use matzoh meal instead of bread crumbs; that they tend to cook beef well; that they prefer sweet rather than salt butter and often make traditional Eastern European dishes, such as stuffed cabbage and borscht, and serve boiled vegetables more often than salads; that they eat a good deal of smoked or pickled fish; and so on. Thus even those who are not religiously observant frequently preserve certain Jewish traditions in their style of cooking.

Despite the variety of religious practices, clients perceive a trend away from the greater orthodoxy of their parents, with the result that religion is often an area of difference between generations.

Style of Life

Home visits made it possible to observe present household styles. The furnishings of client households exhibit every taste: some living-room floors were covered with linoleum, others with wall-to-wall broadloom; some families read the *Daily News,* others *The New York Times;* in some homes, the furnishings were the carefully chosen symbols of those newly arrived in middle-class status; in others, they were the casual, much worn acquisitions of those to whom books and records are more important than carpets and upholstery. The television set, however, was a virtual constant, regardless of how much homes differed in other respects.

Despite the variety in tastes, the homes of clients were quite similar in number of people and number of rooms: most families lived in three, four, or five rooms, and most families consisted of three, four, or five persons; most families had two bedrooms, and in the majority of cases, 78 per cent, the maximum number of people sleeping in the same room was two. The overcrowded conditions of tenement living in early immigrant neighborhoods were not typical of the clients.

Although no comparable data exist on the homes of the clients' parents, it is likely that even the homes in which clients grew up did not reflect Eastern European traditions in their possessions. Ties to Eastern European traditions were virtually never expressed in household furnishings or arrangements of clients' homes. On a questionnaire item, 87 per cent of the clients said that their furnishings were mostly things they bought new; only 6 per cent said they were mostly used; and only 7 per cent reported that their furnishings were mostly things given or lent to them. Although assistance and passing on of furnishings among kin is important, the symbols of Eastern European traditions and ethnic identity were not attached to material possessions. There were virtually no objects of traditional or family significance; no one, for instance, pointed with pride to their grandmother's samovar. Indeed, only 23 per cent of the clients indicated that they had received any form of inheritance (material goods, property, or money) from kin. The one place where ethnic traditions were expressed in material possessions was in the objects associated with keeping kosher, such as two sets of silverware and dishes, but even these were often new.

Whatever the extent of the shift from parental styles may actually be, the present household arrangements and furnishings of clients do not symbolize ethnic identity of Eastern European traditions, except for those items directly connected with religious practice.

Education and Occupation

Like other new immigrants, the Eastern European Jews who poured into America in the decades around the turn of the century were often funneled into the city's pool of unskilled labor; but unlike other immigrants, the Jews often brought with them from Europe a variety of skilled trades. They were tailors, milliners, hatmakers, shoemakers; many others were retailers, having been peddlers and small store owners in the *shtetl*. These skills and the aspirations accompanying them enabled many who began as unskilled workers in the garment and retail trades to move up more rapidly in the occupational hierarchy than other immigrants were able to do.[20] In a discussion of the unusual speed with which Jews as an immigrant group have moved into middle-class status, it has been suggested that this preference for self-employment is a result of the Jew's desire not to be dependent for advancement on a possible anti-Semitic employer; we can also see it as the product of discrimination in European countries which forced Jews into service and trade occupations. With increasing assimilation, however, the third-generation Jews have been moving into large companies and new professions; instead of medicine and law, Jews turn increasingly to journalism, literature, engineering, architecture, and academic life.[21]

Many clients perceive that they and their friends have changed from the more typically immigrant occupations of their parents and their parents' friends. Although data were scanty on the occupations of parents, probably in part as a reflection of the feeling of clients that their parents' status was low, it is evident, both from genealogical data and from the information given on parental occupations, that many clients have shifted away from the occupation of their parents, even though upward mobility undoubtedly occurred during the careers of many of the clients' parents.

The shift from unskilled and skilled trades to small retail proprietor, to employed white-collar workers and professionals is frequently demonstrated in genealogies collected from clients. One genealogy illustrates this rise over time from the occupations of the parental generation (Table 4).

The trend away from the occupations of the parental generation is clear in this typical genealogy. Not all those within the same generation have moved to the same degree, but when one keeps in mind that generation and age overlap the shift away from the occupations of early immigrants is striking.

Most client husbands were working at the time the mail questionnaire was returned; of the 184 husbands who answered the question, 8 per cent said they were not presently working, and of these, two were retired and seven were disabled; of the remainder, five were out of a job, two were on seasonal layoff, and one was a student.

Sufficient information exists to classify 172 client husbands' present or most recent main occupation according to the United States census categories; 59 per cent, or more than half, describe themselves as holding jobs that fall into the white-collar category. These data correspond to the picture of the shift from the unskilled and semiskilled occupations of the parental generation (Table 5).

*Table 4.   Generational Differences in Occupation Found in
Genealogy of One Family*[a]

Husband's Kin

Parental Generation:
Fish dealer, Men's clothing accessories,
Carpenter, Haberdasher, Policeman,
Custom peddler, Retail or in men's
clothing, Paint store, Dress cutter,
Grocer, Furrier (three)

Husband's Generation:
Garage business, Physician, Schoolteacher, Plant nursery, Book business,
Chemist, Furrier, Clothing, Picture
framing business, Farmer, Piece goods
fabrics, Academic research Ph.D.,
Accountant in Bureau of Internal
Revenue, Real estate operator, Buyer in
men's clothing

*Children's Generation,
Husband's Side:*
Lawyer, Teacher, Accountant (two)
Engineer, Physician, Cab driver, "Cum
laude" Ph.D., Dentist (two), Furrier,
Government employee

Wife's Kin

Parental Generation:
Soda business self-employed, Real
estate owner-landlord, Garment industry (two) presser, Grocery business,
Cloak operator, Fabric merchant,
"Literate in Yiddish," Skilled plate glass
workman, Cutter in men's hats, Tailor
store, Furrier (two), Presser in ladies
dresses, Accountant and very well-
educated Hebrew scholar

Wife's Generation:
Wholesale candy business, accountant
(two), Government employee, Grocery
business, Accountant in real estate,
Cutter in ladies garments, Self-employed
fabrics merchant, Electrical supply
salesman, Salesman, College graduate in
army, Liquor store proprietor, Self-
educated writer for TV, Master plumber,
Partner in drygoods concern, Butcher
and furrier, Fur salesman, Jewelry
salesman, Trucker and salesman for
shoe store, Cloak operator, Furrier,
Chiropractor, Musician in symphony
orchestra, Chauffeur, Camera and
photo supply salesman, Schoolteacher

Children's Generation, Wife's Side:
Engineer, Garage business, Clothing
manufacturer

[a] The classifications of occupation are recorded verbatim from interviews.

The rank of client occupations can also be estimated by income.
At the time of the study, slightly more than half the client husbands earned $99 or less each week; one-fourth, between $100 and
$125 weekly; and a similar proportion, more than $125.

In roughly a third of the cases the family income was even
higher because the wife was working; 14 per cent of the wives
worked full-time and 20 per cent held part-time jobs. Compared

Table 5. *Census Classification of Client Husbands' Jobs*

	PER CENT
White Collar	
Professional, technical	16 ⎫
Managerial, proprietor	17 ⎬ 59
Clerical and sales	26 ⎭
Blue Collar	
Craftsmen, foremen	16 ⎫
Operatives	17 ⎬ 41
Service and labor	8 ⎭
Total	100
	(172)

with some other data on the Jewish population of New York City, the clients were not disproportionately in the lowest income brackets.[22]

Clients clearly differ from their parents in education. Whereas two-thirds, 66 per cent of the husbands, and the same proportion of the wives, did not have any college education, the clients do not compare unfavorably with the Jewish population as a whole in the proportion who have had some or a complete college education.[23] Only 14 per cent of the husbands and wives as compared with 54 per cent of their parents had no formal education or only grammar school education. In addition, for 31 per cent of the parents, clients reported that they had European education, meaning in most instances that they had training within the Jewish community. Only 12 per cent of the parents of clients had some or a complete high school education, and only 2 per cent had any college training. Education is clearly an area of great difference between clients and their parents. Changes in style of life, in neighborhood, even in religious orientation to some extent, have occurred simultaneously for clients and their parents. Most parents of clients, however, were not able to obtain formal education as extensive as that of their children. But the gap of education remains one of the greatest gaps between the generations.

One might think that part of the clients' problems might stem from having received fewer advantages than their siblings; and as a result, that they would be typically less mobile than their siblings.

This assumption, however, does not appear to be true to any great extent. When comparing the relative ranking on a prestige scale[24] of the occupations of husbands and their brothers, in nearly a quarter of the cases, all their occupations were in the same prestige level. In 40 per cent of the cases, some or all of the clients' brothers were in a higher prestige occupation, but in a large proportion, 30 per cent, all or some of the clients' brothers were in lower-ranking occupations. In 7 per cent, the occupations of their brothers were mixed; some higher, some lower, some the same as that of the client husband. A fairly high proportion of clients therefore had at least one brother who is more successful. But over half had some who were on the same level or lower than they were. Since these represent gross prestige categories, it is entirely possible that husbands more frequently perceived their brothers to be in higher prestige occupations than these categories show. Nevertheless, from an outside view, the terms of overall ratings, the clients were not markedly lower than their brothers in occupational prestige.

The kin relationships of the client families must be seen with reference both to their own sociocultural characteristics and to those of their kin. As we have seen, these are families of immigrant backgrounds, who are involved in the process of cultural transition and assimilation. Despite the complexity of charting changes from one culture to another, when a firm baseline exists neither for the culture of origin nor for the one which the immigrant is assimilating, marked differences between the clients and their parents are evident at a number of points, including occupation, education, and religious beliefs and practices.

Immigration has significance for the differences in the social world of different generations in another way; although most clients have remained in close contact with their own parents throughout their lives, many clients grew up without contact with their grandparents, their parents having been the ones to leave home.

Generation itself is a loose concept that may in some instances overlap with age and social and cultural changes may occur simultaneously within more than one generation. Nevertheless, the social and cultural experience of clients and that of kin in their parents' generation diverge markedly. Marked differences between generations may, in turn, have consequences for solidarities among kin of the same generation.

Kinship behavior is relational; it occurs between individuals and groups; it is a product of interaction. The values, social positions, and personalities of all parties are important for its outcome. Analysis of differences in kinship patterns between generations is complicated, since the behavior being analyzed stems from the characteristics of more than one generation. Thus one cannot say that frequent residence of young married couples in the home of the wife's parents is only the result of characteristics of the young couples such as dependence on their parents; it derives equally from characteristics of their parents. Some characteristics, such as attitudes and values, may be referred to the individual, but their significance for behavior will be manifest in interaction with others. Here comparisons of the older and the younger generations are meaningful. But in other areas the most important analysis of generational differences lies in the study of interaction between generations.

We will consider elsewhere (see Appendix) the degree to which our sample is representative of the client population. The client group is not necessarily typical of other groups, either other Jewish families of Eastern European origin or descent, others of this age group, or nonclient families. Clients interact with their kin to an extent and in ways that are not determined entirely by the clients but by their kin as well, many of whom are nonclients. Therefore, the extensiveness of involvement with kin cannot be assumed to stem uniquely from the problems that led the client families to seek casework help. Indeed, as we have seen, difficulties in relationships with kin were rarely part of the initial presenting problem.

Although we cannot say that similar results would be likely in other groups, the observations on the clients have certain general relevance. Some of the characteristics of these clients, particularly generational differences as these affect kin relationships, may have parallels in other ethnic groups. In addition, the kinship patterns of this group contradict certain assumptions that have been made about kinship in urban industrial societies; namely, that extended kin groups break down and that the nuclear family becomes isolated in urban milieus; and that social mobility, desired in industrial societies, is impeded by extensive kin ties.

In the analysis that follows we will examine in detail the relationships with kin that have been found among client families, and the ways in which caseworkers seek to alter these relationships. In some areas, kinship patterns of these clients appear markedly similar to what is known about Eastern European Jewish traditions; in other respects, the kin relationships of clients appear to be the unique product of immigration and assimilation with the consequent breaking of certain ties and strengthening of others. Generational differences and the continuous process of acculturation affect kin relationships. Since casework intervention involves changes in kinship structure, an understanding of the changes that are already occurring as a result of other forces is of great importance.

NOTES TO CHAPTER 2

1. Seligman, Ben, "The Jewish Population of New York City: 1952" in *The Jews: Social Patterns of an American Group*, edited by Marshall Sklare. The Free Press, Glencoe, Ill., 1958, p. 2.

2. Weinryb, Bernard D., "Jewish Immigration and Accommodation to America," *ibid.*, p. 9.

3. Kramer, Judith R., and Seymour Leventman, *Children of the Gilded Ghetto*. Yale University Press, New Haven, 1961, p. 129.

4. When speaking of Austria, clients sometimes referred to the Austro-Hungarian Empire before World War I. Austria and Germany after World War I were not considered Eastern Europe for our purposes. In an earlier questionnaire administered to 441 agency clients, it was established that, of the 1,480 parents of clients on whom data were collected, the overwhelming majority were of Eastern European origin. Eastern European-born parents of clients made up the following proportions of the total: Russia (including Lithuania and Latvia), 37 per cent; Poland, 22 per cent; Hungary-Romania, 8 per cent; and Yugoslavia, less than 1 per cent (three cases). Other European birthplaces included: Austria, 9 per cent; Germany-Vienna, 2 per cent; elsewhere in Europe, 5 per cent. The non-European-born parents of agency clients were distributed as follows: United States, 15 per cent; Palestine, less than 1 per cent (five cases); and elsewhere, 1 per cent.

5. Zborowski, Mark, "The Place of Book-Learning in Traditional Jewish Culture" in *Childhood in Contemporary Cultures*, edited by Margaret Mead and Martha Wolfenstein. University of Chicago Press, Chicago, 1955, pp. 118–141.

6. *Ibid.*, p. 121.

7. Wolfenstein, Martha, "Two Types of Jewish Mothers," *ibid.*, p. 438.

8. Zborowski, Mark, *op. cit.*, p. 120.

9. Landes, Ruth, and Mark Zborowski, "Hypothesis Concerning the Eastern European Jewish Family," *Psychiatry*, vol. 13, November, 1950, p. 462.

10. *Ibid.*, p. 454.

11. *Ibid.*, p. 452.

12. *Ibid.*, p. 454.

13. *Loc. cit.*

14. *Ibid.*, pp. 458–459.

15. *Ibid.*, p. 459.

16. *Ibid.*, p. 460.

17. Kaplan, Milton, "Private Enterprise in the Bronx" in *Commentary on the American Scene: Portraits of Jewish Life in America*, edited by Elliot E. Cohen. Alfred A. Knopf, Inc., New York, 1953, p. 244.

18. Zborowski, Mark, *op. cit.*, p. 134.

19. In a study of 905 male members of eight Orthodox synagogues in the Midwest, Polsky reports that despite the Orthodox requirement of daily synagogue attendance, "Some 70 percent attend the synagogue only several times a year and on the important holidays; approximately 20 percent attend at least once a week; only 10 percent, or 92 individuals, scattered in eight Orthodox synagogues, attend daily." Polsky, Howard W., "A Study of Orthodoxy in Milwaukee: Social Characteristics, Beliefs, and Observances" in Sklare, Marshall, editor, *op. cit.*, p. 329.

20. Wagley, Charles, and Marvin Harris, *Minorities in the New World*. Columbia University Press, New York, 1958, p. 216.

21. Glazer, Nathan, "The American Jew and the Attainment of Middle-Class Rank: Some Trends and Explanations" in Sklare, Marshall, editor, *op. cit.*, pp. 138–146.

22. "In 1951, according to one study, 12 percent of the Jewish households of the city had incomes of more than $10,000 as compared with 5 percent of the non-Jewish population . . . 20 percent of the Jewish households and 49 percent of the non-Jewish households earned less than $4,000." *Ibid.*, p. 141.

23. "In New York City, two studies, in 1948 and 1953, showed that about one-sixth of the Jews over 18 had completed college, compared with a little more than about one-twentieth of the non-Jews—and this even though considerably fewer of the Jews were native-born." *Ibid.*, pp. 140–141.

24. Occupational prestige rankings were made using a technique reported in Clarke, Alfred C., "The Use of Leisure and Its Relation to Levels of Occupational Prestige," *American Sociological Review*, vol. 21, June, 1956, pp. 301–307.

PART TWO

The Kin Relationships
of Client Families

CHAPTER 3

The Kinship Values

of Client Families

Kinship is important not only in remote or primitive societies; even in a large metropolis of an industrial society the family may be deeply enmeshed in, and may derive important supports from, its network of kin. Because these kin relationships are often also a source of conflict, and because, as will be seen more fully later, casework intervention often attempts to change these relationships, an understanding of the family's involvement is important.

In this and the next two chapters we will discuss highlights of our findings on the involvement of client families with their kin. This chapter discusses kinship values, or what clients believe are appropriate relationships with kin. Chapter 4 considers the actual involvement of client families in their network of kin relationships; the extensiveness of their kin ties, the proximity of kin and communication with them, and the binding power of assistance and reciprocity. Chapter 5 examines kin groups and assemblages in which client families participate, including ad hoc kin assemblages, family-kin businesses, and family circles and cousins clubs. Chapter 6 considers how conflicts with kin reflect the ways in which kin relationships are organized in other respects.

The emphasis in this study diverges somewhat from many

ethnographic descriptions of kinship "systems." This study was concerned primarily with understanding the present interaction of clients with their kin rather than past relationships in the family of childhood, because this focus was considered more pertinent from the casework point of view. The dimensions of the kinship system that were studied in most detail also reflect the characteristics of the society, the particular social and cultural positions of the families studied, and their life-cycle stage. In addition, the portions of our data reported most fully in this volume are those we feel will be most helpful to workers.

A number of areas of the kin relationships of client families were studied. The contacts with kin ranged from daily face-to-face meetings and telephone conversations to gatherings that occur only on special ritual or ceremonial occasions. A variety of levels of data were obtained, including opinions about what relationships ought to be, reports of actual behavior, and observations of behavior. Diversified procedures were employed in obtaining the data, including precoded questionnaire items and open-ended questions, as well as interview and observational techniques. A more detailed discussion of the procedures may be found in the Appendix.

From these observations a picture was drawn of the regularities that typify the kin relationships of client families. A model of the most typical client kin relationships has been constructed, that is, the kinship "system" in which these families participate.

Kin relationships of a group constitute a system when regularities are found among the members of the group. In addition, the idea of system implies that one area of kinship behavior will affect another; where a family lives in relation to kin, for example, will affect the way in which marriage partners are selected. Thus system refers not only to similarity in attitudes and behavior among different members of the group, but also to how a particular family's kin relationships in one area are tied up with that family's kin behavior in other areas.

Various types of regularity in kin relationships have been examined. As we have seen, descriptions of kin relationships in less complex societies are often more clearcut, since the relationships between those in specific kinship positions are conditioned by traditions that spell out, with few alternatives, the expected kinds of obligations, behavior, and emotion. An individual who does not behave accordingly is likely to receive negative sanctions. In more complex societies, however, norms governing relationships among kin are less definite and consistent. Different individuals within a family's kin network may have different views about how relationships in a particular position should be conducted, and about the rights and obligations of kinship. The norms that exist are often less detailed, leaving more "room for manoeuvre within the limits of organized negative sanctions."[1]

To obtain a view of regularity in kin relationships, both values and the actual choices in behavior have been examined. On one level, for example, a given proportion of families believe it is nice for a young married couple to live near their kin. On another level, a given proportion of families actually live within walking distance of one or more of their kin. In both cases the finding consists of a statistical regularity. But an analysis of a kinship system goes beyond recording the most frequent forms of belief and action. Regularities in social behavior occur because individuals interact with each other and thus to a degree follow each other's expectations. Even when the norms of kinship are not entirely consistent and different kin react to the same event in different ways, their sanctions are nonetheless real; relationships with kin are seldom neutral. Therefore, an analysis of kinship system is concerned with reactions or sanctions that a family will receive if it acts in a particular way. If, for example, a family chooses not to reside near kin, what will the reactions of others be?

In the analysis of kinship bonds an attempt was made to build up a model of the similarity of behavior from one area to another. The model consisted of a compilation of information on the particular kin with whom the husband and wife in the client family had most contact in a variety of activities. The regularity, in this instance, consists in the finding that in most areas wives have more frequent contacts with their own kin than with their husband's. Here again, however, there are alternatives; some wives have more contact with their husband's kin than with their own kin, and in some areas the proportion of wives who have more contact with their own kin is smaller than in others. Thus the systematic features of a kinship system do not occur with complete uniformity; in all areas alternatives are found. This is, moreover, a system only in that it is a description of regularities in kin relationships among these particular families.

CONTENT OF KINSHIP VALUES

Early interviews suggested a number of critical areas for the values of clients about kin relationship. These areas include: marriage procedures, residence, obligations for kin interaction, mobility, kin and nonkin institutions, husband-wife versus parent-child bonds, differentiation of the nuclear family from kin, and obligations toward aged parents. Clients' values were compared with those of another group of clients in the special Service to the Aged. The Aged are not necessarily comparable to the actual parents of the clients. Nevertheless, the differences between the Aged and other clients were taken as a rough approximation of differences likely to exist between clients and their own parents.

Clients and the Aged were given a series of statements in the questionnaire and asked to indicate whether they agreed, disagreed, or had no opinion. Responses reveal values about ideal behavior. Taken together with interviews, these values also reflect areas of potential conflict. To avoid repetition, data on the values of clients and the Aged have been placed in Chapter 8, where comparisons are also made with caseworkers. (See Appendix for a fuller discussion of methods.)

In all areas of values, clients hold divergent views. In addition, the views of a given client are not necessarily consistent from one area of kinship behavior to another. But in most areas the majority placed a high value on obligations of kinship.

A variety of factors in an individual's social experience influence his values, and more detailed examination of variations within the client group, for example, with age and sex, might be useful for certain purposes. The data on values are presented for the client group as a whole, however, because the primary concern was with portraying the kin relationships that typify the client group. Moreover, the client group was comparatively homogeneous in age of husband and wife and age and marital status of children. Since it included very few individuals who were either extremely young or extremely old, comparisons of age and generation were made with another group, that is, the Aged, rather than within the client group.

Marriage

The clients believe that ideally marriage should take place within the Jewish group. Most clients agreed that *"In general, Jewish people should not marry outside their faith."* This view was often expressed in emphatic terms by clients. Parents ideally have the right to oversee the selection of their children's marriage partners. This right is in a sense a logical correlate of the strong prohibitions against marrying certain categories of individuals.

Ideally, parental guidance of their children is aided by the residence of children in the parental home until marriage. The majority agreed that *"Children should not leave home before they get married."* Reasons given in interviews for agreement with this statement were that children are not fully adult until marriage and that parents should continue to guide the child's conduct at least until the time of marriage, including the dating process and the selection of the marriage partner. One woman explained:

> There is a certain sanctity in the home. . . . I think the parents should be around to see whom their children befriend and what type of associates they have, and generally I think it is a more wholesome thing for a single child to remain at home.

There were strong emotional reactions to the idea of children leaving home, including the notion that a child must be "crazy" or a "juvenile delinquent." Others stressed the importance of home life as a reason that children should remain with their parents until marriage, saying that "They are better off staying at home and having a close family life."

Those who felt that it was all right for children to leave home before marriage often limited this to special circumstances such as education, better employment, trips, and vacations. Such extenuating circumstances generally meant that geographic moves were necessary. This approval explicitly did not mean residence outside the parental home within the same community, that is, "They should not have a room outside the home." Such residence would reflect badly on the home: "Then you start figuring out they have trouble at home."

There may be different standards for daughters and sons. Exceptional circumstances under which a son might leave home before marriage would not necessarily apply to a daughter. For some, the idea of a daughter leaving home was unthinkable.

> If I had a son, who could better himself in some job or wanted to see the world, I wouldn't want him to go, but I wouldn't stop him. . . . As far as daughters are concerned, I couldn't think of them leaving home . . . until they are ready for marriage . . . unless a situation arises where you can't—that is, situations which arise which I can't even give an example of.

Even those who definitely felt that children should leave home before marriage assumed that parents play a strong role in guiding a child's activities but felt that, for example, "They stunt the child's growth."

Arranged marriages, a part of the Eastern European tradition may remain vividly in the memories of some clients, but they were clearly not part of the current ideals. Although the general values did not include the idea of arranged marriage, they did emphasize the role of parents in assisting in the selection of marriage partners through the residence of children in the home and influence over their social life.

For some, marriage would seem to imply a greater continuity in the daughter's ties with her parents than in the son's. A fair number of clients agreed with the idea that "It is true that a daughter is a daughter all her life, a son is a son until he gets a wife," a proverb mentioned in initial interviews. Although some disagreed with this as "an old saying, a proverb which has not much sense," others seemed to feel that it was reasonable that the mother-daughter tie would be stronger after marriage than that between mother and son.

Residence

Combined households are definitely not an ideal, but geographic proximity to kin is of value for many. A fair number agreed that "*It is usually nice for a young married couple to live near their parents.*" Even those who thought that the nuclear family should function as an independent unit felt, from the parents' point of view that children should live near their parents, because seeing their children as adults is one of the rights and joys of being a parent:

> I would like them to be somewhere in the vicinity . . . but out of town I would say definitely no . . . this is your life. As parents, you have brought up your children. You want to see the fruit of your labor, it's the development of your own. . . . Now they are married, you want to see their houses.

Even from the parent's point of view, however, the potential for conflict in close residential proximity is apparent. Descriptions of a good mother stress that in doing her duty she will necessarily be inclined to interfere even with adult children, since almost by instinct a mother has a longstanding habit of guiding her children:

> It's so natural for the mother to open her mouth and say, "Don't do it." She's been doing this for over twenty years. Not that the child has been taking this, but her duty to the child is to guide the child. To give advice to the child. Just because the child has put on a wedding ring, that is not going to break the habit. It's instinctive in the parents to do this. . . . The mother's job, she guides; it's primarily her job to guide all day long. From the moment they are up until they go to bed.

Quite naturally, "The parents see too many things they don't like and they talk about them." Therefore, it may be preferable to "cut that cord" and avoid interference through moving away. Otherwise, parents quite naturally "like to throw in their own ideas when it's really not necessary." The position of the mother is understood precisely because she is seen to be continuing her job as a mother out of habit and instinct.

Despite the potential for conflict, nearly half of the clients agreed that *"It's good for a young mother to have her own mother close by to help her learn how to take care of her baby."* One woman explained:

> I have my own mother who helps me . . . without her I would be too scared. I always leaned on her and depended on her, and she told me my mistakes and everything.

One qualification to the idea that it is good for a young mother to have her mother close by was that parents from Europe have different education, habits, and "they don't change"; so that this may limit the quality of the mother's advice on child rearing, since the younger generation has to "pick up new habits with progress, with education."

The majority agreed that *"If a mother and married daughter live in the same household, there's usually trouble."* Possible troubles, while usually framed from the child's point of view in terms of interference, were also expressed from the point of view of the parents as imposition. It was claimed, for example, that a "selfish and demanding" daughter might "impose upon her mother by making a baby sitter out of her." The potential for "making emotional demands," being "grasping," and being "dominating" were recurrent themes. The inevitability of the mother's continuing to guide and advise her adult daughter was seen as a particularly acute problem in combined households:

> Two women living in the same house cause a difficult problem, unless one goes to business and stays out of the other's work. Naturally, the older one likes to think that she knows how and she knows what, and the younger one, of course, will resent the advice unless she has experience.

Another problem of combined households was that there were too many authorities supervising the child, that the adults in the household might be "like a bunch of wolves." Combined mother-daughter households were also regarded as a possible infringement on the authority, dignity, and independence of the male.

Although combined households were not an ideal, if they occurred at all, matrilocal forms of combined households would usually be preferable. The majority agreed that *"A widow would usually prefer living with a married daughter than with a married son."* In views about residence patterns, there thus appeared to be a definite slant toward the wife's side.

Obligations for Interaction

Despite dim views about the prospects of combined households, strong values support obligations to interact with kin. These obligations are reflected in the idea that geographic proximity to kin is desirable and are also expressed more generally. Cutting oneself off from kin is considered reprehensible and selfish, and those who attempt to reduce contacts with kin may be severely sanctioned. The majority agreed, for example, that "*It's selfish for someone to cut himself off from his relatives.*" Someone who cuts himself off from his kin would be "antisocial." One should stay close to one's relatives because "they are by blood closer to you." Some linked obligations to remain close to kin with Jewish ideology, describing strong reactions of kin for failure to maintain ties even in cases of presumable legitimate reasons. Descriptions of the difficult position of anyone who became remote and the fact that kin "don't understand" were common. This is connected with the idea that "ideology stresses in the Jewish family the fact that you are related, in some form or another, you must be close."

Face-to-face interaction is sometimes seen as the only way of showing love. Apparently there may be little understanding of attachments maintained at a distance. As one wife explained, it is expected that attachments will be validated through continuing daily contact:

> The only way of showing love for one another [in that family] was by being with one another. They can't understand that a son can love his mother and not see his mother for a month . . . in order to show love you have to be with her every minute.

The strength of obligations to maintain ties with kin was also expressed in agreement with the statement, "*Regardless of what brothers or sisters may have done, one should never stop talking to them.*" Nearly three-quarters of the clients agreed with this.

Another expression of obligation to keep in touch with kin was found in agreement with the statement, "It's a thing of pride and joy to have a family circle or cousins club." Although a high percentage had no opinion, very few disagreed. Clearly, therefore, there are strong obligations for interaction with kin, and strong sanctions for those who attempt to cut themselves off from kin or reduce social contacts.

Mobility

Since values of clients strongly support obligations to maintain close ties with kin, the question arises of the implication of kin ties for mobility.

It has generally been considered that Jewish culture places strong values on mobility, and particularly on education. Over half of the clients agreed that *"No sacrifice is too great for the educa-tion of a son."* Most clients did not feel that geographic proximity to kin should take precedence over mobility for the sake of occupa-tional advancement. The majority disagreed with the statement, *"It's better to take a good job near your parents and relatives than to take a better job where you will have to move away from them."* However, the clients disagreed less frequently than respondents to a similar item in another research study.[2] Almost one-quarter be-lieved that it is best to stay near parents and relatives even if this interferes with job opportunities.

The memory of the disruption of family ties during immigra-tion was one reason given in interviews for thinking that occupa-tional advancement was not worth the cost of moving away. This was "like burying them alive." Others pointed out that "to make a big change or transition would be very hard" and, as one man said, "I like to be near my relatives." Some who felt that they definitely could not move away from kin phrased this as being "devoted" to kin:

> If you are cold and indifferent, you might as well move away from them. Any strangers who will give you the same benefits as your relatives ... with my relatives, relatives are much more important.

Even those who favored leaving for the sake of success stressed the difficulty of breaking away from attachments to kin, fears of moving, fears of a strange community, a strange city or state, and the problem of making new friends. All these unknown factors become more acute because people like to be with kin: "People have attachments to their relatives." Some explicitly felt that being close to relatives one loved was more important than material achievements, that "Perhaps sometimes you're satisfied with a little less and being close to the people you love." Those who gave pri-ority to occupational advancement, even when it meant moving away from kin, sometimes saw this in terms of greater obligations to the nuclear family than to kin: "Your first interest is you, your husband and your children, and then come the relatives." But even so, moving away from kin was seen as a hardship: "You're going to miss them." The fact that ties of kinship should not interfere with success was reflected in agreement to another statement, *"It should be enough satisfaction to parents if a son is a success even if he moves away from them."* Some noted that with modern means of transportation geographic distance did not make it totally impossible to see children although it did limit contact. However, even those who favored geographic separation for the sake of success frequently stressed how difficult separation would be:

> It does you good to feel that your children are really making their way in life, but by the same token you will miss them very, very much.

Thus success is valued and achievement is seen as a reason for parents' happiness. One should be happy no matter where the children are, "as long as you realize they're making their dreams, their professions."

From the point of view of a daughter's making a successful marriage, the issue is sometimes considered more complicated. Here the importance of ties between grandparents and grandchildren was stressed, "There's a question of grandchildren involved." This emphasis possibly reflects the expectation that the mother-daughter tie will remain strong so that the grandmother will have particularly close access to her daughter's children.

Education and success are highly valued. If there is a real inconsistency between values about occupational advancement and remaining near kin, a majority of clients would give priority to occupational achievement. But even those who stress the importance of success most often viewed moving away from kin as a hardship. In reality, the choice of moving for the sake of success or remaining near kin is not likely to be as clearcut as in the hypothetical question, and obligations of kinship may reduce geographic moves when the advantages of mobility are uncertain. Occupational success, moreover, may not always require geographic mobility, particularly in a metropolitan area. As indicated in some interviews, the demand of kin for time and attention may interfere more with occupational achievement than inhibition of geographic movement.

Despite the emphasis on success, status differences should ideally not disrupt ties of kinship. Almost all clients agreed that *"Even if some relatives are much better off than others, that shouldn't stop them from getting together as often as they can."* Status differences, therefore, should ideally not disrupt contact among kin: "There shouldn't be any snobbishness among relatives." Moreover, contact with kin of different social positions may

be one way to keep from narrowing one's own circle of acquaint-
ances, since "you shouldn't focus your attention entirely on people
in the same class." Despite these ideals, some felt that actually
status differences would reduce common interests and, therefore,
might reduce contact: "When relatives don't have common interests, they just don't get together." Nevertheless, the predominant
view was that kinship ties should transcend status differences. The
obligations to interact with kin are clearly strongly held even when
such other important priorities as occupational success are at stake.

Kin and Nonkin Institutions

Many of the clients indicated that they would give priority to
kin over friends or impersonal institutions in many areas. This was
found in questions about whether one would prefer to turn to kin
or a bank to borrow money, the trust one would have in kin as compared with strangers, how business dealings with kin would work
out, and the comparative importance that would be attached to the
relationships with relatives and friends.

Strong feelings surround obligations to contribute assistance to
relatives when needed, and equally strong feelings exist about the
failure of anyone to contribute his share. Even those who were
otherwise opposed to frequent contacts with kin felt that bonds of
kinship should make it possible to give and receive assistance when
in real need. Failure to assist, like failure to maintain contact, was
termed selfish. As one client said, "If you're in desperate need, I
don't see anything wrong with turning to relatives."

At the same time, economic relationships with kin are expected
to be fraught with conflict. Most clients disagreed with the idea
that "*If you have to borrow money, it's better to do it from a relative than a bank.*" However, nearly a quarter of the clients did feel
it was better to borrow money from a relative than from a bank. In
interviews some indicated that they would not have to pay interest
to relatives, and some felt that they might not be able to obtain
credit from a bank. Nevertheless, the problems of such borrowing
were mentioned frequently. If difficulties in repaying debts should
arise, emotional involvements would only complicate them, with
the possibility that the relationships of relatives might be broken
up:

Such a touchy subject. From a bank you have everything written out—as far as payments, as far as to what you are expected to pay, what would happen to you if you don't pay, and there is no emotional involvement. But when it comes to relatives, and you have emotion involved, then you break up a friendship, and I don't like to break up a friendship with relatives.

It is therefore better to avoid borrowing from relatives and running "the risk of losing the relationship that you established with your relatives." Nevertheless, there are "circumstances where the families are close, and borrowing is just helping somebody out." But there are problems. Borrowing is a way to make enemies and you always run the risk that if anything goes wrong, "they'll always hold it up to you." Moreover, borrowing money from relatives may result in their knowing too much about the family's affairs, thereby infringing on family privacy. They will "know why, when, and all the reasons," whereas with a bank "nobody has to know my business." The anticipation of conflicts in economic dealings with kin was evident in the fact that nearly half of the clients agreed that "*When relatives go into business together they're likely to end up enemies.*" The potential conflict in business dealings with kin was expressed in terms of "the demand" that they would make on a person. Some claimed that these demands would be "so great that it would be impossible to have a good relationship with them." Problems of maintaining objectivity with kin, in view of the personal element of the relationship, were also mentioned as a source of business conflict with the idea that it would be easier to "think twice with an outsider."

It may be difficult to maintain objective contractual rules and regulations with kin, not only because of the personal element but also because additional kin may be drawn into the conflict. "With relatives, when there's an argument, it's a family affair and everybody has to know about it." With a stranger, on the other hand, "You can simply put down the rules and regulations and what is expected from each other."

Evaluation of performance may also be complicated by personal relationships with kin. Tensions that arise in evaluation may "push the people apart." It may be more or less impossible to remove this personal element with relatives, whereas with an outsider it is easier to keep it a "business proposition."

Some of the problems anticipated in business dealings with kin were specifically tied to the personal element of kinship but others anticipated problems in any business partnership, claiming that "Partners always end up the same—either you break up or you are angry, you are enemies."

Despite the anticipation of conflict in business dealings with kin, many clients felt that kin could be trusted more than outsiders. Many agreed that *"In business dealings it's usually safer to trust a relative than an outsider."* Some indicated that the trust of relatives, however, may be based as much on mistrust of outsiders as on the expectation of smooth ties with kin. Nevertheless, there were positive statements about the trust that one may give to relatives in joint business ventures. When one leaves, for example, one may feel "perfectly at ease that they are leaving the place in the other's hands . . . you can trust each other." With relatives personal knowledge forms a basis for trust, but also means that "You have to put up with his idiosyncracies and he has to put up with yours, but at least you know each other." Thus despite the probable demands of kin and the possible conflicts in economic and business dealings, a substantial number would still prefer to place their trust in kin rather than in outsiders.

Nearly a third of the clients agreed with the statement, *"Friends cannot give you the love you can get from relatives."* Some expressed strong disagreement and annoyance with this statement, pointing out that relatives were too demanding and friends were therefore preferable, but even in this disagreement they noted that kinship was a basis for counting on others and for "taking things for granted." Many felt likewise that *"One usually has more in common with relatives than with friends."* Even those who felt they would have as much in common with friends as with relatives emphasized that ties of kinship are binding. While one might terminate a friendship because one did not have much in common or did not like the friend's behavior, with relatives allowances would have to be made because the relationship would be harder to terminate. As one woman explained:

> If I come in, I ask Marty how he is. But Marty doesn't ask me how I am. . . . I'm interested in him . . . but he doesn't ask me . . . If he wasn't a brother-in-law, the next time I saw him I wouldn't ask him either. But I was brought up with the idea of relatives' closeness . . .

the closeness of the family. So if he comes up, I'll ask him again but if he was a stranger I'd never ask him again because he's not interested in me. . . . In a Jewish family, it's this here business of ideology.

Thus not only do strong ties and obligations of kinship exist, but there are many areas where a good number believe that priority should be given to kinship over other institutions.

Husband-Wife versus Parent-Child Bonds

Since many clients believe that the mother will instinctively continue to guide her children, particularly her daughters, even after they are adults, a potential conflict exists between the mother-daughter and the marital bonds. Most clients ideally gave priority to the marital over the mother-daughter tie. Nearly three-quarters of the clients agreed that "*A woman should take her husband's side even if her mother doesn't think he is right.*" Some clients saw a "question of loyalty" between mother and husband, and felt that "loyalty comes first to a husband instead of to a mother" since "she has to live with her husband." This is a reason for strengthening the marital rather than the parent-child tie.

The marital bond may not, however, be given priority in actual behavior; it is strongly voiced in part because of the potential for deviation. Some informants believed that the wife should not take sides with either her mother or her husband, but should make independent judgments, thereby implying that the marital bond does not automatically take precedence over the parent-child bond:

I don't think a woman should try to side with her husband or with her mother. She should try to do what she thinks is the right thing.

No, I wouldn't think that she should go along with her husband. Of course, she shouldn't give her mother too much satisfaction, either. Not just because she picked him as a husband . . . that shouldn't be the case. You've got to listen to two sides of the story to see which one is right. . . . I know how my daughter is. She would say, "Ma, my husband knows what he's talking about. He knows his business." A daughter should think twice before she makes such a remark as "Ma, you're old-fashioned. Ma, you are this and that. I know what my husband is doing." You don't talk like that. It hurts. We have more than ideas, things like that, you know. But, all right, a sensible little woman would make her own judgment and think it over, not just make a crack judgment.

Clients also expressed their belief in the ideal priority of the marital over the parent-child bond by disagreeing with the idea that *"A woman can often get more warmth and understanding from her mother than from her husband."*

From the mother's perspective, most clients gave priority to the marital bond. This was reflected in disagreement by nearly two-thirds of the clients with the statement, "It is more natural for a mother to get more pleasure from her children than from her husband."

From the point of view of the son, again most clients gave priority to the marital over the mother-son tie. The majority disagreed with the idea that *"A man can often get more warmth and understanding from his mother than from his wife."* However, some clients gave priority to the mother-son tie.

Differentiation of the Nuclear Family from Kin

Ideally the nuclear family is expected to function as an independent unit, but a persistent effort may be required to achieve independence because of expectations that a strong mother-child bond will continue into adulthood.

Ideally parents, not grandparents, should make child-rearing decisions. Almost all of the clients agreed that *"Parents should make all the decisions about child rearing even if grandparents don't approve."* Thus the nuclear family is viewed as ideally independent in decision-making and child rearing. As one man said of the role of grandparents, "Just because he [the grandfather] brought me up, he can't tell me how to bring up my kids." This man's wife, however, felt that grandparents "can suggest" and that this guidance should be used as a resource even if it is not accepted.

Nearly half of the clients agreed with the statement, *"A woman can usually get better advice about child rearing from books than from her mother."* Some felt that "mother is not always right—so you have to consider both." That is, one should shop around for the best advice, but this does imply giving consideration to the mother's ideas. Some felt that differences of cultural background between mothers and daughters would considerably limit the applicability of a mother's knowledge. As one woman explained,

"Her ideas about child rearing were much different from mine." Thus the scope of the mother-daughter bond is limited in some areas, but both expect the mother's role as adviser to continue.

Nevertheless, most clients disagreed with the idea that "*A mother has reason to be hurt if her daughter doesn't listen to her advice about taking care of the house and children.*" Although ideally the mother should not be hurt, informants indicated that since she would naturally think it her duty to advise her daughter because of her greater experience, she would feel hurt if the daughter did not listen.

> Well, she [the mother] thinks she knows best, she knows the method, but the daughter would not listen to her. She knows that her daughter is doing wrong. It's like slapping somebody on the face and they would not listen to you.

The view that the mother should not be hurt if her advice is not heeded by a married daughter seems to be in part a reaction to that very experience:

> I don't think she has plenty of reason. I think it's silly. My mother puts entirely too much stock on cooking and house care, and she learned to accept the fact that I have gone to work and the children are neglected. She says, "*Nebikle*" [poor little one], she says. . . . "I haven't got what to eat." If I broil a piece of meat it isn't good enough, I have to make soup, so I do without the soup. So, I say to her quite often, "Look, mama, mind your own business. What do you care? This is my house and my business, and I'm running it my way." And she might get slightly hurt, but she overcomes it very quickly.

Despite cultural differences between mothers and married daughters, many assumed that without the mother's advice the daughter would make mistakes.

> My daughter had made plenty of mistakes. Then later she said, "Ma, you are right, you are all right." When I told her, "Sarah, you shouldn't do this," she said, "Oh, ma, you were right. I was wrong and I didn't listen to you." Then I'd say, "All right." You know, the same thing will be all over again . . . a sort of cycle, you know, a vicious cycle.

More moderate responses indicated that a child could take the advice if she felt it was worthwhile. Yet the democratic right of children "to make their own decisions—including the right to

make a wrong one once in a while" was invoked by some informants as a reason that the mother should "let her children grow up."
This again assumes that the mother will advise and that ample
rationale is required for not accepting her advice. Moreover, it
assumes that it is very hard for the mother to let her children
grow up.

Despite the ideal of the independent functioning of the nuclear
family, particularly in child rearing, many believed that the nuclear family should alter its religious practices for the sake of
grandparents, thus acknowledging a significant influence of grandparents on the life of the family. More than half of the clients
agreed to the statement, *"Even a nonobservant couple should keep
a kosher house for the sake of more observant parents if it means a
lot to the parents."* Some felt that modifying religious practices for
the sake of parents would be hypocritical if the children did not
accept the beliefs. Others, however, believed that children would
naturally follow the way of their parents in religion. In addition,
many pointed out that, even in cases where the children themselves
were not religious, parents who kept a kosher home could not eat
in their children's home. One woman, for example, described her
father's reaction to her nonkosher home, indicating that he said,
"I can't even have a glass of water in your house" and that she felt
very badly about it. Some felt that keeping kosher for the sake of
parents was "not much of a sacrifice anyway," especially since "you
could eat whatever you liked outside the house." Many felt that
they would want to make their parents happy in this way, emphasizing the nonmaterial return to parents "after all they have
done for you," implying that parents have a right to demand this
form of observance. Thus keeping kosher is one way of showing
love and respect for parents who deserve this pleasure, with the
idea that "Love would do it . . . because of respect for the parent."
Some indicated that parents, particularly the mother, might impose such demands on her children in martyr fashion by indicating
that if they did not follow her wishes, they felt she did not deserve
it. As one explained, "My mother made me feel that she doesn't
deserve that much pleasure."

Therefore, the predominant ideal is that in child rearing the
nuclear family should operate independently of grandparents. But
it is anticipated that grandparents will consider it their role to advise, so that this independence may be difficult to maintain. Fur-

ther, in religious practices it is clearly expected by many that the nuclear family will alter its functioning because of relationships with grandparents. Sharp differentiation of the nuclear family from kin is thus not automatic or unequivocal. The ideal of independence of the nuclear family is something that must be achieved by persistent effort; independence is not in isolation but amidst kin.

Obligations Toward Aged Parents

In keeping with feelings of obligation in other areas of kinship, most clients had a strong sense of responsibility toward aged parents. Nearly three-quarters of the client agreed that "*A family should be willing to sacrifice some of the things they want for their children in order to help support their aged parents.*" If problems of support of aged parents do arise, there are fairly clear expectations that the distribution of responsibility among siblings should take economic means into account. There was general agreement among the clients that "If you have more money than your brothers and sisters, you should be willing to contribute more to the support of your aged parents."

Definite obligations to support parents if necessary do not mean, however, that such support is ideal; parents ideally should not be dependent on their adult children. More clients agreed than disagreed with the statement, "It is humiliating for parents to be supported by their children in later life." Thus the older generation should ideally remain independent and not need the support of their children:

> If the parents could possibly see their way through without their children's help, it is the most wonderful thing in the world to be on your own feet, to be independent.

If parents are in real need one should help them, but Social Security and other forms of welfare assistance should make this support unnecessary. "At this time you don't have to come to your children." Social Security in this view reduces the dependence of the aged on their children, and therefore strengthens bonds within the nuclear family. Ideally one should be able to help one's children first. A sense of community responsibility to assist in the support of the elderly and the existence of many Jewish institutions for the aged are probably related to these views.

Ideally, therefore, financial assistance should go from parents to children, not from children to parents; obligations to parents are met by giving, in turn, to one's own children:

> By the process of the generations coming down, the first need is from a parent to his child, but in that way I will be repaying my parents. Because the generations as they go along . . . responsibility is for the ongoing generation primarily.

Reciprocity to parents, however, is not seen to occur entirely through giving to one's children; parents are entitled to some direct return but ideally this is not in the form of economic assistance. Almost half of the clients agreed that *"Parents are entitled to some return for all the sacrifices they have made for their children."* Some reacted strongly against this statement with the idea that assistance to parents was "not because the parents have sacrificed; you don't do it because your parents have sacrificed for you, because they give birth to you, you do it because they are your parents." Or, as another client said, "The parents putting away money in the bank so they have 'my son, the doctor,' this isn't sacrifice for the child." Many reacted with strong negative feelings against the idea of a sacrificing mother. But even those who reacted against the notion of sacrifice still felt that parents should receive some direct return from their children, "just for the sake of common decency."

The ideal form of return is joy in seeing the success of one's children. Many spoke in terms of giving their children "pleasure." Giving one's parents pleasure entailed giving them the opportunity to observe their adult children, "to see the interest on your investment." This form of pleasure necessarily strengthens the bond of kinship.

The bonds of kinship, however, are not often distributed equally to the families of husband and wife. Some degree of *lateral skewing* is expected; that is, a tendency to emphasize ties to one side of the family more than to the other. In this case, even in the ideal, a stronger tie is anticipated between mother and daughter than between mother and son. Nevertheless, typically, clients have a strong sense of obligation for continuing involvement between parents and adult children; thus there are strong bonds outside the nuclear family of marriage.

VALUES AND KINSHIP POSITIONS

Husbands and Wives

Similarities and differences between husbands and wives in kinship values can be significant. However, among clients, husbands and wives compared as groups had almost the same values. None of the differences between husbands and wives was great and does not represent consistent differences in extent of kin orientation. The cases in which a husband and his wife agreed with each other were examined. There were only four items in which more than 30 per cent of the husbands differed from their wives in agreeing, disagreeing, or having no opinion about the issue. Moreover, these differences do not appear to be related consistently to overall patterns of kinship values. Although more refined statistical analysis could be employed in comparing husbands with wives, as a group the similarity of their responses is striking.

Clients and the Aged

Differences in kinship values between the clients and those in the Service to the Aged are striking in their consistency. The Aged may or may not be similar to the actual parents of these clients but the differences suggest generational differences that are likely between the clients and their own parents.

In almost all areas, the Aged were consistently more kin-oriented than other clients. They were more frequently in favor of marriage within the Jewish group and more frequently favored residence of the children in the parental home until marriage. They were more likely to consider residential proximity to kin desirable, and although they could foresee problems in combined households, they did so slightly less frequently than other clients. They more frequently felt it selfish to break ties of kinship, considering it essential to maintain contact with siblings regardless of their behavior. They were also more likely to think family circles and cousins clubs desirable. Education was more frequently stressed by the Aged, but at the same time they were likely to believe that it is better to remain near relatives than to move away for the sake of advancement. They also stressed the ideal priority of the marital over the parent-child bond, but they were more likely to view the mother-son and the mother-daughter bond as a greater source of emotional warmth and understanding than the marital tie. More frequently the Aged felt that a mother had reason to be hurt if her daughter did not take her advice about housekeeping and child rearing, and although most of the Aged also agreed that parents should make all the decisions about child rearing regardless of the opinion of grandparents, they held this view less frequently than other clients. They also felt more often than other clients that the family should modify its religious practices for the sake of parents, so that in both child rearing and religious activities they placed somewhat less stress on the separation of the nuclear family from kin than was true of other clients. And although they felt financial support from children would be humiliating, they placed greater stress on the obligation of children to give their parents some return, ideally pleasure, for the care they had given them.

Insofar as differences between the Aged and other clients reflected generational differences that exist in the actual social network of clients, they suggest significant factors in their kin relationships. It seems entirely likely that marked differences in kinship values are experienced by clients in relation to their own parents, as suggested by the data on the Aged and also by interview material. Despite the many levels on which values may operate and the complexities of interconnection between values and actions, values are preferences that are felt to be morally justified. They are the basis for expectations about behavior and a basis for judging and sanctioning it. Even clients who are not strongly kin-oriented undoubtedly are often sanctioned by more kin-oriented relatives who feel they have a moral right of social contact and access to the family.

The source of the kin-oriented values of many clients is difficult to determine. Perhaps these values are more typical of families living in an urban industrial environment than was previously supposed. There are also some striking similarities to Eastern European Jewish kinship traditions.

Although these traditions are undoubtedly vivid and meaningful for many clients, the process of transition from one culture to another is complex, especially since both the old and the new cultures are themselves undergoing change. More important than the continuity of predominant client values with Eastern European Jewish traditions are the effects of value similarities and differences between the clients and the individuals with whom they actually come in contact. The extent to which an individual has changed his values from those of his parents and others of his parents' generation may be critical for his interaction with others as well as for his views of himself. Our interview and questionnaire data suggest that kinship values are, in fact, in the process of transition and that clients do come in contact with those holding rather different views.

The values that clients hold are more kin-oriented than those presumably characteristic of the predominant middle-class kinship system in America. It is probably true that earlier characterizations have been overstated, but if the clients interact with those whose kinship values are similar to the Aged, they are probably in an in-between position—between those with values more similar to Eastern European Jewish traditions and those holding predominant American middle-class kinship values. In any case, the predominant client view firmly stresses the obligations of kinship.

The values that have been examined are not exhaustive of kinship values. Those related to other areas of kinship behavior could have been included, for example, values about inheritance. But interviews pointed to the areas examined as particularly significant.

The predominant view, which emphasized the strength of kinship obligations despite ideal independence of the nuclear family, is not held by all clients. Some disagree with certain aspects, some with others. The predominant values are themselves not necessarily consistent. For example, the value of achievement may be inconsistent with the value of remaining geographically close to kin. The consistency or inconsistency of values is a matter of viewpoint and data. These inconsistencies are apparent from an outside point of view; they may not appear inconsistent to participants in the culture.

Even though not all clients are alike in their values, a model of the predominant values among the client group is useful. It offers information on the views that are prevalent for many, and it also provides a model for comparison with other groups. It is thus possible to hypothesize social processes of changing values, which have relevance for all clients regardless of their particular present views.

NOTES TO CHAPTER 3

1. Lancaster, Lorraine, "Some Conceptual Problems in the Study of Family and Kin Ties in the British Isles," *The British Journal of Sociology*, vol. 12, December, 1961, p. 324.
2. Strodtbeck, Fred L., "Family Interaction, Values and Achievement" in *The Jews: Social Patterns of an Ameri-can Group*, edited by Marshall Sklare. The Free Press, Glencoe, Ill., 1958, pp. 147–165. Our own data have also been presented in part in Leichter, Hope J., "Kinship Values and Casework Intervention," *Casework Papers —1961*, Family Service Association of America, New York, 1962, pp. 58–78.

CHAPTER 4

The Network of
Kin Relationships

We have seen that the values of most client families clearly emphasize the importance of ties to kin. Neither immigration and assimilation nor living in a large metropolis of an industrial society has fostered values that isolate the family from its kin. We will now examine how these values are manifested in actual relationships. First, we will consider the genealogical extensiveness of kin ties; secondly, the geographic proximity of kin and the extent of communication with them; and, finally, the bonds of assistance and reciprocity.

THE EXTENSIVENESS OF KIN TIES

The number of individuals that a family recognizes as kin and the number of these with whom it interacts indicates the extent to which kinship ties are meaningful. If a family has information about and maintains contact with a large number of kin, values stressing the obligations of kinship are, in fact, accompanied by kin involvement.

Where and how kin boundaries are drawn is also important. Since more individuals are related by blood and marriage than are actually recognized as kin, there must be criteria for inclusion in a kin network. The definition of an individual as a kin is social, not purely biological. The following data on these topics were collected from genealogies, interviews, and questionnaires.

Boundaries of Kin Knowledge

Knowledge of kin does not necessarily mean that significant social relationships exist, but it indicates the importance attached to kinship and to keeping up information about kin. Deceased as well as living kin can be important, since deceased kin may be a link to living kin. Knowledge about deceased kin is part of the social image and the social identity of an individual and a family. Particularly when deceased kin were highly prestigious, they may continue for generations to heighten the prestige image of the family. Where deceased kin were notorious in other ways, they also contribute to the social identity of the individual and family.

In collecting genealogies it became evident that images of kin were an important part of the individual's perception of himself and his family. Some stressed people of high status in their genealogies and gave sketchy information on those of lower status, for example, in descriptions of occupations. Some attempted to cover up information on kin who were for some reason socially unacceptable; for example, cases of mental illness, business failure, and physical deformity. Clients were often surprised by the size of their genealogy and indicated satisfaction with having a large network of kin.

Both interview and questionnaire data indicated clearly that despite immigration and urban life, most of the client families have information about a large number of kin. The amount of kin knowledge varied from those known vaguely to exist, but who could not be traced through any definite link, to those on whom a great deal of social placement information could be given.

Figure 1 contains two genealogies that were obtained in interviews with one family. The data on the husband's kin were given by the husband, and those on the wife's kin were given by the wife. The total number of individuals recognized as kin by this family is 587, clearly a very large figure. Moreover, even a genealogy as extensive as this is not necessarily complete, since the criteria for recognizing an individual as a kin are variable. Probing to determine the limits of an individual's kin knowledge by questions about the kin who are present at specific gatherings almost always brought up kin not initially included in the genealogy.

Not all the genealogies collected were as large as those in Figure 1, but many approached it. These genealogies were chosen for illustration because they show the amount of kin knowledge that is possible, and because more limited genealogies can be visualized as segments of them. With the separate genealogies of husbands and wives from all those families in which genealogical data were collected in interviews combined, the average number of kin recognized per family for the ten families was 241. In these ten families data were obtained for both the husband's and the wife's sides of the family. There were three cases where information was given on only about 100 kin, these having 93, 102, and 109 kin, respectively. All other genealogies contained over 200 kin. Thus even though families differed, all recognized a fairly large number of kin.

The proportion of recognized kin who were living varied somewhat from family to family. Thus families differ in the extent of their interest in kin who are no longer living. On the average, about 20 per cent of the recognized kin were deceased. All but two families had over 90 living kin on whom they gave some information, that is, more than 90 kin potentially available for interaction.

The contours of these genealogies had certain typical patterns, which are apparent in the genealogies in Figure 1. Typically, relatively little is known about ascending generations and few attempts are made to trace ancestry to distant relatives. An exception to this was one Hassidic family interviewed, but which was culturally so different from other families that these data were not tabulated with the other data. In this case the client alleged he could trace his ancestry back to the Bal Shem Tov, the eighteenth-century founder of Hassidism. But this type of genealogy, which is typical in other societies, for example, among the traditional Chinese, was not found in any of the non-Hassidic client families. For most families the information on the clients' grandparental generation was scanty or nonexistent; very few were able to report occupations of this generation, and few were certain about the number of siblings of grandparents. Most had almost no information about great-grandparents. In the genealogies in Figure 1 the data on the husband's grandparental generation is thin by contrast to the amount known about his parents' generation, his own generation, and descending generations. He does know something about his maternal grandparents, but nothing about their siblings or ascendants beyond this. Among his paternal kin there is knowledge of multiple marriages of the grandparents, but nothing about siblings of grandparents or their descendants, and nothing about great-grandparents. In the wife's genealogy the existence of grandparents is known, and the existence of siblings of the maternal grandparents and their descendants is known. Information about siblings of paternal grandparents is incomplete, and nothing is known about their descendants. There is no information at all about great-grandparents. In the genealogies of both husband and wife, there is greater lateral extension than generation depth.

By comparison with data from other studies, the number of kin known by these client families is large. Compared with one study conducted in London, the total number of recognized kin for these client families is larger.[1] The client genealogies, however, tend to show greater lateral extension and less generation depth. The size of the clients' network of known kin is also large by comparison with the study made among Vassar undergraduates, but again clients tend to have information on fewer generations than the Vassar students.[2] By comparison with still another study, the client sample is less able to trace lineal ancestry.[3]

Boundaries of Kin Interaction

Knowledge of kin is not purely of genealogical interest even though significant social relationships do not exist with all the living individuals who are recognized as kin. Most families have some form of social relationships with a high proportion of their living kin. The variations in the size of the family's kin network, depending on the criteria employed in defining it, are even more significant for social interaction with kin than they are for knowledge of kin. The number of known kin varies, depending on the amount of knowledge about the kin that is taken as a criterion of "knowing," that is, merely knowing of their existence, knowing their name, knowing more about them.[4] But there are even greater variations in the size of the network of social interaction when one examines the kin with whom different types of activity are carried out.

Data on the kin with whom various forms of social interaction occur were obtained through the research questionnaire for two degrees of intimacy of social contacts: (1) *effective kin,* those kin seen only at big family gatherings, or those with whom some effective social relationship exists, and (2) *familiar kin,* those kin seen other than at big family gatherings, who are to some degree familiar. These criteria were used to estimate the greatest extension of the boundaries of the kin network.

It is evident from the data on the number of individuals recognized as kin, the number of kin seen only at big family gatherings, and the number seen more often than at big family gatherings that most of the client families have large kin networks. Data on cognatic kin obtained through the questionnaire procedure indicate that only 11 per cent of the families had 15 or fewer kin that were effective, while 59 per cent listed from 16 to 45 kin, and 20 per cent listed from 46 to 60 kin. Nine per cent of the families listed 61 or more kin. Thus most families have a large number of cognatic kin with whom they maintain some degree of effective social interaction. The actual number of kin is undoubtedly larger than that represented merely by the categories of cognatic kin included in the questionnaire.

Most families indicate a difference between the number of living individuals recognized as kin and the number with whom some degree of effective social interaction is maintained, thus exercising the principle of selectivity in interaction among kin. Very few families saw all of their living kin at big family gatherings. Fifty-nine per cent of the client families, however, indicated that they had contact at big family gatherings or on more frequent occasions with three-quarters or more of their living kin. There were no families within the client group who had totally cut themselves off from all social contact with their kin; all had some effective communication with at least some kin.

Without comparative data it is impossible to say how the number of familiar and effective kin compares with other groups. But when one thinks, for example, of the obligations to attend weddings, bar mitzvahs, and funerals in a network containing from 16 to 45 cognatic kin and their spouses, it is clear that it is incorrect to think of a nuclear family as isolated. Clients not only recognize a large number of individuals as kin, and have some information about them; in addition, they maintain some degree of social contact with a great many kin.

Defining Network Boundaries

Drawing the boundaries of the kin network means making choices of considerable significance about the allocation of time and resources; it is impossible to devote equal time and attention to all kin. This is clear in one man's description of his problems in keeping up contacts with kin:

> It's tough to keep closer. . . . We just don't see one another as often as we would like. Like myself, come the week-end, I have to run to my in-laws, and I have to run to my mother, so I am too tired to run to my cousins unless it's an occasion.

But the basis for selecting kin with whom to interact is not always clear to all involved because it varies with the activity, and because the genealogical relationship between kin depends on the perspective of each individual. Considerable ambiguity and a basis for conflict result.[5] Even with kin such as parents and siblings, who are closest genealogically, the decision of inclusion and exclusion may be a problem from the perspective of a spouse or someone slightly more distant. The shifting and uncertain criteria for defining boundaries of the kin network are clear in explanations of which kin were included at particular events.

A description of which kin one woman invited to her daughter's engagement party reveals several implicit criteria. The bridegroom had three siblings, all of whom had to be included because of the principle of genealogical equivalence. On the other hand, the grandfather of the bridegroom and the mother's sister were included not by virtue of genealogical closeness alone, but because they lived with kin who were closer genealogically. A principle of representativeness, or balancing the various sides of the family, also operated; but this principle was complicated by the lack of geographic proximity of the client's brothers. Therefore, a principle of substitution was employed; the client's uncle and his wife, who were in geographic proximity, were substituted for her brothers, not on the basis of genealogical closeness, but in order to maintain balance. The number of kin in the same genealogical position is also relevant; all the husband's kin were included since there were not many. Finally, the physical facilities influenced the limits of the total number who could be included. As she explained:

I made a dinner, and, of course, it had to be completely kosher. I had service for 12, but we were 18. We managed, you know; God bless the salad plates.

When the boundaries of the network are fluid, varying with the individual perspective and the occasion, and when so many criteria are employed in deciding where to draw the lines for a specific event, it is not surprising that all parties do not always see the criteria in the same light. As one woman explained, no matter what you do, "You insult somebody anyhow." The intensity of emotion attached to boundary definitions is great, since basic ties of kinship are expressed in each event in which an individual is included or excluded; in addition, these events are often public. In the following description about participation in a wedding, the woman felt that a high moral prerogative was attached to the principle of "genealogical equivalence" and was deeply offended at its violation:

There are only three grandchildren in the family . . . two grand-daughters walked [in the wedding procession] . . . and my daughter didn't. . . . No one else was taken out . . . my daughter was most certainly insulted and hurt. . . . Everyone walked up to me and said, "How come Shirley wasn't in the ceremony?" and I said, "Well, she just doesn't rate" and I was very angry about it.

The definitions of boundaries in a group and network differ in a significant way. In a group the boundaries are the same regardless of the particular individual member who is the reference point; individuals are members by virtue of their relationship to the social unit, not just to each other. In a network the boundaries are different from the perspective of each individual; the individuals that are considered kin by one person are not necessarily the same as those considered kin by close relatives of this person, even though they have certain kin in common. Kin within a network do not necessarily have any significant relationship to each other except that they are both related to the specific individual who was the reference point. The only individuals in a society who can have the same network of kin are unmarried siblings. Husbands and wives may come to be incorporated in each other's kin networks, but they bring to the family different perspectives on the issue of who are kin.

The boundaries of the network also differ according to the criteria employed and according to activities: the network may include all those whom the individual is able to name as kin or all those living within a given geographic area, but these kin may be different from those with whom the family exchanges economic services. For every kinship event decisions must be made about who is and who is not to be included as a kin. Thus considerable energy is expended in the process of boundary definition, and inconsistent definitions among kin easily cause conflict.

Despite the elusive nature of the boundaries of the kin network and the incumbent problems, most of the client families can be considered to have large kin networks by almost any of the varying criteria that can be employed. Most have information about a large number of kin, more than has been found in other urban groups. Their genealogies are characterized by a high degree of lateral extension and comparatively little generation depth. In addition, some degree of interaction is maintained with a high proportion of the recognized living kin. Most interaction and closest ties of sentiment are with kin who are closest genealogically but the urban environment by no means restricts all forms of effective social interaction to this narrow genealogical range. On the contrary, the genealogical extension of effective and familiar kin is great for most families. Thus, in fact, as well as in values, clients have an extensive kin network.

THE OMNIPRESENCE OF KIN: PROXIMITY AND COMMUNICATION

Geographic Proximity

Both the household and geographic proximity outside the household are relevant for determining what constitutes proximity to kin. In either case it is necessary to determine the boundaries of the household and of geographic areas that are meaningful for social interaction. Boundaries of the household do not necessarily correspond to physical structure. In large apartment buildings or new housing projects, and in two- and three-family houses, the physical boundaries of the house or apartment may not correspond to boundaries that define the unit for many household activities such as cooking and shopping. Even structural boundaries are not always fixed; for example, in one of the client families the wife's parents lived in the adjacent apartment and a hole was cut in the wall to allow the parents easier access to the family's home.

Defining meaningful geographic boundaries outside the household is even more complex, particularly in a metropolitan area. Although neighborhood and subcommunity divisions exist within a metropolis, they are not always clearly separated from each other. Moreover, modern means of communication and transportation facilitate integration of various subparts of the metropolis, making it a whole community for many purposes. Thus the definition of meaningful geographic boundaries must rest on criteria other than geography alone.

The most meaningful geographic boundaries may be those that serve as cutoff points, limiting access of kin to each other. But here the criteria vary greatly from one individual to another, for example, the definition of what is within walking distance. One woman explained that her married daughter lived within walking distance and she frequently walked over to see her; but, on the other hand, the mother said: "I couldn't walk it, I'm too tired; it's within walking distance, but I'm too tired." Any given geographic cutoff is, therefore, to some degree arbitrary.

Several boundaries were selected for analysis on the basis of recurrent distinctions made by clients in interviews. Although they are somewhat arbitrary, and the subjective meaning may vary from one client to another, they serve as a baseline for making comparisons, at least roughly, among clients: (1) the New York City area, (2) walking distance, (3) the same building, and (4) the same household.[6] These categories were treated as mutually exclusive. According to these criteria, all of the client families have at least some kin that are within geographic proximity.

Kin in the New York City Area. None of the research families was completely without kin in the area that they defined as New York City; all mentioned one or more blood kin, implying that all of the families have at least one kin family within the area.

Most families have many more kin in the New York City area. Eighty-six per cent of the research families had 16 or more, and 54 per cent had 31 or more blood kin within the New York City area; many of these kin were married and had families.

Having kin available within the same community, at least for client wives, has been a lifelong experience. Seventy-eight per cent of the client wives had never lived in a city or town where they did not have relatives.

Although clients may reside in the New York City area in order to take advantage of the opportunities it offers, interviews told of clear instances where residence there was specifically for the purpose of remaining close to kin. One woman explained that, although her brother had greater job opportunities in California and went there briefly after returning from the Army, he decided he could not stay because "he was devoted to my mother." This woman explained concerning herself: "I don't know if I could go away . . . there is a responsibility to my mother for support." In this instance, a second brother had moved away, so geographic proximity clearly served as a basis for extensive interaction on the part of those who did remain in the New York City area. As the client explained of herself about her mother:

> She calls me twice or three times a day, and if I have time, I talk to her. It does me good, too. Everybody likes to talk and to have somebody listen.

It may be possible to maintain close ties with kin when they are not within the same metropolitan area but this may be more difficult, particularly if ties with kin are expected to be validated by continuous contact. As the client cited above explained, when her brother did leave New York for a brief period, her mother "felt very badly, very upset, and very disappointed."

Kin Within Walking Distance. Distinctions intermediate between the New York City area and walking distance exist. For example, borough demarcations may seem like "a different country." Parts of Long Island were often described as far away, and it is not clear how often this was considered to be within the New York City area. But walking distance was a particularly crucial cutoff. Having kin within walking distance implies that contacts are possible without prearrangement. In such cases kin often meet in the street or are frequently brought together by religious practice. One woman explained about her grandfather:

> He went to a synagogue on our street, and he always came to our house on the way, to have coffee my mother had for him.

Living within walking distance makes possible some degree of overlap of household activities, such as joint shopping and exchange of many other services. One woman, for example, explained that while her husband was working late she had regular meals with her mother, who lived nearby. And during one interview, a married daughter and her husband came to the client's home to borrow sections of *The New York Times* and to pick up some meat which the client had purchased for her married daughter. She had this to say:

> I had the meat for her. She was supposed to meet me at eight o'clock at the butcher's, and she lives at the other side of the parkway, which is quite a walk. Then she overslept, so she called me up and told me she overslept and could I get it for her or she'd be late for school. So I bought it, and I had to run back and put it in the refrigerator. . . . She doesn't have too much time and she feels that if she goes to the butcher's around her way, they will fool her. So she wants me to buy the meat for her. . . . Well, there's a butcher right around here . . . so I bought her meat. Usually she tells me what she wants, and I buy it. She should have enough for two weeks, and she freezes some of it. . . . This way I buy her a supply of meat, so she has it.

A high proportion of the client families, 53 per cent, have at least one or more kin households within walking distance. Nearly a quarter had two or three kin households within walking distance; and a few, 6 per cent, had more than three households within walking distance. For some families having kin within walking distance is clearly the result of a conscious decision to live near kin. One woman who lived in a middle-income housing project hoped very much to obtain an apartment in the same project for her mother and father. She did not wish to have them in the same building because this would give the children too much chance for going to her mother's; however, she did wish to have them in the project where her mother could be within easy reach. She said her mother "is really very anxious to come . . . they will be living with school things and the things that children do. I'll be in and out of her house to see if she needs anything." In this case the elderly parents clearly preferred to live near kin, even though it meant that the husband would have to commute some distance to his work. Thus values of geographic proximity to kin are supported by behavior.

Kin in the Same Building. Living in the same building with kin constitutes a further degree of geographic proximity that exists for at least some of the client families, 13 per cent of whom have one or more kin households in the same building.

The significance of living in the same building varies, of course, with the type of building; living in the same large apartment building may not involve the same degree of proximity as that of kin who share a two- or three-family house, particularly if the house is owned by some of the kin. In either case, however, the ready access and overlap of household activities possible when kin are within walking distance also arises when kin are in the same building. Access and privacy may be even more difficult to control when kin are in the same building, particularly when this allows children access to each other's homes. One woman described how difficult it was to keep separate households when they lived in the same three-family house with her brother-in-law's family. Her brother-in-law's son "would just push right in . . . the kids went up and down the stairs to play all the time." Despite the fact that the "kid stuff" that ensued was sometimes difficult to handle, this woman also noted with pleasure the close social relationships that were possible among the adult kin in this instance. Thus although only a small proportion of the research families have kin in the same building at present, this practice is compatible with the values of many and does entail considerable household overlap.

Kin in the Same Household. Living in combined households with kin is clearly not valued by most clients. At present only 8 per cent of the client families are living in the same household with kin. Most of these do so because kin have moved in with them. However, when examining past residence with kin, the picture is different, providing a clear indication of the importance of looking at family patterns in terms of particular stages of the life cycle of the domestic group, and changes throughout the life cycle. Sixty-one per cent of the client families have had at some time some form of combined household with kin, in contrast to values about combined households.

Combined households with kin occur in a variety of ways. The client families may have moved in with kin, generally with their parents; or kin, usually their elderly parents, may have moved in with the client family. Different reasons predominate for the two forms of combined households. For client stays in the home of kin the most frequent reason given by clients was lack of housing, accounting for 42 per cent. Kin living in the client's home occurred most frequently because of illness, pregnancy, old age, or incapacity, which accounted for 41 per cent of the stays, compared with only 19 per cent of the times when the client stayed in the home of kin. Financial problems and unemployment were most often given as reasons for the clients staying in the homes of their relatives. Military service was another reason given more frequently for staying in the home of kin than for having kin in the client's home. These differences in part reflect the stage of the life cycle in which these two types of residence are most likely to occur.

One question was whether the Eastern European tradition of the *kest* would be carried over in residence patterns of the clients. Matter-of-fact descriptions of temporary residence with the wife's parents after marriage were frequent. For example, they stayed there because "they didn't have their own apartment yet," but only 4 per cent of the clients gave explicitly as their reasons for staying in the home of relatives that they had just been married or were preparing a home, so that residence with kin is apparently not perceived in traditional terms even if it does occur immediately after marriage. The frequency of living with kin because of lack of housing reflects the fact that many of these families married during World War II when housing shortages were acute. Thus the behavior of living with parents after marriage was similar to the traditional form, but it was usually perceived as an emergency measure, not as a desired mode of residence.

The relatively small percentage of families currently living with kin and the fact that most stays with kin in the past were of short duration correspond with views that combined residence is not desirable. However, the fact that so many of the families have at some time had the experience of living with kin does not correspond with expressed values. Because the reasons for living with kin were generally ones of necessity, this may have strengthened views against it. Descriptions of actual residence with kin were generally negative, and in some cases led to the conclusion that combined residence was undesirable. One young man explained his experience when he and his wife lived as a young couple with her parents:

The mother is still trying to be a mother to the daughter and, therefore, of course, be more than just a grandmother to the child. . . . It's a matter of stripping a man of his dignity, of his independence. This is his home. This is his to take care of. A parent-in-law must cause conflict because a parent is concerned with her daughter, and she really shouldn't be in the sense that she should feel "Look, he married her, let him take care of her" . . . the closeness, I don't think it's good, and there's bound to be trouble.

Many descriptions were given of comparable difficulties of having an elderly parent in the home. Strenuous efforts may be made to prevent interference and maintain the independent functioning of the nuclear family, but continuous contacts and problems such as kitchen space make this difficult. Complaints about problems of interference with child rearing, questions about who should do the cooking, quarrels because an elderly parent, particularly a mother, felt unwanted if she was not allowed to perform the household activities to which she was accustomed, were common. One woman summed up the problems of living with an elderly mother by saying, "Our nerves are no good from getting on each other's nerves."

But not all descriptions of combined households mentioned problems. In some instances the assistance given by a parent was mentioned as essential in managing the household. One woman explained about her mother, "I go to business and she keeps house and prepares dinner . . . without her help it would be impossible for me to keep house and go to work."

Combined households are clearly such an intimate form of proximity that they can influence the entire gamut of family activities. One woman, for example, described the derogatory remarks her mother would make when she sang in the morning, saying, "What did you do last night?" The effects of joint residence with kin on family relationships are so pervasive and complex that they are difficult to estimate. Many factors are influential, including the outside relationships of family members and the number of friends to whom an elderly person can turn. Particularly for residence of elderly parents in the home of their children, which is not seen as temporary, problems undoubtedly outnumber advantages. It is significant for the outcome of joint residence that it is not considered normal or ideal, as it is in some societies where individuals are socialized early in life, to be able to accommodate to joint living.

In view of the short duration of most combined households, the difficulty of living in the same home with kin may not be as significant as the fact that the frequency of combined residence reflects strong obligations of kinship. These ties remain even when residence is shifted from joint households to preferable forms, such as living within walking distance or close by. As one woman explained, after her mother moved out to a separate apartment, she continued to drop in almost every day on her way to or from shopping. "I would like to be hospitable to her—she is very good to me —she has always been very generous of giving . . . so she may as well come up here because she loves the children and misses them terribly."

In short, all of the client families have kin within a reasonable degree of geographic proximity: 100 per cent have kin within the New York City area; 53 per cent within walking distance; 13 per cent, in the same building; and 8 per cent in the same household. When kin are within walking distance, a great many forms of household overlap are possible. Living within the same household may not be seen as desirable, but many of the client families have had this experience. For all client families, some kin are readily available for contact.

Communication with Kin

Despite the fact that all of the client families had some kin within the New York City area, the availability of kin for interaction cannot, as we have seen, be determined by arbitrary geographic boundaries alone. The forms of communication that are possible among kin are as important as the actual geographic distance. In any society a variety of modes of communication are possible. The forms of communication vary with other characteristics of the society, but particularly with its technology. In most primitive societies communication is face to face. In an industrial society, however, other forms of communication are available.

The telephone is a most important technological invention in our society. Although obvious, its significance has not been fully recognized in theories about society and has not been amply studied. The use of the telephone not only mitigates against diminished contact through distance, it may actually intensify contacts. It makes it necessary to examine geographic proximity of kin in a different light. In an urban area like New York City, the telephone is available at almost all times and places. Within an urban area, particularly within the area of local telephone calls, kin are accessible for interaction, even if they live at some distance, for example, in another borough.

Another example of the role of technology in communication among kin is the ease of correspondence possible with modern means of transportation. Here also technology makes available means for increased communication with kin. Letter writing, sending greeting cards and pictures help symbolically to maintain emotional ties of kinship and they may serve as means for effectively sanctioning kin, as was indicated in interviews.

Among client families, telephoning and visiting were of particular importance as means of communication. Visiting was facilitated by subway transportation.

Communication by Telephone. Kinship values clearly entail the obligation to maintain contact with kin by telephone as well as other means. The telephone is the most readily available mode of contact with kin, and there are definite expectations that it should be used. Failing to communicate by telephone is as much a breach of kinship obligations as any other failure to interact.

The general importance of telephone contact among kin is indicated by the fact that 95 per cent of the client wives maintained telephone contact with kin; of these, 47 per cent listed one or more relatives with whom they talked at least once a day.

In six of the interview families both husbands and wives kept "Kin Contact Logs" or diaries of all contacts with kin during a one-week period. Of all instances of contact with kin listed, there were nearly twice as many telephone contacts as face-to-face meetings. There were 112 telephone contacts listed and only 60 instances of other forms of contact, all of which were face-to-face, because there were no mentions of letter writing.

The importance of telephone contact, as well as the extent to which some families are enmeshed in a network of kinship obligations and continual contacts, is illustrated in a kin contact log of one wife, which is reproduced exactly as she kept it.*

This Kin Contact Log demonstrates the extensiveness of tele-

---

*All names and other identifying information about clients in this volume have been altered to preserve anonymity.

phone contact. There were 14 occasions of telephone contact as opposed to five face-to-face visits, a proportion similar to that found in other kin contact logs. It also illustrates the variety of content in telephone interaction, as well as the extent to which the family may be engaged with kin. Phrases such as "daily chat" make clear that the telephone is expected to be a significant mode of communication. Interview statements indicate views about obligations for telephone interaction with kin; for example, the idea that the relationship will not continue if telephone contact is not kept up: "Somehow if you don't keep calling them, you just drift away." Obligations are often so strongly felt that telephone contact is maintained even when inconvenient:

> She [eldest daughter, now married] calls me up every day and she wants to tell me things. But we find we're so busy, like if I call her she says, "Mother, I'm sorry, I'm cooking and I can't talk to you!" . . . or she says, "I have to write out three papers, and I can't talk." Or she calls me in the office and I say, "Honey, I can't talk to you, I have to catch the mailman." . . . But we do manage to squeeze in a conversation every day."

In other instances, similar obligations for maintaining telephone contact were felt even when the actual tie to kin was not considered personally meaningful or interesting. Even "duty calls" may be made as frequently as once a week or more often. The expectation that one should maintain contact with kin is also indicated by reactions in instances where this is not done. One man explained that his parents had "a bad habit, they call me only when someone dies."

Content of telephone communication. Despite the frequency of telephone contact with kin, it might be presumed that it would be limited in content, not covering the same areas as face-to-face communication. But the variety of subject matter in telephone communication is almost limitless; it includes highly emotional and personal content. Moreover, the possibility of discussing routine household matters while they are occurring contributes to the intimacy of telephone contacts. One client, when asked what she talked to her married daughter about on the telephone, explained: "Oh, anything and everything. She calls me up and she says, for instance, 'I made stuffed cabbage.'" Telephone conversations were reported that included such content as details of daily household

Kin Contact Log

Day	Relative(s)	Telephone		Visits			Time		Reason for the Contact
		I Called	They Called	Here	There	Other (state where)	From	To	
Mon. 10/3	Sister-in-law Rose [husband's sister]—rest of her family remained in car.			X			5:40	5:50 p.m.	To bring a few dollars she owed us, and some outgrown clothing I am to hand down to some other relatives (on my side of family).
Mon. 10/3	My mother	X	X				10:30	11:45 a.m.	I knew she would call me around 1 p.m. so I "buzzed" her phone (one ring) and she then called me. I felt this to be a more convenient time as I was planning to leave for an interview after lunch. (We talk on the phone daily—just to say "Hello, how are you?") We got into the habit of her making the call so that it would be on her bill. Also, even when I have a specific reason for contacting her, if she should be dozing, the one ring won't awaken her.
Tues. 10/4	Rose [sister-in-law]		X				10:45	11:30 a.m.	She was upset by a letter from the Income Tax Bureau and had to "tell some one"—we "visited" by phone after discussing what they might want from her.
Tues. 10/4	Mother	X					12:40	12:50 p.m.	Daily chat.
Wed. 10/5	In-laws. Spoke to Martha [husband's sister]	X					8:15	8:20	To ask if Ruth's shoes were ready and we'd pick them up on way to school.
Wed. 10/5	Rose [sister-in-law]		X				11:45 a.m.	12:00 noon	To tell me further developments on Income Tax affair.

Day	Relationship	Planned	Unplanned	Time	Purpose
Wed. 10/5	Mother	X		12:45 1:00 p.m.	Daily chat.
Thurs. 10/6	Mother	X		12:40 12:50 p.m.	Daily chat.
Thurs. 10/6	Mother-in-law	X		5:40 5:50 p.m.	To offer us fresh-baked cake, and ask advice re insurance from hurricane damage.
Thurs. 10/6	In-laws		X	8:30 9:30	To get the cake and discuss the insurance matter.
Fri. 10/7	Mother	X		11:35 11:50 a.m.	Daily chat.
Sat. 10/8	Mother	X		11:55 12:05 noon	Daily chat.
Sat. 10/8	Mother	X		12:06 12:07 noon	Afterthought to above.
Sat. 10/8	Mother	X		9:40 9:50 p.m. p.m.	She knew Ruth [daughter] was "baby sitting," and she wanted to "keep her company"—We had come home early though.
Sun. 10/9	Mother	X		12:30 12:40 noon	Daily chat.
Sun. 10/9	Mother-in-law Father- " " Sister- " " Harriet Nephew- " "		X	12:45 2:55 p.m.	Afternoon visit—but we had an engagement so they left and were to have dropped in in the late afternoon.
Sun. 10/9	Parents		X	4:30 5:00 p.m.	Hadn't visited in about 2 weeks.
Sun. 10/9	In-laws		X	5:30 5:35 p.m.	To get something early in the afternoon and continue the visit—"nobody home" except nephew-in-law.

life, arranging and discussing services and visits, giving and receiving information and advice. Minute details of household life are often discussed on the telephone more fully than in face-to-face contacts. Detailed discussions of household activity included such things as what one is going to have for dinner, recipes, prices at the local butcher, new draperies for the living room, purchase of an electric mixer, a sale at a department store. Discussions of visits and services included arrangements to pick up food a relative had cooked, arrangements to carry out household repairs. Advice and information were given on the telephone in almost all areas of family life. In one interview, for example, the client explained that she did not talk about anything "special" on the telephone with her sister, it was just "family talk." By this she meant such things as an x-ray report from her sister's doctor and a detailed discussion about whether or not her sister had arthritis.

It was clear in many interviews that not only are everyday details of life discussed on the telephone, but also subjects to which there are highly emotional reactions, including intimate advice, family tragedies, and even heated arguments such as the following:

> [My father's second wife] wanted $45 a month and I just can't do it! But my brother-in-law tried to wheedle it from us. He called my husband on the phone, and my husband was saying he'd be glad to do it but we just haven't got it. My husband was practically pleading with him. He said, "If I could possibly find a way to get it, I would be glad to do it. If I could get $15 more I would, but it's impossible." It got so heated that I had to grab the phone and scream at him. I told him in plain King's English, "Don't you know what 'We haven't got it' means?"

Who communicates with whom by telephone. Women talk with kin more often than men; almost all wives communicate with kin by telephone but fewer husbands do. Only 70 per cent of the husbands indicate that they have some contact with relatives as compared with 95 per cent of the wives.

There are similar differences between husbands and wives in the periodicity of telephone contacts with kin. Of the wives, 47 per cent talk with one or more kin every day, whereas only 15 per cent of the husbands talk with kin this frequently. There are similar differences in the frequency with which husbands and wives talk to kin "at least once a week," "every few weeks," and "less often than every few weeks." Wives talk with a larger number of kin than husbands do, and they talk with kin more frequently than do husbands, but in both cases a high proportion maintain at least some contact with kin.

Moreover, wives are to some extent delegated the task of "representing" the family in kin contacts. They are responsible for relaying what goes on with kin to their husbands, so that husbands are also involved in kin interaction on the telephone through their wives. Husbands are not totally exempt from maintaining some contacts with kin on their own. In one case, for instance, the wife reported that relatives just "don't understand" when the husband does not call them on the telephone. She justified his behavior, however, by saying that he works "such irregular hours." In addition, she pointed out that she carries on the intermediate role in relaying information about kin to him, "I give him all the information. He knows what is going on."

In addition to one member of the nuclear family relaying conversations with kin to others, a great many telephone conversations are undoubtedly overheard, or even participated in by more than one family member. Home observations and house drawings show that in most instances telephones were not in private places within the home; there is an expectation that conversations will be heard by more than one person. One client received a telephone call during an interview and returned to elaborate on it, thereby assuming that the interviewer had naturally listened to the entire conversation.

The telephone significantly increases the potential for communication among various kin within the kin network. For example, gossip is possible among kin even though they are not in daily face-to-face contact. The way in which the nuclear family is sanctioned by kin is also affected by the fact that kin are in communication with each other and can support each other's sanctions.

How kin within a network may communicate with each other is indicated by the following instance in which the client received information from several kin on a kin gathering that she had not attended: "Anna was telling me about it, Gertrude told me, my sister, Estelle, told me part of it, and Frieda. Whoever I talked to gave me some information." The fact that kin within a network can readily communicate with each other by telephone increases their opportunity for interacting with each other and supporting each other in their sanctions. One husband, for example, explained that he was sanctioned by his mother-in-law with whom he lived, because his father telephoned his mother-in-law to report information about him:

> [My father] says to me, "How much do you make . . . and how much do you gamble?" . . . So I told him I was making a hundred, and I gamble a hundred and a quarter a week. Now, I was being facetious, and my father is stupid, so he picks up the phone and calls my mother-in-law and says, "He makes so much, he gambles so much." Now, that comes back to me, "You're gambling."

This relaying of information by telephone among kin indicates that in an urban industrial society communication other than by face-to-face contact is vital. Similar orders of interaction among kin and sanctions such as gossip and direct reprimanding may all be carried out by means of telephone contact with kin who are not in continuous face-to-face contact.

Initiative and access in telephone communication. One significant feature of telephone communication is the pattern of initiative and access that it makes possible. The telephone provides immediate and easy access to members of the family—no elaborate preparations are required. There are ritual procedures by which it is possible to cut off a telephone conversation, such as asking to call back later, but the initial contact has been made. Other than measures considered extreme, such as having an unlisted telephone number, the family receiving the call has minimal control over entrance into its life. Although this is an everyday experience of most people in our culture, its significance for relationships among kin in an urban setting has not heretofore been adequately taken into account. Even if a family chooses to reduce interaction with kin, the ready access by telephone is difficult to control.

Communication in Face-to-Face Visits. Although telephone communication is more frequent than face-to-face visits among kin, face-to-face contacts remain significant, particularly in view of the high proportion of clients having kin in the metropolitan area. There are definite expectations that contact by telephone should be maintained, and the ready access to kin by means of the telephone undoubtedly helps to increase the frequency and intensity of communications among kin, but telephoning is not generally considered sufficient to replace face-to-face contacts entirely. As one client explained, calling "is not as good as seeing each other, but it still maintains the relationship."

There are also definite obligations for visits among kin. Values that stress obligations to maintain contact with kin support face-to-face visiting. In some instances these obligations were interpreted as daily face-to-face contact. As one woman explained, these obligations might even include the idea that "a son should see his mother every day." Although many individuals in the group, including this client, would not agree with so extreme a statement of obligation to visit kin, the obligation to maintain some kind of visiting relationship to kin was widely held.

A variety of types of visits with kin occur, including: those on formal ritual occasions, such as bar mitzvahs, weddings, and Thanksgiving gatherings; meetings of organized kin groups such as family circles and cousins clubs; informal visits that are prearranged such as Sunday visits with the family; informal visits that are not prearranged such as dropping in unannounced or meeting in the subway. Visits may also occur in the process of giving assistance or carrying out services for kin.

All these visits offer opportunities for face-to-face contacts among kin. The form of communication that occurs varies with such things as the intimacy of the relationship between kin, the number of people present and the formality of the gathering, the type of access that a particular visit involves. There is perhaps more situational variation in face-to-face than in telephone communication.

Although the clients live in an urban area where visits with kin might be presumed to take on a formal quality, and where the ready use of the telephone makes it possible to arrange visits in advance, 63 per cent of the wives indicated that kin drop in unannounced. This informality implies an intimacy of the relationship with kin as well as ready access of kin to the life of the client family. Both interview and questionnaire data indicate that if kin drop in unannounced, they have considerable knowledge of the family's affairs. Dropping in unannounced is comparable in some respects to the access possible through the telephone, since it takes the initiative away from the family being visited.

The Importance of Communication with Kin. Communication with kin is clearly possible both by telephoning and by face-to-face visits; it does not appear to be restricted by the urban environment. Moreover, the means of communication that are available as a result of technology and geographic proximity result in communication of emotionally important information to kin.

The fact that communication with kin includes areas of great emotional importance is indicated by the frequency of communication with kin about the agency contact and the problems that brought the family to the agency.

The common experience of being agency clients served as a baseline for comparing the kin involvement of different families. Both the problems that bring families to the agency and the experience of coming to the agency are clearly matters of considerable emotional importance.

In 76 per cent of the families either the husband and/or the wife indicated that some kin knew about the problem that brought them to the agency. In 82 per cent of the families either the husband and/or the wife indicated that some kin knew of the agency contact. A high proportion of the families had communicated with some kin about these experiences.

Kin were often instrumental in the process of referral to the agency. Although referral occurs in a wide variety of ways, kin were the most frequent single source, with friends and neighbors a close second. In one of the families interviewed, for example, the wife heard of the agency through her sister; in addition, she later passed the information on to her niece, who also became a client.

Communication with kin about the problem and the agency contact, however, was selective; most families who communicated about these matters did so with "some" and not with "most" of their kin. Of the wives who said kin knew they were coming to the agency, 85 per cent indicated that "a few close relatives" knew; whereas only 15 per cent indicated that "most of the relatives" knew. Similarly, of those wives who indicated that kin knew about their problem, 91 per cent claimed that "some kin" knew, whereas only 9 per cent claimed that "most" of their kin knew. When asked whether they had specifically avoided telling some of their kin that they were coming to the agency, in 71 per cent of the families either the husband or the wife indicated that such communication was avoided. Another indication of the selectivity of communication was the difficulty encountered in attempting to gain entry to family circles and cousins clubs for the purposes of participant observation, when client members did not want all of the kin in the organization to know of their agency contact. The reasons most frequently checked for not telling kin about the agency contact were: (1) "it wasn't any of their business," and (2) they did not want kin to know that they "had a problem." Therefore, it was expected that at least some kin would have negative reactions if they knew about the agency contact. There were, in fact, reports of such negative reactions of kin to the agency contact. In those families where kin did disapprove of the agency contact, the reasons most frequently given were: first, the family really "didn't have a problem" and, second, they "felt we should be able to work it out ourselves."

Selecting those kin with whom there is communication and withholding information from other kin is a means of avoiding negative sanctions or loss of face. This process of selection is apparently reasonably effective, because families reported that the reactions of those kin who did know about the agency contact and the problem were most often positive. When relatives did know about the problem, 73 per cent of the wives indicated that their response was "sympathetic"; 20 per cent said that "some were sympathetic, some critical"; and 6 per cent indicated that "most" relatives who knew were critical. In 81 per cent of the families the husband and/or the wife indicated that none of the relatives with whom they communicated about the agency contact disapproved of it.

In the case of more than half of the wives, and an even higher proportion of husbands, moreover, relatives are said to know more about the family than do friends. Thus communication with kin is about important matters and it is also fairly extensive as compared with communication with others.

The urban environment does not impede continuous communication with kin for most of the client families. All clients have some kin in general geographic proximity, and many have kin as close as within walking distance. This geographic proximity allows extensive overlap of household activities and informal visiting. But the geographic cutoff points, such as living within walking distance, are not necessarily the limits of contact with kin. The extent of telephone communication indicates that urban technology can increase the modes of access to kin, making possible intimate, daily communication even when constant face-to-face interaction does not occur. As a result, constant communication of vital matters is maintained between most of the client families and their kin. Kin are geographically close and telephone communication further implements their proximity. The result is that for most clients kin are omnipresent.

THE BINDING POWER
OF ASSISTANCE AND RECIPROCITY

Assistance is a crucial factor binding kin relationships. Economic aid and the gamut of major and minor services—baby sitting, shopping assistance, giving information, help with household repairs, helping with household tasks during illness—are but a few of the main forms of assistance that are regularly exchanged between client families and their kin. Assistance in the form of emotional support is also crucial, but here we will first examine what may be termed instrumental assistance; that is, concrete acts that are directed to carrying out specific tasks. As will be seen, the exchange of instrumental assistance is intimately bound up with emotional ties; instrumental assistance may be symbolic of emotional support. Like other areas of kin relationships, exchange of assistance is interpersonal; it is governed by fundamental and powerful norms about obligations between kin. Severe sanctions may be imposed for failing to live up to these obligations.

In practice, almost all of the client families have relied on kin for assistance. The importance of assistance among kin is reflected in actual behavior as well as in values. Although the specific forms of assistance vary considerably from family to family, related in part to different needs at different life-cycle states, some form of assistance was received from kin in almost all families; 95 per cent of the client families had received services and/or monetary aid from kin. As shown in the analysis of kinship values, there are strong obligations to assist kin.

Alternative Sources of Assistance for the Nuclear Family

Values about the particular external system to which it is appropriate to turn for specific kinds of assistance are reflected in differences in the frequency with which families turn to kin as opposed to other external sources for various types of assistance.

Some of the questionnaire items on assistance also included checklists to indicate the relative frequency with which the particular form of assistance was received from kin and other sources. These included kin, friends, and institutional sources such as hired help, employment agencies, banks, and social workers. Checklists covered a variety of specific forms of assistance. For each type of assistance, the frequency with which the client families checked kin, friends, or other sources was ranked (Table 6).

Table 6. Rank of Frequency with Which Nuclear Families Rely on Kin, Friends, or Other Sources for Assistance[a]

Form of Assistance	Kin	Friends	Other Sources
	RANK OF SOURCE		
Care of children if orphaned			
Husband	1	3	2
Wife	1	3	2
Making a household move			
Husband	1	2	–
Wife	1	2	–
Decision making on major purchases			
Husband	1	2	3
Baby sitting			
Wife	1	2	3
Shopping and errands			
Wife	1	2	3
Gifts of household furnishings			
Wife	1	2	–
Getting jobs			
Husband	2	3	1
Helping financially			
Wife	2	3	1
Cooking and housecleaning			
Wife	2	3	1
Child-rearing advice			
Wife	2	3	1

[a] In some instances the checklists did not include all three of these sources. Some questions were asked only of husbands or only of wives because an effort was made to avoid duplication, and the question seemed more appropriate for that individual; for example, assistance in getting jobs was asked of husbands.

There are no areas in which families turned to friends more frequently than to kin. Kinship and friendship are both personal ties, but kinship ties are defined as nonvoluntaristic and permanent, whereas friendship is voluntary and is not defined as having the same order of permanency. Moreover, there are stronger expectations for help among kin and stronger sanctions supporting these expectations; expectations of friendship generally do not include intimate instrumental aid. The cultural expectations of assistance among kin are reflected in the legal system; there are no comparable laws supporting assistance among friends.

Assistance among friends is often considered embarrassing. One woman whose close friends helped her family when her husband was out of work reports, "I feel badly even thinking about it now." In this instance the family also received assistance from kin and banks. The feelings of embarrassment were particularly strong in relation to friends, which in part reflects the family's feeling that they had lost status through being put in a position where they could not reciprocate. Because most types of instrumental assistance among kin and friends result in obligations of reciprocity, frequently involving conflict of expectations and embarrassment, it is often considered preferable to turn to kin rather than to friends.

Variation exists in the frequency with which families turn to kin and other institutions for various kinds of assistance. In response to a question about whom one would want to take care of one's children if they should be orphaned, "If something should happen to you and your husband (or wife) whom would you want to look after your children?" the highest proportion of families, 91 per cent of the wives and 96 per cent of the husbands, indicated that they would turn to kin. This question, although hypothetical, pertains to an issue of considerable emotional importance. Almost all families felt they would turn to kin, reflecting a high degree of consensus in kinship rights and obligations surrounding such circumstances. Families undoubtedly felt they could count on kin to feel obligated. Moreover, there is a kin relationship not only between the parents and their kin, but also between the children and their kin, so that orphaned children would themselves be turning to kin. There are other institutions such as placement agencies that could take care of the children but no client indicated that she would turn to this type of resource rather than to kin.

Another reason for turning to kin is that, despite the extensive elaboration and nonfamilial institutions in our society, there are certain kinds of assistance which for the most part other institutions are unprepared to handle. The "migration" of second-hand furniture and clothing among kin is an example of an important kind of instrumental assistance, occurring through complex forms of exchange and reciprocity:

> WIFE: Some [children's clothes] just get outgrown before they're worn out, and that's what travels around. I've gotten clothing from Marty's [husband's] cousins for Sara [daughter] and ones which weren't good for Sara, I handed them down to a cousin of mine . . . and the child felt as if she fell into a pot of gold.
>
> HUSBAND: In all probability this cousin got it from a hand-down, too.

There are few formal institutions carrying out this type of assistance, at least, few defined as an acceptable institutional resource.

Similarly, there are virtually no institutions that offer significant assistance in shopping and errands, another area in which kin ranked above other sources.

Assistance during illness is another area in which the family often turns to kin. Despite the development of modern medical institutions, kin may be the most readily available source of certain kinds of aid during illness. The residentially segregated nuclear family is not structurally well equipped to care for illness, since few individuals are available within the household to assist in caring for the ill. Many minor illnesses hardly ever require hospitalization but may disrupt the life of the nuclear family almost as much as more serious illnesses; for example, if the wife is in bed. Moreover, even if parents, a father or particularly a mother, are hospitalized, their roles within the household are unfilled. In a residentially segregated nuclear family there is no ready substitute within the household; so despite the use of medical institutions, the nuclear family may still require additional assistance.

When relatives are geographically close, they frequently come to the family to help carry out tasks associated with the care of a minor illness, or to substitute in the duties of the ill. Answers to the question, *"Have relatives ever helped you out during an illness?"* indicated that 58 per cent of the families had received such assistance. From interview data, however, it seems likely that even more families have received assistance from kin during minor illnesses but that those responding to the questionnaire defined illness as relatively serious illnesses, which many had not had. Many examples of assistance during illnesses were cited in interviews: shopping, letting children stay overnight, coming in to do cleaning and housework, sending cooked food, and other forms of help with the daily running of the household other than the actual care of the ill person.

Homemaker services of social agencies, private nursing, paid domestic help are nonfamilial sources of assistance; these may be a counterpart to the modern hospital, also associated with the structural characteristics of the family in our society. Housekeeping assistance, however, may be expensive and institutional sources of support for the expense are not highly developed; medical insurance policies, for example, do not generally cover homemaking costs. Although it depends on the life-cycle stage, most kin cannot come in on more than a temporary basis without leaving their own families unattended. Nevertheless, they are a significant source of assistance during illness.

Kin may also have access to external institutions when the nuclear family does not. For example, one relative borrowed from his credit union and lent the money to the client, who was not able to obtain credit himself.

Kin are the closest, most intimate part of the social network of most of the clients, having the greatest access to their lives. It is natural to turn to kin unless there are circumstances that make it preferable to turn elsewhere. There were several areas where families more frequently turn to other sources than to kin.

First, there is a tendency to turn to external institutions if the particular type of aid can be obtained better through a specialized institution than through kin. For example, in assistance in getting jobs, kin often do give information, but unions and placement agencies have wider sources of information.

Child-rearing advice is another area in which more families indicated that they turned to sources other than to kin. The immigrant status of their parents and generational differences in values about child rearing create problems in relying on parents. However, interviews indicate that frequently relatives give "a lot of advice even though it's not asked for"; kin feel it is their right and duty to offer child-rearing advice so that there is no need to seek advice. Nonetheless, most families indicated that if they were seeking advice they would turn to other sources. The most frequently checked source was books. No one indicated that he relied on a social worker.

Another reason for turning to external institutions arises where assistance from kin might threaten the status of the husband or the wife. Child-rearing assistance or child-rearing advice given in front of children may undermine the status of the parents. As one husband explained, "In-laws spoil children with too many gifts, and condone conduct that is not up to our standards."

Competent performance is crucial to woman's status as a wife and mother. Kin may sometimes assist in cooking and housecleaning, for example, if the wife is ill, with no threat to her status. Under other circumstances the assistance of kin in cooking and housework may be perceived as jeopardizing the status of the wife. Kin asked to perform a menial task may also feel their status threatened. This threat does not occur in joint households or even adjoining apartments where the women have some sort of specific division of labor; it does not necessarily apply to bringing in food cooked in another household, more easily seen as ritual assistance or gift-giving.

Financial assistance from kin may threaten the status of the husband and wife. Values data indicate that, despite the strength of kinship obligations, most families prefer banks or other nonkin sources for financial assistance, although a high proportion of families actually have turned to kin for economic assistance. The values may therefore reflect the fact that families who have done so have experienced consequent difficulties in their relationships with kin. Interviews indicated that financial assistance from kin is a threat, with the potential for breaking up relationships among kin. Not only is the fact of having to borrow from kin a possible source of status loss, but the problems that may be encountered in paying back loans to kin, particularly as compared with the definite expectations for such payments in loans from a bank, were seen as a potential source of difficulties. Some have concluded that they should do "no more giving and no more receiving." Since it is essential to maintain relationships with kin, financial assistance from kin is a source of problems; nevertheless, it is extremely frequent among the research families.

Reciprocity in Assistance Among Kin

Instrumental assistance reinforces emotional ties among kin, particularly since assistance among kin is reciprocal. Just as the families we have interviewed rely on kin, so do other families in their kin network. In other words, kin are interdependent for instrumental assistance; reciprocity is basic to interdependence.

Reciprocity in exchanges among kin was clear in questionnaire data. Not only had 95 per cent of the families received some form of economic or service assistance from kin, but 94 per cent of the families had also given some kind of instrumental assistance to kin. No one family necessarily gives and receives the same amount, or gives and receives the same things from the same people. But as a group, families are both giving aid to and receiving aid from kin.

This equivalence of assistance given and received applies not only to all forms of assistance, but also to specific kinds of assistance. The proportion of families having given and received a particular kind of assistance was examined. Where the difference was less than 10 per cent between the proportion giving and that receiving, this was considered "equivalent." Giving and receiving assistance was equivalent for the following kinds of assistance: assistance during illness, baby sitting, child-rearing advice, help during a household move, cooking and housework, household repairs, job hunting, advice on major purchases. Equivalence did not occur with monetary assistance and gifts of household furnishings where the clients received more than they gave, and shopping and errands where the clients gave more than they received. These differences undoubtedly reflect life-cycle differences to some extent. Despite these specific discrepancies, the overall similarity in the extent to which families have given and received various kinds of assistance from kin indicates a high degree of reciprocity.

Forms of reciprocity and the process through which reciprocity occurs are significant in understanding relationships with kin. The discrepancies in monetary assistance, household furnishings, and shopping and errands can also be understood in light of the process of reciprocity.

From the perspective of particular client families, reciprocity does not always mean reciprocity in kind. One may reciprocate for one form of assistance through giving a very different kind. In one interview the family explained that there was a kind of specialization in reciprocity with their kin. The husband's father, a shoemaker, repaired shoes for the children: in return, the family drove the father and mother in their car:

> WIFE: Well, I don't say it's exactly equal, 50–50, but I mean I feel that when we're able to do something, we do.
>
> HUSBAND: I mean, I think we do the things we can do and they do the things they can do.

When reciprocity is not in kind, a system of exchange cannot operate unless there are values that make it possible to reckon the equivalence of various kinds of assistance. Complex scales for determining equivalence in exchanges among kin clearly exist and are a vital concern for the clients. The following statement measures equivalence in gift-giving on a number of dimensions:

> We had a catered affair. . . . We had 42 pounds of fish, we had chopped herring and pickled herring. . . . It was really very nice . . . and my sister gave him $25. . . . This was five and a half years after her friend's son was bar mitzvahed. . . . And she gave him the *same*. . . . Just for a sandwich thing. . . . Not even a sandwich . . . tidbits at somebody's house. . . . $25 to a stranger whom you don't even know. . . . And she gave her own nephew $25 at this kind of an affair. . . . It hurts me deeply. . . . It rankles.

Several variables enter this calculation; first, the style and expense of the particular form of entertainment; second, the kin or nonkin form of relationship; and third, the monetary value of the gift. The exchange was entirely monetary, but an equal amount of money did not mean equivalence in the overall balance considering all criteria.

If different individuals are to agree about the equality of an exchange, there must be equivalence in terms of a large number of variables, some of them difficult to measure. If one individual uses criteria different from another's, a perceived discrepancy in evaluating the exchange and a potential conflict are likely to result. The calculation of equivalence is often exceedingly explicit, but the total balance is not always absolutely clear in view of the complexity of measurement.

Time is a variable in any exchange. Since it exists in all acts of exchange, it must be evaluated in each instance. The time within which an act of reciprocity is expected to occur varies with the circumstances and the form of assistance. In gift-giving on ritual occasions such as weddings and bar mitzvahs, immediate return is not expected; return is expected when a comparable occasion arises for the other person. Examples were given of exchanges that took place over extremely long periods. Some time lag always exists. The fact that kin relationships are defined as permanent makes possible long time spans in reciprocity. If reciprocity is not given at the time that it should be, a sort of increment or debt accrues as a result of feelings of shame or guilt, and the final act may entail a larger return than it would have before the delay.

Once in the middle of a cycle, one cannot depart without leaving an imbalance in the state of exchange; if the next step is not taken someone is left owing a debt or having a debt owed to him. Cultural norms support expectations of continuation of the cycle of reciprocity.

Reciprocity is not always directly to the individual from whom assistance was received; frequently it involves third or fourth parties. Reciprocity through a third party is illustrated in the case of one client whose father died, leaving her mother alone when the client was a young child. The father's brother was supposed to assist in the support of his widowed sister-in-law but he apparently did not "help my mother and me" very much and "always felt kind of guilty." Finally, years later, when the client married he reciprocated to the client's father who had started him off in business by making "the wedding for us . . . a very nice catered affair." This kind of reciprocity to third parties requires a clearly defined relationship among all those involved, which is more likely among kin than it would be, for example, among friends.

Who reciprocates to whom, as well as the content of reciprocity, is influenced by the life-cycle positions and the socioeconomic status of the various parties. Life-cycle stage influences not only needs for assistance—for example, whether or not a family has children and needs help with child care—but also their resources for giving assistance to kin. A family at a later stage of the life cycle may, for example, be more able to give financial assistance than one at an earlier stage of the life cycle, assuming that the socioeconomic status is relatively similar in both of these families. On the other hand, younger families may be able to give certain kinds of services to older people such as shopping and doing errands because of their greater physical abilities. For instance, one woman reciprocated with her mother for monetary gifts by shopping and running errands:

> It's only lately that I've been able to convince her . . . to let me do this—because she always would feel it's imposing on me. . . . And yet, it's necessary for me to be able to do these little things for my mother, so that I can take the money, because she pushes the money on me anyway, with some rationale.

Socioeconomic status or class differences also influence the resources of families and the kinds of reciprocity in which they can engage. A kin who has means may give financial assistance to those who are able to reciprocate only through their services. Thus one might chart the content of exchanges in terms of status positions, with financial assistance going down from those of higher status to those of lower status, and various services going upward to those in higher economic positions. A similar kind of charting could be made for many exchanges between those at different stages in the life cycle, such as children giving pride or *nakhes* to their parents.

Initiative in exchange is influenced by the idea that kin have a right to give assistance and start a process of exchange whether solicited or not. Kin are obligated to give assistance if it is necessary; they also have a right to give it. It is generally difficult to find a reason for not accepting assistance from kin. The right to give is defined as one of the basic rights of kinship. Coupled with expectations that one should reciprocate, this right to give contributes to the binding power of kinship.

Although we have examined mainly instrumental assistance rather than ceremonial gift-giving, the line between the two is indistinct. Assistance among kin is often defined as gift-giving. Even financial assistance is generally not given on a contractual basis, that is, with interest. Nearly half of the families who claimed to have received financial assistance from kin indicated that it was "more of a present than a loan"; when it was defined as a loan it was generally without interest. Only 3 per cent indicated that interest was involved in their financial assistance to kin. Those who give more than they receive, however, gain the power of the indebtedness that others have to them. In the example above, the daughter who shops for her mother is anticipating both that the gift of money will be given by her mother and that it cannot be refused. By anticipating, and so to speak, reciprocating in advance, she is attempting to prevent an imbalance in the system of exchange and power.

A basic mechanism in the strength of kinship bonds is the perception that gift-giving gives one person a hold over the other, which is clearly revealed in the following discussion of the husband's mother:

> WIFE: Every now and then she has something or other that she makes and nobody else does and she sends it over. . . . She'll say that nobody will eat it if they've had it for a day or two.
>
> HUSBAND: That's what I mean. If this happens time and time again and you make so much and nobody—I mean you'd think you'd make less, but that's not the story. She deliberately makes all this [food] because she knows she will give some to us. That's what I think. . . . How stupid can you be? I mean—if you make a certain amount and it's always left over. . . . And you complain that the kids and nobody is eating it, why do you keep making it? She knows that she will give it to us. . . .
>
> INTERVIEWER: How do you feel about it?
>
> HUSBAND: I don't mind. . . . I mean if she has to give it I take it, if she hasn't got it. . . . I mean if she had it and she gave it to somebody else it might bother me. Today she's in a peculiar situation. She's very sick, and she's getting older and she cannot do as much as she'd like to—physically, so I think her only hold on us is the little that she can do that way, so she comes over with, "Look, I did just as good as you." That might not be the ideal thing to do, I mean let her, maybe it's better that she thinks she is doing this for us.

Here the mother is perceived as having a hold on the family through the food she gives them; an economic service is closely tied in with an emotional bond. The strength of emotional dependency in kinship is built up through assistance and reciprocity. Cultural norms that one should reciprocate for assistance give legitimacy to expectations of dependency on kin.

How it is possible to manipulate the process of exchange to gain power both psychologically and in terms of sociocultural expectations is illustrated in the following example, in which the husband is talking about his mother-in-law who lives in the same building.

> When she was able to, she would be the "good mother." "What? Do you need tomatoes? Do you need tomatoes? I have tomatoes! You want apples? I have apples in my house!" So she'd give Marilyn all these apples and then half hour later she'd say, "You know, I need tomatoes." After she had just given us hers she would expect me to go out and buy some for her. But in the meantime she has become the good one because she has given those apples to her.

The client families turn to kin for many types of instrumental assistance. There is an underlying obligation of kin to assist each other. Other sources may be preferred if assistance from kin would threaten the status of husband or wife, or if more expert sources are available elsewhere. But alternative sources do not always exist, and where they exist they are not always accessible. Thus almost all families turn to kin at some time.

Reciprocity strengthens kinship ties and binds kin together. Clients rely on kin for many kinds of assistance. The right of kin to give and thereby to initiate exchange processes adds to the hold of kinship. Ritual and economic, psychological and social mesh in exchanges among kin; cultural norms define expectations of reciprocity as legitimate. The sequential processes of reciprocity and the resulting imbalances increase the binding quality of kinship ties, making them difficult to change. Termination of a contractual exchange, as in business, where the relationship is not defined as permanent and there is less imbalance in the exchange may be easier. A cycle of action and reaction in kin exchange exists that cannot be interrupted without leaving some kind of imbalance in the system; those involved in this imbalance will react to it. Thus reciprocity reinforces the ties of kinship.

In assistance, as well as in the extent of geographic proximity and communication, and the extensiveness of kin ties, almost all client families are deeply involved with their kin.

NOTES TO CHAPTER 4

1. Firth, Raymond W., editor, *Two Studies of Kinship in London.* The Athlone Press, London, 1956.
2. Codere, Helen, "A Genealogical Study of Kinship in the United States," *Psychiatry,* vol. 18, February, 1955, pp. 65–79.
3. Young, Michael, and Hildred Geertz, "Old Age in London and San Francisco: Some Families Compared," *The British Journal of Sociology,* vol. 12, June, 1961, pp. 124–141.
4. Firth makes a similar distinction between "recognized" kin and "nominated" kin, *op. cit.,* p. 42.
5. Leichter, Hope J., and William E. Mitchell, "Feuds and Fissions Within the Conjugal Kindred." Paper read at the Annual Meeting of the American Anthropological Association, Minneapolis, November, 1960.
6. A more detailed presentation of the research findings based on these four boundary criteria appears in Mitchell, William E., "Proximity Patterns of the Urban Jewish Kindred," *Man,* vol. 65, September–October, 1965, pp. 137–140.

CHAPTER 5

Kin Groups
and Assemblages

Kinship can be studied in terms of the kin ties of a particular individual or family, as was indicated in Chapter 4; various kinship groupings can also be examined in terms of their organization as systems. A shift of perspective from the individual to the group becomes necessary because many social groups, particularly those that have persistence over time, have characteristics that cannot be understood merely from knowledge of their individual members. Moreover, relationships between kin may be influenced by their joint participation in a kin group, and knowledge of the structure and functioning of kin groups therefore is an important factor in understanding the relationships of client families with kin.

We will discuss three types of kin groups in which client families participate: ad hoc kin assemblages, family-kin businesses, and family circles and cousins clubs. In each case the organization of the group itself affects the relationships between the clients and their kin.

As we have seen, the kin of each client family constitute a network, not a group. But groups exist within this network. If the client family participates in one or more kin groups, kin in their network are probably also coming in contact with each other.[1] If the kin of a client family come in contact with each other in various formal groups, the clients are not interacting with completely separate individuals, but the kin may influence each other in their relationships with the client family.

Previous theories have held that corporate kin groups, more extensive than the nuclear family, could not exist in an urban industrial society. Contrary to these assumptions, such corporate kin groups have been found both in family circles and cousins clubs, and in family-kin businesses. Questions are thus raised about the implications that these groups have for other areas of kin relationships.

AD HOC KIN ASSEMBLAGES

Ad hoc assemblages are one type of extended kin grouping. They are kin groups because their boundaries are the same from the perspective of all members, but they are not permanent. They occur on a temporary ad hoc or occasional basis.[2]

These assemblages are a basic form of kin interaction. At some time almost all families participate in them. They encompass a variety of gatherings: (1) informal social meetings and formal family reunions, (2) calendrical ceremonies, that is, those occurring at particular times during the calendar year such as Thanksgiving and Passover, (3) life-cycle ceremonials such as weddings, bar mitzvahs, funerals, and (4) crisis gatherings where kin meet to help solve a particular problem such as illnesses and feuds. They include both invitational gatherings such as weddings and non-invitational gatherings where initiative is left to those attending such as funerals.

Ad hoc kin gatherings serve to define the boundaries and bonds of the kin network since they constitute a visible statement of kin choices and obligations; they augment the nuclear family's potential kin network by providing occasions where links in the kin network are made; they tend to strengthen kinship ties by giving them ritual and ceremonial expression; they provide an arena for joint social participation of family members; many kin gatherings are an occasion for the incorporation of a husband or wife into the spouse's kin network; finally, they serve as a significant reference group for the family. These basic functions will be examined and illustrated.

Fifty-seven per cent of the families that filled out the questionnaire indicated that they celebrated the previous Thanksgiving with relatives. In view of assumptions made early in the study that Thanksgiving was a nearly universal American holiday, and in light of cultural traditions of it as a kin occasion, it may seem surprising to find that only 57 per cent of the families celebrated this event with kin, particularly in contrast to other areas of behavior in which the client families are heavily involved with their relatives. In light of interview and other data, however, this does not appear so surprising. The lack of cultural familiarity and emotional meaning of this gathering to the parents of many clients became evident in interview data. Here, as in many other areas of kin relationships, a gap in cultural values between generations is apparent. Thanksgiving celebrations are generally sponsored by the clients' rather than their parents' generation. Nevertheless, Thanksgiving is an occasion for the participation of more than one generation. It offers, therefore, an occasion for ritual and social expression of the solidarity of kinship ties across generations.

Boundaries of Thanksgiving Gatherings

The choices involved in selecting kin for ad hoc gatherings vary with the type of gathering. Size of the gathering is important for the selection process. Limitations on size, such as financial and space limitations, may make it necessary to search for acceptable objective criteria whereby boundaries may be drawn with minimal offense, for example, the exclusion of children. Size and kinship definitions of the occasion, however, go hand in hand. Certain events such as weddings may entail expectations of more inclusive participation. Thanksgiving, on the other hand, appears to be generally defined as a small and intimate gathering. In 98 per cent of the gatherings fewer than 18 people attended, including all children and the sponsor or sponsors. In a few cases the gatherings were larger but, for the most part, they were celebrations of two, three, or four nuclear families.

One question about how Thanksgiving gatherings serve to define who are and who are not kin for a family concerns which kin are present at the gathering. Here the significance of a systematic perspective becomes clear. Data on Thanksgiving gatherings were obtained from client wives, who were asked to write down which kin were present. But in order to understand these data it became necessary to analyze them from the perspective of the sponsor of the gathering, who sometimes was the client, and sometimes not.

From the perspective of the sponsor, the genealogical range of kin present at Thanksgiving gatherings was generally limited, although in some instances it extended considerably. Of all the kin present at Thanksgiving gatherings, over half were fathers, mothers, brothers, and sisters of either the sponsor or the sponsor's spouse. Others were usually linked through these kin. However, even though most Thanksgiving gatherings are among intimate kin, the genealogical links are different from the perspective of each individual, so that here also a choice process goes on. There are no automatic criteria for deciding which kin to celebrate Thanksgiving with; rather, this must be decided by each family for each occasion.

When one examines the size and genealogical extension of ad hoc kin gatherings from the perspective of all participants, not merely from that of the sponsor, their function in linking and augmenting the kin network becomes apparent. For all participants, sponsors, and guests, ad hoc gatherings of various types constitute an occasion to demonstrate the solidarity of kinship bonds. Since, as we have seen, the boundaries of the kin network shift, depending on the criterion, each kinship event is significant in defining who are and who are not kin. The sponsor or the individual in whose honor the gathering is held largely determines who attends. At both invitational and noninvitational gatherings those who attend do so by virtue of their relationship to the sponsor. As a result, two individuals who are genealogically remote may meet at a gathering because each has close kin ties to the sponsor.

How ad hoc kin assemblages serve to augment the network of kin contacts of the nuclear family is demonstrated most clearly in large gatherings. But the same principle may be observed in Thanksgiving dinners, even though contacts of genealogically distant kin are less likely to occur in small gatherings. Two Thanksgiving examples should help to clarify this point. In each case the client attended a gathering with kin who were more closely related to the sponsor than they were to her.

In Figure 2 the top genealogy is a case in which client and her husband and children celebrated Thanksgiving at her sister's home. Not only her sister's husband and children, but also her sis-

ASSEMBLAGE A

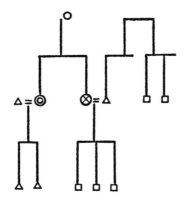

ASSEMBLAGE B

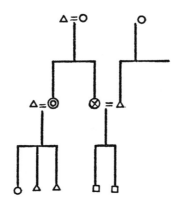

⬤ the client who gave the information; ⊗ the sponsor of the assemblage; △ male;
◯ female; ☐ sex not mentioned; | parent-child tie; — sibling tie; = marital tie

*Figure 2. Genealogical Diagram of Kin Present at
Two Thanksgiving Assemblages*

ter's husband's cousins were present. In terms of genealogical position alone, these cousins would not be likely to be defined as relatives by the client but their joint participation at ad hoc assemblages was on a basis of kinship.

In the bottom genealogy, the sister's husband's mother was present at the Thanksgiving celebration in the client's sister's home. Again, the sister's husband's mother is genealogically not likely to be defined as a kin of the informant, but they met because of common ties with kin.

Large Kin Gatherings

Such contacts between kin who are so removed genealogically that they may not even define each other as kin, but who are both related to a mutual kin, are frequent in large kin gatherings. Weddings are a particularly useful example because the bride's and the groom's kin are being linked for the first time. At one moderate-sized wedding discussed by a husband and wife in an interview, the husband's father's two sisters and his brothers and their wives were present. The wife's mother's sister and brother were also present. These kin of the husband and the wife had not been brought together before the wedding, but they met at the wedding because of having kin in common.

Augmentation of the kin network through kin assemblages was evident in comparisons of genealogies and lists given of ad hoc assemblage attendance. Those listed for a particular ad hoc gathering were checked to see whether they were present in the genealogy already given by the client. In the majority of cases, particularly for more intimate ad hoc gatherings, those present were listed in the genealogy. But in a number of instances some kin were present at ad hoc assemblages who were not included in the genealogy. This example illustrates the fluctuation of the boundaries of the kin network and the potential importance of ad hoc assemblages in augmenting these boundaries.

Although large gatherings such as weddings, bar mitzvahs, and funerals offer clear examples of contact of distant kin, in some respects they may be less significant in the definitions of kinship ties than small gatherings such as Thanksgiving, where this type of contact occurs less frequently. When it does occur, the intimacy of the occasion may make a future relationship more likely.

Moreover, some intimate calendrical gatherings are likely to be repeated from year to year, even though they do not have a formal stable organization, and this repetition tends to strengthen the idea that those present are kin.

Joint participation of genealogically distant kin at the same gathering does not ensure that they will have a continuing relationship apart from kin gatherings, but it does constitute a contact with individuals on the basis of kinship. This contact augments the family's social world and is a potential basis for further relationships, since it offers an opportunity for establishing and renewing contacts. Interview data indicate that ad hoc gatherings do carry over into continuing relationships and may heighten kinship solidarity.

When kin come together, particularly at a time of crisis or heightened emotion, the event may be particularly significant in developing feelings of solidarity. One couple, for example, explained that the husband's brother had started telephoning his kin regularly following his son's bar mitzvah:

> Friday night at eight we know that's his call. . . . He calls the entire family. . . . He calls his father, his sister, and his brothers . . . ever since his son was bar mitzvahed . . . because his family got together and he had a wonderful time, and ever since then he started to make the calls. . . . I think it's nice.

Frequently it was reported that ad hoc assemblages led directly to more formal or more frequent interaction among the kin present. One of the commonest reasons given for organizing cousins clubs was that a group of cousins got together at an ad hoc assemblage, frequently a crisis or "rite of passage" gathering such as a funeral, wedding, bar mitzvah, or the illness of a family member. Often, after a considerable period of noncontact, those present felt it was too bad they did not see more of each other, and attempts were made to remedy the situation. For example, the founding of one cousins club was described in this way:

> We started it in 1951. . . . We felt that why shouldn't we get together at least once a month, or once every two months. At least we see one another, and not just on occasions. Why should we see each other just for a happy occasion, or a sad occasion, and why couldn't we get together more often, all of the cousins.

Thus Thanksgiving gatherings, as well as other ad hoc kin assemblages, are occasions for joint social participation of the nuclear family members with their kin; they give ritual support to ties of kinship and afford a basis for making and renewing contacts, which frequently extend beyond the specific event. Moreover, since ad hoc assemblages often augment the range of an individual's kin contact through extending them to those having common ties to a sponsor, they broaden the individual's kin contact and extend his access to varied models of life style and achievement.

Ad hoc assemblages involve joint participation of the husband and wife in a group that is usually a significant reference group and one that is important for the family's prestige. For example, whether a family is able to give its son a lavish bar mitzvah or its daughter an expensive wedding may be an index of its social status. This, in turn, may lead to other invitations that continue to define its status. These gatherings provide an occasion on which the husband and wife are integrated into the spouse's kin network. When a husband and wife celebrate Thanksgiving together with the wife's family, they are acting as a couple and being defined as a couple by their kin. This joint participation of the couple at kin gatherings can contribute to the strength of the marital bond.

Participation in ad hoc kin assemblages may also give psychological support to the individual, since it offers activity and contacts that supplement those available within the nuclear family. For example, one of the wives interviewed derived considerable support through opportunities to sing and participate socially in various kin gatherings, although her husband did not enjoy these gatherings and did not permit her to sing at home. Thus an individual may be restricted in the performance of certain activities at home, but with the support of kin at a gathering, may find expressive outlets that would otherwise not exist.

These gatherings are social relationships in which client families participate with others, many of whom are nonclients. Their own contacts with kin are mediated by the social and cultural expectations of others, as well as the psychological characteristics of the participants. In order to understand how the environment impinges upon the family, it is necessary to look at the organization of this environment in its own terms. Here we have not only another example of the involvement of families with their kin, but also an indication of how kinship organization perpetuates this involvement.

FAMILY-KIN BUSINESSES

Like ad hoc kin assemblages, family-kin businesses can be examined from the point of view of their organization as a social system, as well as from the perspective of the client family. Family-kin businesses are significant because in them, occupational and kinship roles overlap. Many theorists consider the economy one of the major factors affecting family organization. If one wishes, for example, to understand the effect that participation in a family-kin business will have on a family, it is necessary to understand how the business itself functions. The functioning of a business is, in turn, affected by relationships among kin and may affect kin relationships as well. Both the functioning of the business and the relationships with kin that it supports will, in turn, have consequences for the family. Thus one is inevitably drawn outside the family to an examination of the social units that impinge upon it.

Family-kin businesses were found to exist at present, or to have existed in the past, in a relatively large proportion of client families. Of the husbands who responded to this item in the questionnaire, 30 per cent indicated that they were presently or had at some time been involved in a business with kin outside their present nuclear family. In most of these cases the husbands were no longer associated with the business. Here, as with other areas of kin activity, the importance of systematic examination of stages of the family life cycle is evident. Business involvement with kin is less frequent in the client group than other kinds of kin relationships. However, since these business activities constitute an overlap of kinship and occupational roles in an urban industrial economy, they would be theoretically crucial for an understanding of family and kinship, even if they occurred less frequently than they actually do.

A series of interviews examined the types of relationships with kin that are fostered in family-kin businesses, the ways in which joint business activity influences kin ties, and the influences of family-kin businesses upon the client family. Data were obtained in these interviews on the organization and operation of the business, on relationships with kin, and on roles and functions within the client family.

Interviews covered a variety of types of family-kin business: optical, diamond, drygoods, picture-framing, manufacturing elastic braid, fur trade, retail bathroom utilities, butchering, luggage manufacture, textiles, luggage-cover manufacture, poultry sale, garage, bowling alley, luncheonette, juke box distribution, grocery store, dry cleaning, burglar alarm, candy store, contracting, and air freight. In the 63 cases on which questionnaire data were obtained, roughly a third were in retail business, nearly as many were in manufacturing and service occupations. A smaller proportion were in wholesale businesses. Most of these businesses were small regardless of the type of activity. Twenty-seven per cent employed only one or two persons; 58 per cent, fewer than five; 76 per cent, ten or fewer. Someone other than the client husband was the head of the business more often than the client was, but in roughly a third of the businesses the client husband was head or joint head. Most often these were single-generation businesses headed by a member of the husband's own generation. Where they were cross-generational, they almost always included the generation above that of the husband; descendants were almost never involved.

Business Functioning and Kinship Structure

It is difficult to evaluate the influences of kinship on a business, in part because there are no satisfactory criteria for the successful functioning of the business. Moreover, even where the business was clearly seen as unsatisfactory by its members; for example, where it was dissolved, a variety of factors other than kinship may have affected its failure. Small businesses, in general, are often precarious. In addition, these data are seen from the perspective of one or two participants, and their views may not correspond with those of other members of the business. Nevertheless, from interview data it is possible to obtain insights into the effects of kinship on business functioning.

As perceived by participants, family businesses are often fraught with problems and are usually not outstanding successes. The frequent change from one business to another reported in interviews is one indication of the difficulties that arise in some family-kin businesses. The essential problem in some businesses seems to have been the inability to go out of business when circumstances required, but frequently there were reports of a series of shifts of business ventures with various kin, and frequent shifts from one business to another.

The great majority of husbands indicated in answers to questions in the questionnaire that the business was not going well financially; only a few felt that it was doing all right financially. Most felt that there was a lot of tension and conflict. Conflicts among kin were frequent in businesses that were not doing well financially, but were reported in a few cases even in those that were successful. In any case, a conjunction of financial problems with tension and conflict among kin is frequent.

Most husbands reported negative feelings about the experience of working with kin. From write-in answers to the question, "From your experience, what are your feelings about working with relatives?" a preponderance of negative feelings was evident. The material was coded in terms of whether the response was generally "negative," "positive," "mixed," "neutral," or "contingent." In the majority of cases, 33 out of 56 comments were definitely negative with no positive statements at all. In only 11 cases were the comments entirely positive. Cases that were categorized either as mixed or contingent involved some negative statement either direct or implied, and thus in 42 out of 56 cases, or 75 per cent, there was some indication of negative feelings about working in business with kin.

Many vivid descriptions were given of the problems of these businesses. The following is a not uncommon statement of feelings about business problems:

> My business is atrocious. Sometimes I can't convey how bad it is. It's deteriorating like wagon wheels, like horses and buggies. It's a dying industry . . . dying. See, you got yourself an old Persian coat and made a lining out of it . . . but you're not going to buy again. It's the style and mode of fashion . . . it was time to throw it out twenty years ago. It's like if I were to keep a car for 400 years. It's a dying industry, and I bemoan, and bemoan, and bemoan.

Negative feelings of this sort do not characterize all family-kin businesses but they are typical of many. These negative feelings may be a reflection of the fact that this is a client group, many of whom have more pervasive individual and family problems. However, business problems may affect individual and family problems, as well as the reverse.

Lest the feelings of frustration and conflict that characterize many of those who have at sometime been in business with kin give an unduly pessimistic picture, it is worth noting that business families do not differ greatly from other client families in social status, as indicated by income and education. In fact, they were in somewhat better positions than most other clients.

The frustrations found in many family-kin businesses also do not appear to reflect major differences in life style between business and nonbusiness families. More husbands in business families than nonbusiness families indicated that they had moderate or few social activities. But this did not hold true for wives. Both husbands and wives in business families were somewhat less likely to list friends of the opposite sex than in nonbusiness families, but these differences were small. In all other areas of friendship, business and nonbusiness families did not differ. The parents in business families did not differ appreciably in religious orientation, as indicated by identification as Orthodox, Conservative, Reform, or "just Jewish," or as indicated by whether their present style of cooking was kosher or Jewish style, from those in nonbusiness families.

Despite these general similarities in style of life and the indication that, if anything, business families may be slightly less disadvantaged than other clients; there may well be problems of business organization that derive specifically from its being conducted with kin.

Interviews indicated that in a variety of ways the diffuse obligations among kin and the problems of separating occupational and kinship status do affect the functioning of business, sometimes in ways that create problems for the business. Kin relationships do sometimes make it difficult to assign positions within the business on an objective basis; kinship sometimes clouds the objectivity of the hiring process and the setting up of salary and other benefit conditions; obligations of kinship sometimes limit the flexibility of the business, making it difficult to terminate employment when this is required in view of external conditions. The hierarchy of kinship positions that individuals have in relation to each other sometimes carries over into the business hierarchy, making it more difficult to maintain the business hierarchy if it does not correspond to that of kinship. In general, therefore, there are problems of segregating business from other kin relationships.

The assignment of statuses within the business is, in fact, often influenced by the kinship positions of those involved. In this respect, there is a tendency toward informality of procedures, which may typify small businesses generally, not merely those involving kin. Frequently, for example, financial records were handled informally. In 41 per cent of the businesses, records were handled by the participants themselves or did not exist at all. One woman described a situation of this sort, saying there was "nothing on paper ... whatever was left at the end of the week they split up. It was all on a cash basis."

This lack of formal organizational procedure opens the way for the influence of kinship in filling positions originally and in assigning tasks within the business. Hiring was sometimes definitely on the basis of a kinship obligation. One man explained that his father wanted him to go into the business of his brother, but that there was no "special reason why he should want me ... except for the fact that he is doing me a favor." Obligations among kin may also be used as pressures to recruit. For example, in one case a man was pushed to go into business with his family because of illness on the part of some of his kin. Here, his obligation to kin in time of illness was stressed in an effort to pressure him into entering the business.

The nonspecific, noncontractual character of many business relationships is clear in the descriptions given by one husband and wife of the husband's business dealings with his family:

> WIFE: When we became engaged, he was earning the fabulous sum of $60 a week. . . . We felt that as the business grew, so would his salary . . . he was putting in 16 to 18 hours per day. And then the business did grow, and it did prosper . . . and his salary didn't grow. . . .
>
> HUSBAND: Sometimes I didn't even get paid. . . .
>
> WIFE: Before we were married, let me not neglect this, she [husband's mother] merely took $50 a week out of his $60 to buy him clothing, and this went on for months. . . . This $50 per week that she took for his clothing resulted in a half-dozen undershorts—seconds, faded— that I threw out, a magnificent bathrobe that I later discovered cost $2.00 at Klein's . . . a half-dozen shirts.
>
> HUSBAND: They were broadcloth. . . .
>
> WIFE: When he says broadcloth, he's being nice. This does not even lie near broadcloth. She didn't even spend $40 on all his junk.

At a later point, this noncontractual business arrangement was suggested again by the husband's family in an effort to get him to return to the business.

> WIFE: And my mother-in-law came to me and said to me, "We're willing to take him into the business." . . . and I said, "What will the salary be?" And she said, "Your mother would feed you and the baby, and we would feed Abe [husband]." And with a great deal of self-control, I said, "What about rent?" And she said, "Oh, that we'll see about."

Feelings of exploitation were particularly strong in this case, but similar statements were repeated in interviews with other families. As one man wrote in his questionnaire, "A relative expects more from you than any other employer, and gives in return less."

Obligations of kinship not only affect the hiring process, they also affect termination of businesses. Size of business, competitive situation, technological changes, and many other factors were cited as problems for family-kin businesses. At best it is difficult to predict business conditions and know when to change an enterprise. When kinship obligations are involved, however, this may reduce the flexibility of the organization because it makes it more difficult to discharge employees or to leave the business. One man explained, for example, that he stayed for two and a half years in his uncle's business although he hated the job "because I didn't want to insult my uncle and disappoint my father."

Thus there is a potential merging of business and outside obligations among kin. These external obligations contribute to the difficulty of maintaining objectivity and strictly contractual relations within the business. As one man explained, when you work with kin "you are more or less obligated to defend and protect them. You overlook errors and avoid arguments."

These obligations may give an individual a certain assurance and freedom in business. Since kinship ties are conceived of as lifelong, and in many respects unbreakable, behavior may be tolerated from kin that would be intolerable from nonkin. One man explained about working with a relative that "if he were not related, I don't think he would take me." He went on to explain that he was always "complaining and bitching and crying and sobbing" and that his relative "certainly takes a lot of this nagging abuse that I give him." However, the emotional support derived from strong ties of kinship may not necessarily be beneficial for the overall operation of the business.

The hierarchy of kinship positions may also color the business hierarchy, making it more difficult to maintain the latter, particularly when the two hierarchies do not correspond. Relationships between generations, that is, father-son relationships, appear to have a particularly strong carryover into business dealings. One man described his brother's problem in standing up for his rights in business when working with his father:

> One of his troubles was that he worked under my father, because my father is an older person, and he gets quite irritable, and he does things that are wrong in business, harmful, or wasteful. . . . And my brother, well, he wouldn't talk fresh to my father, so he kept on bottling it up. . . . [With another boss] he could tell him off, or something. But you have to have respect for your father. You don't do that. So, it was a difficult situation.

This man might also have had difficulties in dealing with another boss, that is, a father figure, but with an actual father who reacts to the individual as a son, not merely as an employee, there are added pressures, making it difficult to segregate business relationships from other levels of involvement.

Birth-order distinctions among siblings may also carry over into business positions, affecting authority and decision-making. Sometimes it was considered difficult when a younger brother was in a business position senior to an older brother, or when a younger brother had no hope of achieving partnership with his older brothers.

The carryover of kinship statuses into the business hierarchies may not always produce problems. However, it is extremely difficult to disregard the fact that one has a different status with the same people in another relationship. When business and kin relationships involve the same individuals, business dealings are frequently inescapably pervasive in social life. As one woman explained, "When there's an argument, it's a family affair, and everybody has to know about it." Or as another woman claimed, "Things are brought back into the family, and this side's story is told and the other one's story."

This is a two-way process; the entanglement of kin and business statuses has consequences for relationships among kin as well as for the business. From the point of view of business functioning, it means that kin who are not directly involved in the business are told of the business affairs, and consequently apply sanctions to those in the business. In one case, a woman's husband had received financial backing from her mother for a business venture. Her mother felt that she had been exploited, and the wife, in turn, heard of this through her sister. Here, communication among kin meant that the mother's reaction was reported to the wife and had an effect upon the functioning of the business.

This feedback of the sanctions of kin to business activity, and the lack of separation of business and other relationships with kin, adds to the difficulties of making organizational changes. In one case the husband left his wife's father business, and as a result, generally strained relationships pervaded the family social life:

WIFE: The end was [a] very difficult period of time . . . very strained relations. We just felt bad . . . my mother said that time would . . . she thought it would get better. But there was lots of bitterness. My father was quite bitter also, and they had feelings or hopes that Joe would come back. They really never gave up the idea till they saw that it was a sure thing, the break . . . socially it was difficult. I mean we couldn't go places together . . . we would be there at the same time, but we couldn't go in the same car. It was a bad time.

The repercussions of business for kin relationships and the sanctions from kin for business activity may continue indefinitely in social life outside the business. One woman explained that her husband and his brothers had been in business with their father. After the father's retirement, the brothers had difficulty with the business, which eventually failed. The father claimed, and still claims, that the sons ruined the business. They continued to receive sanctions for this at almost every kin gathering; for example, one time when "he blamed them outright in front of everyone, and it was very embarrassing." In this case, because of the lack of separation of business and kinship, the business failure was with them at all times. As the wife explained about her mother-in-law, "She never let him forget it." It is clear that it is extremely difficult to segregate business and kinship relationships when these involve the same individuals. This connection may be a source of support for the business but it also often introduces problems for business functioning.

Family-Kin Businesses and Kin Relationships

The lack of segregation of kinship statuses from business positions not only affects the business but also other areas of relationships with kin. Despite frequent comments that business dealings with kin are a sure way of making enemies, there are indications that business activity with kin tends to lend general support to obligations of kinship and involvement with kin. By definition, those who are in business with kin see each other daily and thus have much kin interaction. Moreover, business dealings often require financial assistance so that one would expect these families to have received assistance from kin. There are indications, moreover, that this involvement of kin in the business carried over into nonbusiness relationships among these kin as well as other kin outside the business.

A crucial factor is reciprocity. Even those families who are not in business with kin have extensive economic and service relationships with their kin, and the values of kinship give strong support for binding obligations of reciprocity. Thus when business ventures entail assistance from kin, as they often do, this assistance creates an obligation for reciprocity and for continuing involvement.

Reciprocity may be in the business itself or in other kinds of assistance or service. One woman described how, when her father retired, he "gave" his store to his brother and sister. A gift of this magnitude presumably involves reciprocity on the part of the kin at some later date.

Husbands who had at some time been in business with kin not only claim to have received financial assistance from relatives outside the business slightly more frequently than nonbusiness husbands, but they also claim to have given assistance of all kinds to kin somewhat more often. The differences are slight but, nevertheless, in view of general attitudes about reciprocity, it is clear that business activity that requires the assistance of kin tends to further the bind of reciprocal obligation.

Reports of conflict pervade many of the interviews with both business and nonbusiness families. The sources of kin conflict are innumerable. Nevertheless, those in business with kin often report that business dealings had been a specific source of conflict among kin. As one wife explained, when her husband went into business with his brother, "We almost lost a brother-in-law on account of it." Business activity may therefore increase not only kin contacts and obligations but also conflicts. It must be noted, however, that any small business, whether with kin or not, by intensifying contacts may provide many opportunities for conflict.

The conjunction of occupational and kinship statuses may affect the extent to which it is possible to express emotion within the family concerning occupational activities. Ordinarily the husband can express within his family the tensions that develop in his work. But when, as in one case, his boss is also his wife's father, it is not surprising that this complicates the possibility of an outlet at home for emotions built up on the job. In this case, the wife felt that she was in the middle, as a go-between, for her husband and her father. Although she was not formally involved in the business, she was drawn into the relationship between her husband and her father; as a result, there was a minimum segregation of business and family.

The wife frequently heard criticism of her husband from his boss, her father. The open channels of kinship communication were used to discuss the business. Such direct criticism of the husband's job performance to his wife can hardly help having implications for the marital relationship; here it was considered an important factor in the couple's marital problems:

> WIFE: My parents couldn't communicate with Joe. . . . They couldn't reach him, and they went to reach him through me. . . . I was between them, and they were talking to me to get to him, and he talked to me to get to them. Yes, I was in the middle.
>
> HUSBAND: She was the "intercom" wife.
>
> WIFE: So I heard now and then that he is a good worker and all the qualities that he did have, but they felt that he was not taking enough of an interest in the business. . . . My father felt that he was not interested enough to really break his head over it.

In this instance, the overlap between business, kinship statuses, and the nuclear family did not necessarily reduce the expression of feelings about the business in the home; on the contrary, it may have actually increased the amount of such expression. But it made it difficult for the wife to take an impartial position. Her position derived, in part, from her handling of the situation, but the structuring of kin and business relationships contributed significantly. The wife could not have been pressured into an intermediary role in the same way by a boss of the husband's who was not also her own father. Moreover, because business and family relationships overlap in the home of her parents as well, not only her father but also her mother was involved in discussions of the business.

Family-kin businesses are another area in which many families living in an urban industrial environment are deeply involved with kin. Certain problems for the functioning of these businesses appear to derive from their kinship structure. The general inability to segregate kinship and occupational roles when these involve the same people means that there is likely to be a great deal of carryover from one area of relationships to another. Even though business activity is a source of considerable conflict among kin, this conflict does not appear to produce complete ruptures in kinship ties. Rather, since business frequently entails the financial or other assistance of kin, it reinforces obligations of reciprocity and tends to strengthen the momentum of kin interaction. The overlap of kinship and business roles affects both business functioning and kin relationships, and both of these, in turn, have consequences for the family.

FAMILY CIRCLES
AND COUSINS CLUBS

Family circles and cousins clubs are corporate kin groups that exist in the kin networks of client families. They may be considered a type of descent group. The organization of these groups, as well as the contacts they provide for the members, is another area in which the family's relationship with kin is affected by the way relationships among kin are organized as such.

These groups differ from a loosely bound network, in that they are definite groups with clearly defined membership boundaries.

They are corporate groups because they have continuity over time, are group-financed, engage in common activities, and have a definite authority structure. These organizations are significant for theory since, according to previous hypotheses, they should not exist in an urban industrial setting. Their discovery therefore implies certain modifications of theory about kinship and society.

Organizational Structure and Purpose

Family circles and cousins clubs have some important structural differences which will be considered later, and also have many common features. Both engage as a group in common activities, most often social and recreational. Most family circles and cousins clubs meet regularly once a month from September through May or June, either in homes of different members or in a private room at a centrally located hotel. The preferred meeting times are Saturday night or Sunday afternoon. The first part of the gathering is devoted to a business meeting. Once a group has completed its business meeting—this may take an hour or longer—the rest of the evening is a party. Refreshments, often elaborate, are served, and there may be modest drinking. During the party, members visit and some tell jokes. If children are allowed to attend, they might be asked to perform for the group. In some groups the older members play poker and the young people dance.

Besides these regular meetings, the group usually sponsors several other activities during the year, and to some of these additional kin who are nonmembers are invited. Many groups have a spring or summer outing at a park or summer resort. In December there is often a Hanukah party for the children or, depending on the degree of religious orthodoxy of the members, a "Christmas-Hanukah" party, with a gift-laden Santa Claus who gives presents to the children. Many have theater parties, cookouts, and an inaugural dinner dance.

In addition to the activities of the group as a whole, there are sometimes activities for special subgroups. For example, some large family circles have a ladies' auxiliary, which carries out special activities of its own such as fund-raising; some have special youth organizations with different forms of recreation from that of the older members. Youth auxiliaries and special youth meetings may be organized, particularly in the family circles, in an effort to maintain the interest of the younger generation.

The amount of yearly dues varies from group to group, as do other details of organization, but all that have been studied impose some financial obligations on their members. Persistent failure to pay dues theoretically results in exclusion from the organization, although this does not always happen. Aside from dues, many groups also have a "good and welfare fund" or a "sunshine club," which raises money at each meeting by donations or a raffle. These funds are used for gifts or cash presentation to members celebrating some important family event, for example, a wedding anniversary, the birth of a baby, a bar mitzvah, or a graduation from high school or college. Some organizations hold property in the form of burial plots. However, these organizations do not hold major economic resources in common or engage as a unit in earning a livelihood.

Most of these organizations have a formal distribution of authority. Elected officers usually include a president, vice-president, treasurer, recording secretary, and social secretary. Some groups also have a corresponding secretary and a trustee responsible for the care of the organization's documents, or a sergeant-at-arms who is sometimes empowered to levy fines against those members who become too vocally dominant during a meeting. The election of officers is usually held every year or two.

All of these organizations keep some records, with a constitution, the minutes of meetings, and financial records as the usual minimum. Others may have a recorded family history, complete with information on all known ancestors with a genealogy map showing where they immigrated from. Some also regularly issue a newsletter.

The attention given to these different documents varies with the group. For example, a constitution might be written in ungrammatical English on notebook paper, or it might be typed on legal bond paper and phrased in the elegant jargon of the lawyer member who was drafted to write it.

One of the family circles studied—we can call it the Goldman Family Circle—has an eight-page constitution of the formal legal type. This family circle is 32 years old and has 83 members. The Goldman Family Circle's constitution starts with the following statement:

The object of the organization is to create a close relationship between the members and to carry into effect programs that will mutually benefit the entire family.

Proceedings are also formal during the business meeting and the presiding officer may attempt to follow Robert's Rules of Order. But there is often considerable levity. For example, a statement from the minutes of one cousins club reads: "Due to all the hollering and noise, our newly-elected president wanted to throw in the sponge and call it quits, but we moved her down."

In examining kin networks we have seen how the boundaries of the network differ from the perspective of each individual. Family circles and cousins clubs, however, are clearly bounded groups. They differ somewhat in their criteria for membership, but in both groups an individual may become affiliated if his mother, father, husband, or wife is a member or eligible for membership. Husbands and wives may belong to the same group and have equal rights in each other's groups; an individual may also belong to more than one group, which sometimes happens. Unlike many societies, not all families have descent groups within their kin networks. Data from the research questionnaire indicated that 31 per cent of the client families have one or more kin groups with which they could affiliate. Of those who could affiliate, 62 per cent actually did. If an individual does affiliate, the chances are good that he or she will be an active member, that is, one who attends meetings fairly regularly. Moreover, a fairly high percentage of those who are active members have at some time held office.

The multiple affiliations that are possible with these groups reflect the character of the larger society. In a highly urbanized setting a person may hold membership in several groups and the other members of each group may not even be aware of his other affiliations. The functions of the groups are highly specialized and the groups do not, for example, control the transmission of property. Therefore, multiple affiliations do not present problems for their members as they might in other types of societies. Multiple affiliations may even be reflected in a type of competitive familism on the part of different segments of the kin network. For example, one cousins club was started because a successful club existed on the husband's side of the family and, as a result of the wife's attendance at her husband's kin group, she felt she wanted to have a similar organization on her side.

An individual who affiliates with an organization through a spouse has rights equal to those of members who are affiliated through a blood relative. One woman, for example, was an officer in two descent groups on her husband's side: she was secretary of the cousins club on her husband's mother's side, and president of the family circle on his father's side. Thus membership in a descent group does not necessarily pull the marital pair in opposite directions, with different loyalties, as it may when husband and wife are not members of the same kin group.[3] On the contrary, their joint participation and equal rights as members may serve to support the marital tie.

Although family circles and cousins clubs are similar in many respects in their criteria for membership, they differ in others. In a family circle, all of the lineal descendants and spouses of lineal descendants of the acknowledged ancestral pair are eligible to affiliate regardless of age or generation. The cousins club restricts its membership horizontally to a set of first cousins and their spouses, although in many cases their children become eligible for membership at the age of twenty-one or when they marry, whichever is earlier. Thus generation and age are criteria for membership in cousins clubs, whereas this is not true of family circles.

Cousins clubs tend to emphasize the ties within generations, whereas family circles emphasize ties across generations as well. Because age and marital status, as well as generation, are criteria for membership of children, the exclusion of the children's generation is not as strict as that of the parental generation. In one cousins club, a daughter wished to attend but was not permitted because it was "strictly cousins . . . no children under twenty-one, and no parents." The reason for this exclusion of children was: "They wanted to have the freedom of expression and not be hampered by the children; if they wanted to get silly and make a joke, they shouldn't be embarrassed." But even though children may be allowed to become members after they are twenty-one, the exclusion of younger children may be strict. One woman had attempted to bring her children to the cousins club when they were young and "that strict rule was put in" by vote, preventing children from attending meetings.

From the perspective of the group, the question of how individuals affiliate becomes one of how the group maintains its continuity over time. Multiple memberships do not appear to create problems for the individual, but from the point of view of the group, potential size of the group may become unwieldy.

Genealogies of organizations indicate that in almost all of the family circles some potential members do not actually affiliate. Thus an individual's choice not to belong to the organization is one way the group's size may be limited. The group's size may also be limited if it splits into smaller segments, as sometime occurs. Cousins clubs at least for a period do not have the same problem of limiting size as do family circles because they automatically exclude many individuals on the basis of generation. If a cousins club did not ultimately admit the younger generation to membership, however, it would die out with the founding generation. But including younger members means that over time the cousins club also becomes potentially large and, in a sense, similar in organization to a family circle. Those cousins clubs studied contained only a few members of the younger generation and it remains to be seen whether these organizations will terminate with the founding generation or become more like a family-circle type of intergenerational structure. The problems of expansion and group continuity are therefore somewhat different from the point of view of family circles and cousins clubs.

A variety of reasons were reported for choosing not to affiliate or to continue active membership with both family circles and cousins clubs. These included lack of time, the expense of maintaining membership, and lack of interest in kin and preference for friends, that is, a general shift away from kinship values. The same type of motivation from the perspective of those within the organization regarding dropouts was phrased as, for example, selfishness, lack of interest in the family, and emotional problems. Some reasons for nonparticipation may be related to status differences between members who drop out and the majority of the group. One woman, for example, stopped going to her family circle for reasons apparently related to status. Her husband was a cab driver and there was only one other cab driver in the group, but efforts were made to prevent the drivers from sticking together during meetings and the husbands, who resented this, did not enjoy attending the meetings.

Individuals of high status may also drop out because of lack of interest in the organization and a feeling of difference between themselves and other members. However, there is no evidence that social status is a systematic basis for dropping out, so that these organizations might become single-status groups. On the contrary, many of them contain individuals of widely varying social positions.

One reason that some descent groups petered out was that status competition, particularly over refreshments, became so intense that no one could afford to continue his membership. This source of breakdown, however, may be controlled by formal regulations; in one case a rule was passed that "you're not allowed more than bagels and lox, and maybe coffee cake . . . but nobody is allowed to show off."

Generational differences are a major source of conflicts within family circles that sometimes lead to dropouts or segmentation of the group. These differences are often extremely great, since members of the older generation are generally immigrants whose values and ways of life are different from those of their married children. Generational differences, the geographic dispersion of members of the younger generation, and particularly their lack of interest in family circles were often reported.

> We are having problems with our family circle . . . a serious one. Well, it seems that the relationships—many of the people with small children, it is hard for them to get away. Others have moved out to the Island and they are not coming in the way they would like it. So the last meeting they were discussing the drafting of the cousins, you know, really making a business.

Often, in addition to differences of interest and taste, the younger generation are more removed genealogically. As one woman said, "The relationship is so far away that there doesn't seem to be any meaning." The original binding quality of a close relationship among a group of siblings and their descendants tends to be lost over time.

Linking kin, however, may tend to preserve ties even across generations, particularly in family circles. A parent may be able to sanction his child for participation in a way that is emotionally meaningful. One informant, for example, indicated that he continued to go to his family circle meetings, although they held little interest for him, because he did not want to hurt his mother. Since family circles depend on cross-generational bonds, they may be weakened when pivotal kin of the older generation die.

Cousins clubs, however, which are not organized on an intergenerational basis initially, are not subject to the same type of generational splits. It was reported in several instances that a cousins club was founded to take the place of a family circle that had petered out or lost membership because of generational differences. The creation of a cousins club was sometimes seen as a way of preserving the family unity by "a different approach."

A major structural source of cleavage within family circles is, therefore, between generations. Cousins clubs are not subject to this source of conflict but they may have cleavages arising from longstanding rivalry and jealousy, for example, among siblings. One cousins club, for example, split up into segments because of a dispute arising among several sisters, the mothers of the cousins, who were not members, but who actively attempted to break the solidarity among the cousins. In an effort to retain the unity, a point was made of electing a president who "would be favorable to all of them."

Differences in age between family circles and cousins clubs reflect differences in the process by which they maintain continuity. There are some new descent groups of both types, and there are also some old groups of both types. But, on the whole, the family circles studied tend to be older than the cousins clubs. Only 2 per cent of the cousins clubs reported on in the questionnaires were over twenty years old, whereas 31 per cent of the family circles were over twenty years old. Thus despite generational differences that may cause the family circle to split up or peter out, some appear to have a considerable possibility for continuity over time. On the other hand, there are many more cousins clubs of recent origin than family circles. Sixty-six per cent of the cousins clubs were five years old or younger, whereas only 16 per cent of the family circles were started as recently.

Implications of Descent Groups for Their Members

These groups contain nonclient as well as client members and the meaning for clients and nonclients may differ. However, it is

possible to obtain some clues about their meaning from considering their purpose and organization.

A large number of these organizations, particularly cousins
clubs, have begun within the past five years, which is indicative
of their vitality and their probable importance to their members.
These organizations are clearly not merely a holdover from the
past; on the contrary, they continue to have a significant function
since new ones are being started all the time.

Reasons for founding new organizations indicate their meaning for members. A common reason for starting cousins clubs was
that kin met at an ad hoc gathering, particularly at a crisis event or
life-cycle ritual: funeral, illness, wedding, or bar mitzvah. As noted
earlier, this occasion served as a basis for renewed interest in
maintaining contacts with kin and led to agreements to meet on a
more formal basis.

Although membership is by choice, once one is a member, the
formal organization gives a basis for sanctioning members to continue participation. For many there may be wholehearted enjoy-
ment derived from the activities of these organizations. Nevertheless, the sanctions of the group are often strong and meaningful.

The strength of the sanctions that cousins clubs and family circles may impose upon their members is indicated in the following
sequence of events in one cousins club. One member, a young
man who was at the time in the Army overseas, had been sent a
package but failed to acknowledge it with an appropriate "thank-
you note," validating his continued interest in the organization. A
formal motion to censure him was made and recorded in the minutes of the cousins club. (It is noteworthy that these minutes had
been saved for fifteen years.) The young man responded to the
reprimanding note very apologetically and proclaimed his strong
tie to his cousins.

The sanctions imposed by these organizations may not always
be as effective as they apparently were in this instance. But it is
typical for a descent group to apply strong sanctions for participation. In addition, sanctions may be imposed through individual
members. Here linking or pivotal kin, particularly of the older
generation, may be significant.

Interaction in these organizations and among their members
may enter into the process by which an individual defines his own

state of emotional well-being; that is, these groups may serve as reference groups in defining the individual's emotional state. For example, a woman was told that not coming to the meeting indicated that she had an "inferiority complex," but she, in turn, compared her own emotional health favorably with that of her cousin:

> One of my cousins, who is my mother's sister's daughter . . . she told my mother recently, "Louise has an inferiority complex and that's why she doesn't come to the meetings," and my mother told me about it, and, of course, I was hurt. I was hurt about it because I don't think I do. I think I'm a much happier person than my cousin is. She's very unhappy because she was left a widow with two babies. She's only a young woman, younger than I. So, so I'm glad I don't go—the heck with it. It cost a lot of money . . . and there's no reward for us. We didn't care for it.

These groups, therefore, can have considerable emotional significance for their members.

The groups also serve as an important area of social participation for members. They may be an arena in which conflicts stemming from relationships within the nuclear family are acted out and given public expression. One wife, for example, attempted to impeach her husband when he was president of the organization; and later, when the wife was secretary, the husband attempted to impeach her for inadequate note-taking. Although both attempts were carried out with considerable jocularity, there was clearly a double-edged significance. Conflicts that arise within the organization may also affect relationships within the family. In either event, the organization affords an area for social participation in a group that is built upon a network of longstanding emotional ties among individuals, including those with siblings and spouses and, in family circles, those with parents. There are frequent conflicts and competition for status within the organization, often with disputes over what appear to be fairly minor matters like dues. Although this is an emotionally charged arena, it also allows the marital pair to participate together.

As we have seen, one of the reasons for presuming that corporate kin groups would not exist in an urban industrialized society was that these groups might limit the occupational and geographic mobility of their members, thus making it more difficult to make moves to other areas when necessary. This restraint is true in kin groups in other societies and has been considered one reason for their breakdown as industrialization occurred.

The family circles and cousins clubs do not appear to contribute to this kind of conflict between kin and the occupational world. They do not appear, moreover, to hinder the occupational advancement of their members.

Although status differences may be a reason for leaving an organization, these organizations continue to hold members of varying social positions. The occupational range of one family circle, for example, is shown in Table 7.

Table 7.   Occupations of Presently Employed Members of a Family Circle[a]

Occupation	Number of Members
Drugstore owner	2
Taxi driver	1
Pharmacist	1
Certified public accountant	2
Lawyer	3
Dyeing service owner	1
Clerical	1
Real estate broker	1
Manufacturer of surgical supplies	3
Artist	1
Salesman	1
Candy store owner	1
Fur cutter	1
Fabric cutter	2
Partner in wholesale wool remnant business	1
Saleslady	1
Commercial physicist	1
Doctor	1
Stock broker	1
Total	26

[a] The total membership of this family circle is 77. Only 34 per cent (26) work, whereas the majority, or 66 per cent, are women and children who are out of the labor force. The occupations were given by one of the members.

A similar range was found in many, although not all, the organizations studied. Different groups differ in their occupational range, but high-status as well as low-status individuals may continue to hold membership. It is noteworthy that these groups are found within an American subgroup that is generally characterized by a high rate of social mobility.[4]

Interview data indicate a variety of ways in which kinship organizations may actually foster mobility. Because the groups' boundaries are clearly defined, those within the group are unequivocally seen as kin to each other and thus lend symbolic support to ties of kinship. In addition, the descent group provides an opportunity to sustain kin relationships in a way that may facilitate requests for assistance in occupational advancement. For example, in one group, two brothers helped their formerly unsuccessful cousin by setting him up in business. This active assistance was facilitated by joint membership in the cousins club. Since these cousins lived in different neighborhoods and moved in very different social circles, they would probably have had much less basis for social contact without the descent group.

Potential conflict between group membership and geographic mobility is limited, moreover, by the fact that these groups exist in a large metropolis where extensive job opportunities that do not require making a geographical move are more likely than in a small community or rural area. When members are in independent business or professional practice where success depends on remaining in a given location and building up a clientele rather than being able to accept an opening wherever it may occur, geographic mobility may also not be required for success. Although there are many constraints against making geographic moves, when they do occur in the interest of occupational achievement, they are generally accepted by the group's members. An effort is then often made to maintain contact with the group by continuing correspondence and continuing to pay dues, or by formal newsletter. Moreover, since husbands and wives belong to the same groups, their loyalties are not split at times when moves must be considered.

Family circles and cousins clubs may also support occupational achievement by giving instrumental help as an organization: the group's loan fund may help to support children's education, or special collections may be taken up when there is particular need on the part of one member.

Perhaps a more important function of these descent groups is as a reference group. Intense status competition creates a highly sensitive social environment for formal recognition of achievement. These groups also provide some members opportunity for status by association, while providing others status by deference.[5] They also give individuals personal access to a variety of occupational styles and role models that might otherwise not be available.

Since family circles and cousins clubs also exist in a group of immigrant background, they may well have acculturative functions for their members. These groups are not organized on the basis of territory of immigration. Their formal purpose is not to preserve a locally derived culture but rather to preserve ties of kinship in a changing environment. But this preservation does not necessarily mean that these groups are antithetical to changes in other areas of social values and ways of life.

Here the differences between family circles and cousins clubs are of great importance. The bonds of a family circle, which transcends generations, are very different from the single-generation ties of a cousins club in this respect. Most of the cousins clubs studied were founded by a group of first cousins who were usually the children of those who emigrated from Europe. The cousins for the most part were those born in the United States. This one-generation structure of cousins club is rare as a form of kinship organization. It undoubtedly has a special significance in relation to value differences that separate the immigrant generation from their more Americanized offspring. The cousins club is apparently one way to maintain the traditionally Jewish value of family solidarity by organizing generationally, while at the same time excluding an older generation whose viewpoints and life styles are very different. One man explained that he joined a cousins club rather than a *Landsmannschaft Verein* (organization of those from the same area in the country of origin) because "I was looking for younger people; I wasn't looking for older people . . . their ideas are different and they have different ways of doing things; they stick to the old ways of doing things." Thus cousins clubs and family circles differ greatly in their probable implication for the acculturation of their members. Family circles may be subject to cleavage along generational lines because of differences between the generations in interests and styles of life. This implies that in the family circles that survive there is a certain degree of continuity of the values of the older generation, at least for a period. Although both family circles and cousins clubs undoubtedly recognize the achievement of their members in moving toward Americanized ways of life, their impact in this respect is undoubtedly very different.

Cousins clubs serve as a way of uniting the younger generation and maintaining their kinship solidarity. At the same time, they may actually serve to strengthen the bonds of the younger generation against the older generation. This organized bond of solidarity among the younger generation may help it as a group to break away from the ways of life of the older generation, who are generally not allowed to participate in the cousins club.

Individuals, too, may be assisted in making a transition to a new set of values. Cousins clubs may also offer collective opportunities for trying out new types of social activity, often things that the nuclear family would not do alone. Elaborate preparations and much energy may be devoted to collective efforts to ensure that the new type of activity will be carried out in proper style. For example, extensive time may be spent in surveying restaurants to determine the best for a group gathering. Families sometimes stated explicitly they participated in activities that they would not do alone. Thus membership in a cousins club may give support for a family's attempt to alter its style of life:

> They went to "South Pacific." They get tickets every so often, and the club pays for one-half of the couple, and they pay for the other. So when they go out they have a good time. They went to the Roseland Ballroom and went to see "Ten Commandments" downtown. There are lots of things that we don't ordinarily go out of our way to do, but they do it as a group.

Since these descent groups clearly function as an arena for social participation and status presentation of the family, for example, in competition over refreshments, they afford an opportunity for recognition of achievement in style of life as well as in the occupational sphere. The group may give explicit recognition to the style in which the family entertains the descent group. In the minutes of one cousins club, for example, it is noted that "everyone congratulated Cousin Ellie on her beautiful kitchen set and newly painted apartment."

These descent groups, therefore, undoubtedly have an important role in the family's ability to transcend generational differences and move into a new way of life. The functions of the organizations in this respect will, of course, vary greatly from one individual to another. But the major structural differences between family circles and cousins clubs in their emphasis on bonds between, and in, their generations mean that their general functions in the process of acculturation are undoubtedly different.[6]

NOTES TO CHAPTER 5

1. Bott, Elizabeth, *Family and Social Network.* Tavistock Publications, Ltd., London, 1957.
2. Firth, Raymond W., editor, *Two Studies of Kinship in London.* The Athlone Press, London, 1956.
3. Schneider, David M., "The Distinctive Features of Matrilineal Descent Groups" in *Matrilineal Kinship,* edited by David M. Schneider and Kathleen Gough. University of California Press, Berkeley and Los Angeles, 1961, pp. 1–29.
4. Glazer, Nathan, "The American Jew and the Attainment of Middle-Class Rank: Some Trends and Explanations" in *The Jews: Social Patterns of an American Group,* edited by Marshall Sklare, The Free Press, Glencoe,

Ill., 1958, pp. 138–146; and Strodtbeck, Fred L., "Family Interaction, Values, and Achievement," *ibid.,* pp. 147–165.
5. Litwak, Eugene, "Occupational Mobility and Extended Family Cohesion," *American Sociological Review,* vol. 25, February, 1960, pp. 9–21. Litwak discusses the difference between status by association and status by deference, noting the significance of the segregation of visits of family and friends that large-city anonymity affords.
6. These descent groups have been described in Mitchell, William E., "Descent Groups Among New York City Jews," *The Jewish Journal of Sociology,* vol. 3, June, 1961, pp. 121–128.

CHAPTER 6

Kin Conflicts

and Kinship Structure

THE POSITIVE IMPACT
OF KIN ON THE FAMILY

In the two previous chapters we have examined the values of kinship, the family's involvement with its network of kin, and kin groups and assemblages. Throughout it has been clear that kin play a significant role in the lives of client families. Kinship may be a source of many problems and conflict, as we will see in the next chapter, but at the same time the ties of kinship offer many positive supports for the family. In considering change in the kin relationships of a family in one area, the caseworker should, therefore, be attuned to the variety of areas of kin relationships and the implications of kinship structure for the family.

A great many factors combine to influence, and are influenced by, the extent of a family's involvement with kin and the forms that this involvement takes. The psychological characteristics of individual family members are relevant. In addition, the geographic features of the kin network and relationships among kin clearly have significance in determining the quality of the family's kin ties and are reciprocally influenced. The factors that affect, and are

160

affected by, kin relationship include the demography of the network, that is, the birth rate, size of sibling groups, death rate of family members, the life-cycle stage of the family, the geographic proximity of kin, the social and cultural differences and similarities among kin, the values of kinship, and the extent to which the kin network of a family is connected through "linking kin."

Whatever the underlying reasons that predispose to extensive or less extensive involvement with kin and to involvement with some rather than other kin, it is clear that most of the client families, even though they live in an urban industrial society, have extensive contacts with their kin.

The many functions that kin may fulfill for the family have been noted in examining particular areas of kin relationship. It has been evident throughout that kin may impose powerful sanctions upon family members. These sanctions may cover almost any area of life, including formal participation in kin groups, assistance and other forms of relationships among kin, and even the individual's conduct of life within the family. Here value differences between generations, which frequently give kin in the older generation the view that they have a right to express themselves in family affairs, enter into the openness of the family boundaries.

As we have seen, kin may contribute in many important ways to the identity of the family and its members. Kin therefore serve as a significant reference group. Family circles and cousins clubs offer an arena for status presentation and a significant reference group in which achievement may be recognized. Geographic proximity and the availability of communication which technology makes possible, for example, by telephone and rapid transportation, offer kin an opportunity for participating actively in each other's identities.

Kinship may not only support occupational mobility, but also assist the individual in making the transition from the values and ways of life of one society to those of another. This has been noted in relation to cousins clubs but may also occur through individual rather than group participation of a family with its kin. Here differences between generations in values and ways of life are offset by solidarity among those of the same generation. In evaluating the ways and the extent to which a family is involved with kin, it is not only necessary to consider the values of the family members, but also those of the kin and the sanctions they may impose. Moreover, a concept of "structural dependency" is useful here. Structural dependency means that the nuclear family as a unit cannot operate independently of other external systems. The family sends its children to other institutions for education and the family is seldom the main unit of economic production. Thus in many areas the family must inevitably rely on outside institutions. It was clear in the examination of assistance among kin that kin often offer support that might not be available through other channels, for example, in contributing second-hand clothing and furniture to the family, and in giving assistance during minor illnesses. Therefore, in evaluating the impact of kin upon the life of a family, the alternative sources that might give equivalent support need to be considered.

It should be clear from this discussion that the caseworker, to understand the impact of kin and their meaning for the nuclear family, needs to consider the interpersonal factors of the relationships among kin as such. In addition, the way in which kin relationships are structured in different areas, for example, the difference between single-generation and cross-generational kin groups, may make a decided difference. The implications of relationships with different kin for the family may vary greatly, and the effects upon the family of kin relationships that are structured in different ways may alter their meaning. In seeking to change one area of kin relationship, therefore, the caseworker needs to be attuned to the structuring of kin relationships and the variety of functions. Otherwise, in changing one area, which may be closely connected with another, the caseworker may undo vital supports for the particular forms of change that are being made. For example, reduction of ties with siblings and cousins cut the family off from occupational and life-style models and supports, which could aid the members of the family in reducing their own psychological dependence on their parents. In the next chapter we will consider in more detail the ways in which conflicts with kin and marital conflicts about kin reflect the organization of kin relationships.

Levels of Conflicts with Kin

We have seen that client families are intensively involved with their kin and that the supports of kinship contribute in many positive ways to the functioning of the family. But the ties of kinships are by no means always smooth and unequivocal; they are also a major source of strain and conflict. Although problems with kin were implicit in some of our descriptions of kin relationships, we will now focus on them explicitly.[1]

In a client population special problems in relationships with kin may arise. Perhaps similar problems occur in other groups and being a client may merely represent a particular way of coping with problems. In casework treatment, problems in relationships with kin often arise and, although such problems are rarely part of the initial presenting problem, handling them may be a treatment goal. However, the evidence of definite regularities in the social structuring of conflicts with kin underscores the need for viewing these conflicts as more than the expression of the problems of individual clients.

The points at which strain arises for an individual depend on the way in which his social roles are organized, as well as on intrapsychic strain stemming from his previous development. Relationships with others do not occur randomly or as a product of individual inclinations alone; they are affected by the values, ideas, and sanctions of those with whom the individual interacts. For a strain deriving from a social role to be real to an individual, he must have internalized feelings that make the obligations of his various roles meaningful. But the source of strain springs from outside as well as inside the individual.

This sociological perspective may be represented by the concept of *structural predispositions to strain*. This concept means that a given social structure will tend to cause strain in particular ways, stemming from the organization of roles.

Role strain may be defined as the "felt difficulty in fulfilling role obligations."[2] Role strain may arise, for instance, when the obligations that inhere in two or more relationships within a given role, or in different roles held by the same individual, are in some way incompatible or conflicting. Conflicting obligations may arise for the individual when different kinds of behavior are demanded in different roles. Another source of conflict may result when an individual holds two or more roles requiring inconsistent behavior with respect to the same individual, for example, the father who is an employee of his son. Strain may also be built into the organization of social roles when the obligations are such that a choice must be made in allocating time and resources between two competing sets of demands. An example is the working wife who must choose between devoting time to the job and to the home; another is the family that must choose between the requests of the husband's and of the wife's kin to spend a holiday with them. A closely related form of conflicting obligation arises when two roles have obligations that cannot be met at the same time, so that scheduling is required to meet both, for example, visits to two sets of kin. In one sense role strain may be considered normal because most roles have a complicated array of obligations and these are often conflicting.

In this chapter we will examine the way in which interpersonal conflicts among kin are related to strains inherent in the organization of kinship roles, that is, the obligations and expectations between those in specific kinship statuses.

As we will see, conflicts with and about kin are not randomly distributed among all kinship statuses; conflicts with kin in certain reciprocal statuses are more frequent than those with kin in other positions. Moreover, conflicts between husbands and wives arise more frequently about some categories of kin than about others. For this reason the structuring of interpersonal conflicts cannot be said to derive uniquely from the personality problems of the individuals involved, but also reflect the organization of kinship roles.

For present purposes "conflict" refers to antagonism or hostility toward another person that is consciously recognized, whether or not it is openly expressed. It is distinguished from strain, which refers to a felt difficulty of fulfilling role obligations.

Overt conflict is only one form of expression of role strain. Many kinds of strain do not lead to open interpersonal conflict. In one sense overt conflict may be a mechanism for coping with role strain. By allowing the overt expression of feelings, open conflict may, in fact, serve as an integrative force for the group. By contrast with indifference, it implies a definite form of social involvement and may prove a means for resolving differences.[3] Although conflicts may be an expression of strain in the organization of social roles, they are not necessarily a disruptive factor in social relationships.

Conflicts may be conducted within a socially acceptable framework. Hostile impulses may be expressed indirectly, for example, by wit, so that overt conflict does not take place. Socially sanctioned substitute objects may serve to channel the expression of feelings, which would disrupt relationships if expressed directly against the original object. Scapegoating safeguards the original relationship because aggression is channeled away from it. Thus a new conflict situation arises with the substitute object. Nonetheless, the original unsatisfactory situation may remain unaltered or become intensified.

It is often difficult to distinguish between conflict with the primary object of hostile feelings from that with a substitute object. One can make the arbitrary assumption that the original objects of hostility arise in early childhood and thus are likely to be parents or siblings. But such an assumption implies that all other objects of hostility are necessarily secondary objects and makes it difficult to distinguish between hostilities and antagonisms that arise in the course of later relationships from those that are merely displacements of feelings toward parents and siblings. Moreover, even where conflict represents the displacement of hostilities away from the original object, the substitute object may be one toward which some basis of antagonism also exists. Even if it is assumed that almost all conflicts in intimate relationships reflect some displacement, one cannot assume sociologically that the choice of object is random, especially if certain objects are chosen more regularly than others. It is still necessary to account for the choice of a particular object as the focus of conflict.

Moreover, a conflict as a form of interaction must be examined from the perspective of more than one party. In some instances the initial impetus for a conflict with kin may arise from the kin, not from the client family. The client in this sense may be the object of hostile or aggressive impulses of the kin, either an object on whom impulses arising elsewhere were displaced or a direct object. In order to determine who is the initiator of a conflict, one would have to know the sequence of events in any given conflict. Even without this information, it is possible to assume that an interaction between two parties involves some entry into the relationship by both parties, and that both can act as if the other were either the primary or a substitute object of hostility. Even where the choice of object may be considered accidental and another object might serve the purpose of ventilating hostile impulses equally well, the sociological consequences of the choice of object differ from one object to another.[4]

In analyzing conflicts among kin the problem of distinguishing direct from substitute objects becomes particularly complex, since many of those involved have had lifelong relationships in parental and sibling positions, that is, precisely those from which the source of much displaced hostility is often assumed to arise.

From a sociological perspective it is not sufficient to analyze conflict merely in terms of its underlying motivation. Aggressive behavior has, in fact, been shown to be shaped by the organization of the group.

Although hostile feelings that arise in close relationships are likely to be intense, more frequent conflict is not necessarily more likely in closer relationships than in less close ones. The very closeness of a relationship and the mutual feeling involved may induce participants to attempt to avoid conflict.

When conflicts arise more frequently in certain relationships than in others, one cannot be sure, without extensive observational data, what the underlying motivations for these conflicts may be, whether the hostile feelings arose in this relationship or represent a substitute of object, or which party to the conflict instigated it. One can, however, assume that something about the particular relationship makes it a point where the motivations for conflicts are either instigated or where hostile impulses instigated in some relationship find an outlet.

REGULARITIES IN KIN RELATIONSHIPS

In order to understand the way in which conflicts are related to the structuring of kinship roles, it is necessary to consider patterns of interaction with kin generally. Therefore, we will first examine the specific kin statuses and the categories of kin in terms of laterality, generation, and sex with whom there is most interaction. This will serve as a basis for analyzing the relationship between conflicts with kin and the organization of kinship roles.

In considering the boundaries of the kin network we noted that choices had to be made both in the recognition of kin and in the selection of kin for certain activities.

A basic criterion of choice is the priority given to individuals in different kinship categories. The data on kinship values indicate that priorities are given to the marital as compared with the parent-child tie, and that obligations to the nuclear family are stressed over those to others, even though these priorities may not always be easy to maintain.

Another question is which kin are given priority among those outside the nuclear family. A crucial issue here is how the marital partners are integrated with each other's kin and hence how the nuclear family allocates priorities between the husband's and the wife's kin.

Data on choices among kin were derived from the relative frequency of interaction and sentiment with kin in various spheres of activity. These included interaction more frequently than at big family gatherings, telephone contact, giving and receiving of household repairs, giving and receiving of baby sitting, knowing most about life in the family, dropping in unannounced, having a key to the apartment, being in a family business with the husband, living within proximity, and sentiments, that is, those with whom husbands and wives feel they have most in common, and those to whom husbands and wives would want to leave their children if they should be orphaned. In looking at regularities in categories of kin with whom there is most interaction, data from all of these activities were combined. The selection of which areas to include in the questionnaire was not arbitrary. Based on the findings of preliminary interviews, these areas probably cover reasonably fully family activities that involve kin.

For all of these areas of activity, the overall combined rankings of the most frequently mentioned categories of kin, when data from husbands and wives were combined, are as follows: *wife's mother, wife's sister, wife's brother, husband's sister, husband's brother, husband's mother, wife's father, husband's father*. These rankings were in terms of the absolute number of kin mentioned. However, there are more kin in the sibling than in the parental generation available for interaction. Therefore, the kin categories with whom there is most frequent interaction were also ranked on the basis of the proportion of living kin. Viewed this way there is more frequent interaction with members of the parental generation than with siblings, as follows: *wife's mother, husband's mother, wife's father, husband's father, wife's sisters, wife's brothers, husband's sisters, husband's brothers*. It is striking that with either mode of ranking the wife's mother appears first. From the point of view of husbands and wives separately, the wife's mother ranks first for interactions of the wife, whereas the husband's mother ranks first for the husband. From a family perspective, however, in many activities entailing the allocation of family resources there is most involvement with the wife's mother.

The rankings of kin vary, depending on the activity. The wife's mother, for example, is the first in terms of the kin seen most frequently by the wife at big family gatherings and kin with whom she has most telephone contact. But the overall rankings give a picture of the comparative extent of involvement with different categories of kin.

Laterality

As we have seen, kinship systems differ in the relative emphasis they place on ties to the husband's as compared with the wife's kin. The way in which the marital partners are involved with each other's kin has a significant impact on the marriage. In the discussion of affiliation with family circles and cousins clubs, it was seen that the possibility of membership, with equal rights, in one's spouse's kin group prevents the marital pair from being torn by loyalties to different kin groups to the extent that is often true in other societies. Instead, joint participation may offer a definite support for the marriage.

However, in other areas of activity, constant choices are made about the kin with whom to interact, a basic factor being whether the kin are on the husband's or the wife's side.

Table 8 shows that both husbands and wives appear to be most closely tied to their own kin: husbands list more kin on their own side of the family than on their spouse's side in many activities; wives also list more of their own kin for almost all areas of interaction examined.

However, husbands tend to be somewhat more closely tied to their wife's kin than wives are to their husband's kin. For example, in listing the kin with whom they have most in common, wives list 76 per cent of their own kin, whereas husbands list only 58 per cent of their own kin. There are no areas of interaction or sentiment where wives listed more of their husband's than their own kin. Husbands, however, listed slightly more kin on the wife's than on their own side of the family in household repairs received. In a series of questions on assistance where husbands were asked to

Table 8. *Laterality and the Structuring of Kinship Bonds*

Area of Relationship with Kin	Per Cent of Husband's Contacts with Husband's Kin	Per Cent of Wife's Contacts with Wife's Kin
Interaction		
Have telephone contact	86	76
Household repairs:		
Received from kin	44	
Given to kin	64	
Baby sitting:		
Received from kin		76
Given to kin		86
Know most about life of family	51	72
Drop-in unannounced		78
Have a key to the home		86
In family business	75	
In proximity:		
Present household		54
Past household		93
Same building		91
Walking distance		66
Other assistance	41	82
Sentiment		
With whom have most in common	58	76
Feel closest to:		
Own relatives versus spouse's relatives	61	91
To whom would want to leave children if orphaned	58	85

NOTE: This table should be read as follows: Of the kin listed by husbands as those with whom they have telephone contact, 86 per cent were the husband's kin, the remainder were the wife's kin. Contact is used here to refer both to actual contacts and to sentiment. The table is based on the *absolute* number of kin listed, not the proportion of living kin.

check the side of the family with which they were most frequently involved, they checked their wife's kin slightly more often than their own. These areas of assistance included: getting a job, making a major move, making a major purchase, and making household repairs.

Thus there is an indication of somewhat fuller integration of husbands into the wife's family than of wives into the husband's family. But there is an exception. Husbands list 86 per cent of telephone contacts with their own kin, a higher proportion than wives, who list only 76 per cent with their own kin. However, telephoning may be designated as a representative role of the woman, who is therefore responsible for a certain amount of contact with all kin.

Whatever its source, there is a definite skewing in interaction and sentiment toward the wife's side of the family, particularly for the wife. The husband is most intensely involved with his own kin in some areas, particularly family businesses, which are specifically his activity, but he is more closely tied to his wife's kin than she is to his.

Sex

Sex is another basic criterion in terms of which social roles may be organized and kinship ties delineated. Among the clients, women listed more female than male kin in all areas of activities about which data were obtained. The highest proportion of female kin listed by wives were those from whom they have received baby-sitting assistance, those who have a key to their home, those with whom they talk on the telephone, and those to whom they would want to leave their children if orphaned. Wives also listed a high proportion of female kin as those to whom they give baby-sitting assistance, those with whom they have most in common, those who know most about the family, and those who drop in unannounced. The lowest proportion of female kin were listed by wives as those seen more frequently than at big family gatherings and those living in proximity, but even here they listed slightly more female than male kin. This priority of ties to females is also seen in specific kin statuses where wives gave top ranking to their own mothers and sisters.

Husbands also listed more female than male kin in most areas.

Thus both men and women indicated that they had more interaction and closer ties of sentiment with female than with male kin. For wives this represents a same-sex tie; for husbands a cross-sex tie. For specific kin statuses, husbands as well as wives gave top ranking to their mothers. Husbands listed more females than males in most areas of interaction and an equal number of males and females as those with whom they have most in common. However, for those activities where clear distinctions of sex roles exist, such as those from whom they have received household repairs, husbands list more male kin. Husbands list the highest proportion of male kin in the occupational area, indicating that they have been in family business with far more male than female kin.

In activities where the nuclear family is the unit, the ties between female kin as links for the ties of others become critical. In most family activities there is more contact with female than male kin. In examining Thanksgiving gatherings, for example, there was more frequent contact with kin on the wife's side. However, this meant the wife's sisters more often than the wife's brothers; the wife's brothers went to their own wife's sisters' homes.

Generation

The comparative frequency of interaction with those in similar and those in different generation positions also varies from one area of activity to another. Moreover, variations during different stages of the life cycle have a significant effect upon ties of kinship. For example, those in the younger generation, as we have seen, may perform shopping and errands in return for baby-sitting assistance given by members of the parental generation. If those in the parental generation are living, interaction occurs with them in a higher proportion of cases than it does with those in the sibling generation. In this sense the ties to parents are more binding than those to siblings. Nevertheless, in terms of absolute number there are more instances of interaction with kin of the sibling than of the parental generation. Although in part a result of the biological availability of kin, this interaction becomes a social fact of considerable importance.

A notable feature in the generational organization of relationships among kin is the horizontal extension evident in genealogies in which generation depth is limited by cutoffs of immigration. The organizations of cousins clubs also reflect the importance of single-generation kinship ties.

In some areas the strongest ties are those to one's own children rather than to one's parents. Ninety per cent of the husbands and 90 per cent of the wives checked "children" in answer to questions about whether they felt closest to their parents or to their children. The closest ties are ideally those within the nuclear family. A shift occurs when a child becomes an adult and moves into a new family, substituting ties with his children for ties to his own parents, or at least modifying the intensity of these ties.

The ties of kinship extend across generations and are colored by the differences between these generations as well as by the relationship with those in still other generations. For example, the cutoff of the clients' parents from their own parents contributes to a downward focus on children, which is especially strong on the part of the parents of clients.

The regularities in these data show that kin interaction does not occur at random. When examining actual choices, differences in the frequency of interaction with kin in different categories are evident. These differences are related to values about desirable forms of kin contact. Differences varied with areas of activity, but for many purposes there was a preponderance of involvement with the wife's family. Although this involvement certainly does exist in many other societies, it is by no means a universal aspect of kinship.

Aside from the issue of which factors determine one kind of emphasis or another, the question arises of the consequence of choosing to affiliate more closely with certain kin than with others. We will see that the patterns of kinship organization show close parallels to the patterns of conflicts with kin.

REGULARITIES IN
CONFLICTS WITH KIN

There are various levels of conflict. A conflict may be a feeling of dissatisfaction or anger on the part of one party, which is never made known to the other. A conflict may be an act of openly acknowledged dispute between two or more parties. An open conflict may ensue between two individuals as primary parties with others supporting one side or the other, but not becoming active participants in the open conflict. A conflict may bring into active open dispute more than the two initial parties, or it may arise between more than two individuals. Finally, conflict may arise between two individuals about a third, who is not directly involved but seems to be merely a convenient subject for attack.

Despite the complexities of determining the meaning of conflict and the psychological factors in an individual that contribute to the selection of an object of conflict, the frequency of conflicts between those who hold particular reciprocal kinship statuses indicates that in some way the conflicts are engendered by the organization of the roles. Therefore, it is important to examine the categories of kin with whom and about whom conflicts most frequently arise.

A critical question about conflicts with kin is how they affect the marital relationship. Bonds to kin outside the nuclear family may be given differing priorities in different types of kinship systems; in some the tie between adult children and their parents is expected to take priority over the marital relationship, in others the marital bond is considered the "structural keystone" of the kinship system. Relationships with kin may support or strain the marital relationship. Ties to kin may pull the marital partners in opposite directions,⁵or kin may support the marital bond by defining it as essential.

Conflicts with kin may strengthen the unity of the marital pair, for example, when the kin are defined as an outgroup against which the marital partners unite to battle. But conflicts with kin may also disrupt marital harmony, for example, when kin are perceived to make demands on the allegiance or time of one marital partner, which the other partner resents or sees as inconsistent with the demands of the nuclear family. It was important, therefore, to see if conflicts with kin also involved conflicts between husband and wife.

The basic data on which this part of the analysis is based were derived from two open-ended write-in questions to husbands and wives about overt conflicts with kin and about arguments with the spouse over kin. The questions followed each other in the questionnaire and clients frequently treated both as one, describing the same conflict under both questions. Sometimes the conflict described as that with kin also involved a conflict with the spouse. The two questions were analyzed together, and for each instance of conflict a decision was made as to whether or not the conflict involved marital discord.

In examining kin conflicts for their impact on the marital relationship, distinctions were made between: (1) conflicts with kin, including any conflict in which kin were directly involved but excluding those in which marital discord between client husband and wife was also reported; (2) conflicts with and about kin, including conflicts where kin were directly involved and related marital discord was also reported; (3) conflicts about kin, including conflicts between the client husband and wife about kin in which the kin were not directly involved in the dispute. Two of these three types of conflict, conflicts with and about kin and conflicts about kin, involve a marital element. In the first type, the conflict with kin was reported without any indication that the conflict with kin resulted from or led to a marital argument. The term *kin conflicts* is used to refer to all three types of conflict. Those conflicts where marital discord was involved, both with and about kin, have been grouped in the analysis that follows and separated from those in which no marital discord was evident.

Distribution of Conflicts with Kin

In a total of 147 client families, husband, wife, or both answered the conflict questions in the questionnaire with sufficient detail to permit further analysis. The 234 conflict situations they described were classified according to which kin were listed and whether the conflict with kin also entailed marital discord. In all, husbands and wives listed 467 kin in various categories: mother, father, sister, brother, sister's husband, brother's wife, and so on.

The categories of kin mentioned by both husbands and wives were examined and compared with the data on interaction. The specific kin most frequently mentioned in conflict situations is the *husband's mother,* whereas interaction is most frequent with the *wife's mother.*

In terms of generation and laterality, too, conflicts do not arise most often with the categories of kin with whom there is most interaction. Although most interaction occurs with the wife's side of the family, most conflict arises with the husband's side. Table 9

Table 9. Kin Listed by Husbands and Wives in Conflict Situations

	Kin Conflicts Involving Marital Discord			Kin Conflicts Not Involving Marital Discord			Total Kin Conflicts		
	Husbands' List	Wives' List	Both Lists	Husbands' List	Wives' List	Both Lists	Husbands' List	Wives' List	Both Lists
	PERCENTAGES			PERCENTAGES			PERCENTAGES		
Husbands' Kin	71	61	65	76	36	54	74	49	59
Wives' Kin	29	39	35	24	64	46	26	51	41
	(76)	(142)	(218)	(112)	(137)	(249)	(188)	(279)	(467)

shows the distribution of kin mentioned in conflicts. It is striking that in conflicts that do not involve marital discord husbands and wives most frequently list their own kin; but in conflicts that do involve marital discord, both husbands and wives agree that it is the husband's kin who are most frequently involved.

Similarly, although most interaction occurs with members of the sibling generation, slightly more conflict arises with members of the parental generation.

Kin listed in conflicts involving marital discord, specifically the husband's mother, account for the greater frequency of parental generation kin mentioned in all conflicts. For conflicts not involving marital discord, sibling generation kin are most frequently mentioned. The patterns of interaction and conflict in terms of sex are consistent: both are most frequent with female kin.

It is worth noting that the focal point of conflict among client families differs from that found in studies of other western urban kinship systems. For example, among certain English families, the wife and her mother have close ties, but the husband's exclusion by his wife's relatives is a frequent source of marital conflict. There it is the wife's rather than the husband's mother who is most frequently involved in conflicts.[6]

Client's values about kinship strongly emphasize obligations to maintain ties with kin. Clients' values also support the greater involvement of the nuclear family, especially the wife, with the wife's rather than the husband's kin. Thus values that support a lateral skewing to the wife's side coexist with values that emphasize obligations to interact with all kin. It is not surprising that when actual demands for time and resources are made, kin on the wife's side receive priority over kin on the husband's side, who then feel slighted.

It is easier to understand when conflict with kin will not result in marital discord than to enumerate all the conditions under which they will. They will not occur if one marital partner but not the other is involved in a conflict with kin. They will not occur if both partners agree about the lateral priority of obligations and about the relative priority of obligations to the nuclear family and to other kin in any given situation.

An examination of the content of kin conflicts helps to shed light on the way in which role organization contributes to the greater frequency of conflicts involving marital discord that occur concerning the husband's kin.

Content of Conflicts

The vagueness and complexity of many descriptions of kin conflicts made it impossible to classify all conflicts or make refined statistical comparisons. However, by counting those conflicts that could be classified, it became apparent that certain themes recurred in conflicts with the husband's kin that arose seldom, if at all, with the wife's kin. These three recurrent themes help to explain why conflicts are distributed as they are among certain categories of kin.

One of these themes can be termed *rejection-neglect*. Rejection typically involves hostility, criticism, and exclusion from gatherings; whereas neglect more often means failing to meet what are considered obligations to be helpful, solicitous, interested, and the like. Neglect, of course, is interpreted as implying rejection. Rejection or neglect can be felt by the husband, the wife, the marital pair, or any of their kin. The husband's kin may feel rejected when obligations to the wife's kin take priority over obligations to them. An example of one case in which this arose is described by one wife:

> Husband's parents invited husband to Thanksgiving dinner even though they knew my parents had previously invited us. We went to my parents' house.

Another conflict in which the husband's kin appear to feel the wife's kin have been favored at their expense arose over the naming of children. The wife described this by saying:

> My mother-in-law's brother would not call my children by their proper name if they were named after someone on my side of the family.

Sometimes the wife feels rejected by her husband's kin, as in the following example:

> My husband was out of town and I wanted to borrow $5 for a few days because I needed food for my children. I was refused. . . . I shall

never ask for help from them again. I believe my husband's brothers could help me but refused because I am not liked by them.

At other times the wife does battle on behalf of her husband who she feels is rejected by his parents. Thus a wife says:

It began between me and my father-in-law, about him not caring when his son was emotionally ill. He went on his vacation and didn't even call till he was home several days.

A second theme of conflicts, which arises more frequently with the husband's kin, is *interference*. These conflicts include cases of criticism, as well as actual participation in the affairs of the nuclear family by the husband's kin. A common example is the criticism that the wife may receive from her mother-in-law for her care of her husband:

Me and my mother-in-law [about] her son—that I made him ill and that's why he had to go to the hospital.

Another example is the following:

My husband's sister is always making remarks about anything I do that she thinks is not right and he comes home arguing with me. . . . Example: children's underwear not white enough. . . . My mother-in-law always agrees with her.

Another client says:

My husband's brother, because we had borrowed money from him and because we were in business with him—was interfering in our private and family life—I told him off.

These two themes of conflicts with the husband's relatives sometimes involve marital discord and sometimes do not.

The third theme of conflicts is the *comparative loyalty* of the husband to his wife and to his relatives. The comparable issue of the wife's loyalty to her husband versus her kin does not emerge.

Conflicts of this type usually involve marital discord because the wife feels her husband is too devoted to his kin to the detriment of her own nuclear family. One client said she and her husband had an argument about: "Whether or not to visit father-in-law on Saturday in preference to going out together. Husband went alone." The loyalty theme is also quite clear in the following description:

My husband and I had an argument over the fact that one of his sisters talked about me to him and instead of talking to me and letting me in on what was going on he just believed her and got mad at me. . . . Result is my husband's sister and I don't speak to each other now. Yet she was the only one I was friendly with.

The repetition of these three themes suggests a basic strain in the relationship of the wife with her husband's parents, particularly his mother, which is manifested in a variety of ways. Marital discord results when this strain involves a tug-of-war over the loyalties and commitments of the husband. The question of the husband's allegiance has various consequences. For the wife, it means that she must make sure her husband's relatives do not take advantage of his loyalty to them. She must insist that he support her if they criticize her, and reject their attempts to weaken her position as wife and homemaker by intruding. For the husband's relatives, it is likely to mean that they suspect his wife of trying to alienate him from them, of showing preferences for her side of the family over his, of failing to take proper care of him, and the like. The wife is particularly likely to resent their hold on him, because in effect it reaffirms his status as a child in his parents' house instead of a man in her house. Since her prestige depends on his, she is doubly anxious to assert his independence, particularly his independence of his mother, who often continues to treat him as a little boy.

Conflicts with the wife's relatives rarely involve feelings of rejection, neglect, or interference, probably because values support the greater involvement of the nuclear family, particularly the wife, with the wife's kin.

We find little evidence of competition between the husband and the wife's kin for the wife's loyalties. It is possible that the wife's involvement with her kin is felt to be less of a problem both by the husband and by the wife's relatives. Her ties with her relatives are less threatening, or are perceived to be less threatening, to the nuclear family of which she is now a joint head than are the husband's ties to his kin. The wife is both allowed and expected to rely on her mother and sisters for companionship, advice, and aid in her tasks as housewife and mother. Her role as daughter and sister in her family of origin is less in conflict with her role as wife and mother than is the husband's role as son and brother with his position as husband and father. The husband may resent his wife's attachment to her kin, perhaps feel neglected by her, and perhaps feel outnumbered when she and her kin form coalitions to press for a certain decision; however, he feels less threatened by this attachment.

The husband's kin may be involved in marital conflicts more often than the wife's for another reason: the wife is expected to handle many social arrangements involving invitations, telephone calls, and similar contacts with her husband's relatives; she has more opportunities to engage in open conflict with them than her husband has to open hostilities directly with her kin. Much conflict involving the wife's kin is expressed openly only between husband and wife, and since the wife's kin are not directly engaged in it, the wife is not forced to take sides with the same pressure as the husband. And since his relatives have more reason to resent her because they compete with her for him, they are more likely to be involved in conflict than her kin are.

If the husband's divided loyalty were merely an expression of personal problems, such as an unresolved Oedipal conflict, one would expect a similar pattern of conflict involving the wife's divided loyalty between her husband and her father. However, no such pattern emerges. The wife's father is fourth in the ranking of her kin mentioned in conflicts. Therefore, the distribution of conflicts must depend on other factors as well.

One might also presume that conflicts would arise most often where interaction occurs most frequently. However, interaction occurs most frequently with the wife's relatives but conflict arises most frequently with the husband's. Perhaps patterns of conflict depend in part on the extent to which the structuring of interaction is not consistently supported by values. Clients' values that support a priority of obligations to wife's kin coexist with those that support obligations to interact equally with all kin, with the result that the husband's kin feel they are not getting the attention due them when interaction occurs more frequently with the wife's side of the family. The themes of conflicts with the husband's kin reveal this view.

These interpretations of the distribution of conflicts are only suggestive. Conflicts have other kinds of content which we have not discussed. We have examined themes only insofar as they offer clues about why conflicts, particularly those involving marital discord, arise more frequently with the husband's kin. However, it should be clear from this analysis that conflicts with kin, which are one kind of problem that comes up in casework treatment, cannot be fully understood without taking into account regularities in the organization of kinship roles.

NOTES TO CHAPTER 6

1. This subject has also been treated by Candace Rogers and Hope J. Leichter in their paper, "In-laws and Marital Conflict Among Jewish Families," which appears in *Readings on the Family and Society*, edited by William J. Goode, Prentice-Hall, Inc., Englewood Cliffs, N.J., 1964, pp. 213–218.
2. Goode, William J., "A Theory of Role Strain," *American Sociological Review*, vol. 25, August, 1960, pp. 483–496.
3. Simmel, Georg, *Conflict*. Translated by Kurt H. Wolff. The Free Press, Glencoe, Ill., 1955.
4. Coser, Lewis A., *The Functions of Social Conflict*. The Free Press, Glencoe, Ill., 1956.
5. Schneider, David M., "Introduction: The Distinctive Features of Matrilineal Descent Groups" in *Matrilineal Kinship*, edited by David M. Schneider and Kathleen Gough. University of California Press, Berkeley and Los Angeles, 1961, pp. 1–29.
6. Young, Michael, and Peter Willmott, *Family and Kinship in East London*. The Free Press, Glencoe, Ill., 1957.

PART THREE

Casework Intervention

and Kinship Structure

CHAPTER 7

Casework Intervention
in Relationships with Kin

Many client families are extensively involved with their kin, and this involvement is consistent with kinship values. Kin offer positive supports for the family; they impinge upon it whether or not they are a source of problems, and are thus an area of the family's life that caseworkers need to understand. Kinship is also of specific relevance to casework because family therapists are often involved in changing relationships with kin.

Many families have conflicts with and about kin, and the structuring of conflicts is related to interaction with kin in other areas. We will now examine the kinds of problems in relationships with kin that come up in casework treatment, and the directions of change that caseworkers seek to produce to enable us to consider the connection between patterns of intervention and regularities in kin interaction and conflict.

Data on problems with kin and forms of casework intervention come from interviews of the caseworkers of a random sample of agency clients. Interview questions were based in part on prior interviews with supervisors. (See Appendix.)

PROBLEMS BROUGHT UP
IN CASEWORK TREATMENT

Both caseworkers and supervisors reported that many problems in relationships with kin came up in casework treatment. Some of these reports were phrased as hypotheses about problems that characterized the caseload as a whole, or certain segments of it. Others were statements of relationships in specific cases. For the moment both of these levels will be considered together.

The reports of supervisors and caseworkers can be examined: first, for a general description of the locus and symptom of the problem; second, for views about the consequences of this problem for other areas of family relationships; and, finally, for ideas about the factors that produce the problem.

Problems with kin most often concerned relationships with parents of the husband or wife in the client family. Siblings were also mentioned but less frequently than parents.

A great variety of concrete problems in relationships with kin were described, for example, conflict among siblings about the support of elderly parents. But the most commonly described problem was that of overdependence of clients on their parents. It was phrased as: "The woman can't let go," "utterly involved on every level with their parents," "a hostile-dependent relation," and "The client has no guilt about overinvolvement because her needs are being fed." The following are examples of caseworkers' and supervisors' descriptions of problems of this sort:

> Overinvolvement with parents . . . is such a common business that it is hard to think of it as occurring only in certain types of cases. In many cases both the husband and the wife are utterly involved on every level with their parents, both in day-to-day turning to them and in more subtle forms of dependency which are more concealed. Sometimes they say, "The parent is dependent on me," "I take care of the parents in case of trouble." . . . [In one case the husband] could not distinguish his own dependency on [his mother] from his concern for her.

It was often claimed, for example, that the wife resented her mother's interference but, at the same time, accepted her assistance, representing a hostile-dependent relationship:

There is a hostile-dependent relation to the mother [of the wife]. They do not necessarily both live in the same apartment—the mother may live next door and barges in.

Sometimes dependence and overinvolvement were considered to characterize relationships with siblings, for example:

[A woman may be] involved with a large number of sisters . . . on an ongoing basis, and may involve many kinds of antagonisms and hurts, but the woman can't let go.

She uses her brothers in a dependent way.

But dependency was most often noted in relationships with parents, whereas competition and rivalry were mentioned in characterizing relationships with siblings.

Dependency and overinvolvement with either parents or siblings was almost by definition viewed as a problem. If an individual resented involvement with his or her own kin and saw it as "interference," this resentment was usually considered a healthy sign; especially if the ties were being broken to an extent; this break was taken as a sign of the client's "maturity," "strength," or "growth."

Caseworkers and supervisors hypothesized that one consequence of strong bonds between parents and their adult children was weakened marital solidarity. Consequences of parent-child ties for the marital bond were examined both where the predominant tie was with the husband's kin and where it was with the wife's kin. For example, if the wife was seen to have a hostile-dependent relationship with her mother but had incorporated the mother's matriarchal strength, it was claimed that she married "another" weak man. Thus the husband was submerged by a strong wife and a strong tie between mother and daughter. But the husband was not excluded from acceptance by the wife's mother, nor did he feel himself to be outside the family. In describing this kind of case, both supervisors and caseworkers noted repeatedly that husbands did not express the resentment that one might expect them to have: "The husband did not have the amount of feeling about the overinvolvement." If the predominant tie was with the husband's rather than the wife's mother, the mother-son tie was usually seen to exclude the wife. In these cases the wife usually resented the tie.

A variety of chains of reactions between husbands and wives to their spouse's ties with parents were reported. For example, if the husband resented his wife's tie to her family, his resentment might reduce his wife's guilt about the overinvolvement:

> The client [wife] has no guilt or question about this because spouse is reacting to it and feeling that the client is overinvolved.

Another dimension of dependence on one's own kin was seen to be reflected in "scapegoating" the spouse's kin. In such cases the spouse's kin were the target of hostility displaced from the individual's own family of birth:

> Often dynamic personality difficulties get touched on in connection with the relations between the client, parents, and spouse; often these are very hostile. It is easier to blame a brother-in-law or a sister-in-law and protect a brother or sister.

> Where problems with in-laws are very frequent, with a very disturbed wife who uses her husband's family as an outlet for her residual feelings about her own family, that is, her hostile feelings toward her mother and her hostility toward her brothers and sisters, it may be that there is partly a reality factor in the relationship with her husband's family in terms of the way they feel about her, but [it] is partly an outlet for a projection of her feelings about her own family and a vent for her hostility.

> Mothers-in-law and fathers-in-law are very frequently used in this way. With the mother-in-law, very frequently the daughter-in-law will dread the mother-in-law . . . with other in-laws there are less frequent qualms, but they do enter in. Often it is the feeling about the husband's mother as a mother-in-law and sometimes his father as a father-in-law which is a very strong problem. They are not necessarily all hostile feelings, they may be all powerful. There may be no equilibrium with the relations with the mothers-in-law.

Kin relationships were also described as affecting relationships between clients and their own children. Several types of grandparent roles that cause problems were described. In one case the wife let her mother assume the main authority role:

In some cases we see situations where a grandmother, mother's mother, is used as a kind of policeman over the grandchildren. The mother is dependent on the grandmother to criticize. In these cases the kids feel that the parent is a kind of older sibling and the true parent is the grandmother. The father in these situations is usually a confused figure. He is more related to the grandmother than to the mother. The father usually condones the situation or it can't take place. True parental authorities are the father and the mother's mother. In these cases the men often married in order to get a mother figure, sometimes the wife's mother, and they definitely condone the intervention by the wife's mother. The authority is carried by the father and the grandmother.

In a rather different type of grandparental role an alliance forms between wife and children against the husband and his mother. Hostility toward the grandmother may be displaced on the father, resulting in separation of the husband from his children and weakened ties within the nuclear family:

Another type of syndrome is that where the husband's mother and the husband are the critical agents, and there is a splitting in allied fronts. The mother and the children are against the outside. There is friction between the husband and the wife over the degree of the husband's attachment to his mother. The children are in alliance with the mother. They see the father's mother as a hostile and negative force. They may be compelled to adore this grandmother by the father and their hostility toward the grandmother has its open expression as it is directed toward the father. That is, the hostility toward the grandmother is displaced to the father or it may work the other way round, the hostility toward the father is displaced toward the grandmother. The mother protests against the grandmother, but does not admit that she is in alliance with the children against the father and grandmother.

Another troublesome grandparent syndrome occurs when a reversal of authority roles exists when the grandparents are old and must be taken care of. The child may come to have a confused view of the authority of adults through seeing grandparents in a position without authority. Interestingly, this was regarded as different from the "natural" reversal of parent-child roles in old age:

In cases of this sort the kids often see the grandparents—usually living with the family—as intruders, as a second or third sibling. They see the grandparents as being on the kids' level. This produces a real fracture in the kids' attitudes toward authority. For example, one case where a kid would talk jibberish, or what he considered to be making fun of Yiddish, which he did not really know. This was a way of making fun of his grandmother when she was mad, for ridiculing the grandmother. He sensed from his mother's attitude that she treated the grandmother like a child. This is very different from the kind of natural reversal of roles which occurs later in life when parents are aging and the child helps them to get on. In these situations kids may be sorry for the grandparents, and they may fear age and be fearful of the whole aging process.

Competition with adult siblings was also seen by caseworkers and supervisors to affect the nuclear family. It was claimed, for example, that status differences between siblings were sometimes stressed by husband and wife, when one spouse used the inferior status of the other's siblings to deprecate the spouse:

> The wife resented the husband's brothers, especially the fact that they did not speak English. Also, she felt that they were most critical of her. She feels that she is more Americanized, and in her family there are dentists and pharmacists. She sees the occupations of his brothers as being lower than hers.

Supervisors and caseworkers clearly considered a variety of problems in relationships with kin as typical of the client population. They recognized many ways in which kin relationships may foster problems within the nuclear family. This is particularly significant because the clients themselves rarely reported that problems with kin initially led them to seek casework help. Moreover, the unhealthy elements in kin relationships were stressed more than the healthy, undoubtedly in part because the interviews raised specific questions about problems, but also because the casework process is naturally problem-focused. There was little comment on healthy dimensions of kin relationships.

Caseworkers and supervisors accounted for most problems in relationships with kin in psychodynamic, rather than in social structural, terms; they conceived of these problems as resulting from the psychological characteristics of individual family members. They did not usually see them in relation to social values or intergenerational differences in acculturation. The basic explanation given for these problems was immaturity and dependency resulting from earlier development of problems such as "ambivalent development toward adulthood" and "unmet dependency needs," or "a strong unbroken tie between parent and child." For example:

> The type of ties which exist in the present are indicative of a deep, residual problem which is unresolved, in terms of ambivalent development toward adulthood.

Interaction between clients and their kin was often described in detail by caseworkers and supervisors. For example, a description was given of the interaction process by which ties to kin are supported and a couple becomes "trapped" through accepting the assistance of kin, even when a young couple with "healthy motives" desires a break:

> It is only with the younger couples where one has the strength to know what they want, and they don't want interference, that they make the move out of Brooklyn to the Island. But then, sometimes they will get involved, because they will buy a house or something, and be building up a debt which they can't handle, and then the relatives come to help out with money.

In some instances "reality factors" were pointed to as affecting the relationship. For example, competition and rivalry between siblings was seen as a result of "reality circumstances" when several brothers were in business but the business was too small to support all of them. A part of the treatment process may consist in trying to distinguish the "reality" of other individuals' reactions from the client's handling of them:

> The mother may live next door and barge in. In casework this would be treated as a question of how much the mother actually barges in, as opposed to the question of how much the client places herself in a position where the mother inevitably comes.

The predominant emphasis was on psychodynamics of the client's relationships. This was reflected in phrases such as "She uses her brothers in a dependent way," and "Mothers-in-law and fathers-in-law are very frequently used in this way." For both

adult parent-child and adult sibling relationships the present relationship was considered a result of earlier development and was
seen primarily from the perspective of the client.

However, certain social structural hypotheses were implicit in
some of the observations of supervisors and caseworkers. For example, relationships with kin and those within the nuclear family
were seen as structured differently when the couple is primarily
involved with the husband's rather than the wife's kin because the
husband tends to be accepted as having "married into" the wife's
family, whereas the wife is not as easily accepted into the husband's family. For example:

> In those families where the husband is tied, almost invariably he
> marries as dependent a person as himself. Both seek what the other
> can't give, love and mothering. The problem is that he can't get it
> from his mother. . . . The wife is often the hysterical kind, and has
> strong feelings of being rejected. She doesn't know that she wants
> her husband more for his mother than for himself. If by chance
> such a man's mother has died, he is usually overprotective of his
> children. He almost tries to take over the mother role. The wife pro-
> tests but she can't really do it because she is like a frightened kid.

> In cases where it is the girl who is tied to her mother it is really dif-
> ferent. In some cases the mother is a strong matriarchal figure, but
> the wife really is stronger . . . the wife has both incorporated and
> resented the strength of the mother. This is the type of case where
> the wife says, "The main thing I wanted was not to do what my
> mother did, but here I am doing it"; where they repeat the pattern
> so much that they marry another weak man, and this goes on from
> generation to generation.

Another social-environmental hypothesis is implicit in the view
that it is easier to break kinship ties when moving into a new neighborhood, particularly into a new housing project where different
friendship patterns are likely to arise. One supervisor explained
that breaks in ties with kin become more "natural" in new housing
developments:

> There are about 5,000 families in the project . . . [in the Kings Bay
> area of Brooklyn]. . . . They are coming to have different kinds of
> standards, and a different look at what has been. They have an easier
> time breaking old ties with both family and others. A few of these

never knew social life (other than with kin) before, but they are finding it through the group work center and in the life of the projects. . . . They are in contrast to those in the Brighton area, where there is a great deal of isolation of couples, they are not able to find any kind of community life or any kind of social or recreational life —they have healthy motives, but they don't know how to go about it. . . . This is the first awareness of what a kind of family life could be like. Before, people always take the extreme kind of family ties for granted, but this is an indication of what a new kind of family life could be like . . . a whole new way of life is emerging, but this way, they are able to make the break without having to think of making the break. It becomes a conscious kind of breaking of the extremity of the tie, but it is a natural one. For instance, in group [therapy] meetings in most areas, no matter what the subject, they talk about problems with their parents, but in the Kings Bay area they talk about their husbands and children. In Coney Island and Brighton they always talk about their in-laws.

The general observation of the kin relationships that characterize the client population as a whole may be summarized in the statement, "In the large majority you would find close connections with relatives, no matter when." Most often, however, caseworkers' and supervisors' explanations of problems with kin were framed in individual psychodynamic terms, with few explicit interactional concepts.

The patterns described by supervisors and caseworkers may also be conceived as reflecting the structure of the kinship system. A major factor in the operation of any social system is the way in which individuals are motivated to perform their roles and thus the personal needs that are developed and maintained in social interaction. Where strains are inherent in conflicting cultural expectations, for example, between generations, these necessarily also involve psychological problems for the individual. The additional understanding to be gained from conceiving of relationships with kin as a type of social structure is that this highlights regularities that transcend the individual.

If these problems in relationships with kin are seen in broad cross-cultural perspective, in comparison with kinship systems of other societies, the typical features of these problems are highlighted. Casework treatment focuses to a large degree on the way in which the nuclear family is incorporated with or separated from its kin. This emerges in problems about the comparative stress given to adult parent-child and marital bonds. An examination of casework goals for intervention in relationships with kin should make these broad outlines even sharper.

FORMS OF INTERVENTION

The problems in relationships with kin which caseworkers and supervisors reported as coming up in casework treatment were often, although not always, the subject of therapeutic intervention. Some problems with kin were considered too difficult to tackle; others were not considered the client's central problem; still others were subsumed under psychological reorganization of the individual. But in many cases a definite goal of casework treatment was to help produce alterations in the family's current relationships with its kin.

Current relationships with kin are distinguished from past relationships, not because the past and present are separated in treatment, but in order to emphasize that this type of intervention is something more than a consideration of the early life influences of parents and siblings upon the client's personality development. The importance of early developmental influences in the interconnection of the nuclear family with its kin is well recognized as a therapeutic topic. In this section, however, we will focus on intervention in current social relationships.

The kin themselves sometimes but not necessarily were seen by the therapists, but in all cases of intervention in kin relationships, current relationships with kin were examined with the client in treatment. The caseworker for each case in the sample was asked specific questions about what, if any, kinds of intervention were hoped for or carried out.

Caseworkers in the district offices indicated that some form of intervention had taken place or was contemplated in relationships with kin in 46 per cent of the cases in the sample. Because intervention had not occurred or was not contemplated in current relationships with kin, these relationships were not necessarily considered insignificant for the client's problem. Often no intervention was planned because the client was "not motivated," or "lacked insight," or because these relationships were too difficult to handle. This sample included cases in which little progress of any kind was considered to be possible in casework treatment. In the Service to the Aged caseworkers indicated that in 62 per cent of the cases there was, or would hopefully be, some kind of intervention in relationships with kin. The higher percentage in the Service to the Aged reflects the different problems dealt with in this group and the fact that adult children of an aged couple are often directly involved with the caseworker even when the aged couple, or individual, is formally regarded as the primary client. Financial support, a frequent issue in cases in the Service to the Aged, immediately involves questions about obligations to kin. In fact, the perspective from which the nuclear family is defined at the life-cycle stage of aged clients is radically different from that of younger clients.

Analysis of data from caseworkers on directions of intervention with kin reveals certain regularities. The district offices and the Service to the Aged will be considered separately because the patterns in these two groups differ somewhat. Data from caseworkers on intervention were analyzed in terms of specific kin, that is, husband's father, mother, brothers, sisters, stepparents, and other relatives, and similar kin for the wife. Tabulations were made of the number of individual kin with whom intervention of a given kind occurred. For all the client families there were 161 kin reported with whom there was some form of intervention. Although the number of cases is small, the patterns replicate internally and also reflect data on problems with kin obtained directly from clients.

Instances of intervention were classified as follows: (1) *restriction*—any form of intervention that explicitly entailed reduction in current involvement with kin; (2) *expansion*—any form of intervention that explicitly involved increased involvement with kin; (3) *redefinition*—a form of intervention that was described in terms of psychological redefinition of the relationship. A few statements could not be classified under any of these categories and were called "other."

Most intervention (47 per cent) involved redefinition of the relations with kin. "Restriction" was explicitly mentioned with 40 per cent of the kin as compared with 9 per cent of the kin with whom there was expansion. The high proportion of cases of re-

Table 10.   Direction of Casework Intervention by Generation

	Number of Kin	Per Cent of Kin
Restriction		
Parental generation	45	70
Client's own generation	17	27
Other generations	2	3
Total	64	100
Expansion		
Parental generation	1	7
Client's own generation	12	80
Other generations	2	13
Total	15	100
Redefinition		
Parental generation	42	55
Client's own generation	33	44
Other generations	1	1
Total	76	100
All forms of intervention		
Parental generation	88	57
Client's own generation	62	40
Other generations	5	3
Total	155[a]	100

[a] Six cases that could not be classified in the categories above were omitted in all tables for the sake of simplicity.

definition indicates that caseworkers saw problems primarily in psychodynamic terms and did not explicitly discuss other changes that would result. Reports of psychological redefinition often implied restriction of kin interaction, but these were not counted as such unless explicit statements about interaction were made. The coding criteria were strict in requiring both restriction and expansion to be explicit. The much greater frequency of restriction than expansion is clearly consistent with caseworkers' views that healthy, desirable kin relationships involve breaking the "extremity" of kin ties and replacing them with marital bonds.

Further regularities in these forms of intervention emerge in terms of the specific categories of kin with whom they occur. The generation of the kin is related to the most frequent type of intervention. Restriction was most frequent with members of the cli-

Table 11.   *Direction of Casework Intervention by Sex*

	Number of Kin	Per Cent of Kin
Restriction		
Male	19	30
Female	44	69
Sex not specified	1	1
Total	64	100
Expansion		
Male	4	27
Female	9	60
Sex not specified	2	13
Total	15	100
Redefinition		
Male	30	40
Female	45	59
Sex not specified	1	1
Total	76	100
All forms of intervention		
Male	53	34
Female	98	63
Sex not specified	4	3
Total	155	100

ent's parental generation and much less frequent with kin of the client's own generation. Restriction almost never involved descendants. This distinction reflects not only the stage of the life cycle of the client group, but also the fact that many problems are seen to involve dependence on the parental generation. Although there were few cases of expansion, the pattern is consistent with the other data; expansion was almost nonexistent with members of the parental generation; the few cases in which it did occur were with those of the client's own generation. Redefinition was somewhat more frequent with the parental than with the client's own generation or others, but was more evenly distributed between generations than the other types of intervention (Table 10). Thus ties to the sibling generation are apparently not considered to cause as many problems as those to the client's parental generation.

All types of intervention were more frequent with female than with male kin. Sixty-three per cent of the kin whose relationships

to the clients were the subject of casework intervention were female, as compared with only 34 per cent who were male. The type
of intervention did not vary by sex (Table 11).

Intervention is also related to *laterality.* More intervention occurs with the wife's than with the husband's kin: 71 per cent are
on the wife's side as compared with 26 per cent on the husband's
side. This pattern holds true for all forms of intervention. Expansion was never mentioned with the husband's kin and was almost
entirely with the wife's kin, mainly the wife's siblings (Table 12).

Table 12.   Direction of Intervention by Laterality

	Number of Kin	Per Cent of Kin
Restriction		
Wife's side	47	73
Husband's side	16	25
Laterality unclear	1	2
Total	64	100
Expansion		
Wife's side	13	87
Husband's side	–	–
Laterality unclear	2	13
Total	15	100
Redefinition		
Wife's side	50	66
Husband's side	25	33
Laterality unclear	1	1
Total	76	100
All forms of intervention:		
Wife's side	110	71
Husband's side	41	26
Laterality unclear	4	3
Total	155*	100

* Cases that could not be classified as restriction, expansion, or redefinition are omitted from this table to simplify
presentation.

When all forms of intervention are considered together, the
most frequent intervention is in the relationship with the wife's

mother and next with the wife's sisters. The relationship with the wife's father is treated less than half as often as that with the wife's mother. The relationship with the wife's mother is dealt with almost three times as frequently as that with the husband's mother (Table 13).

Table 13.   Intervention with Specific Categories of Kin

	Number of Instances
Wife's mother	43
Wife's sisters	36
Wife's father	20
Husband's mother	16
Wife's brothers	13
Husband's father	13
Husband's brothers	10
Husband's sisters	5
Wife's other kin	3
Husband's other kin	2
Total	161

This more frequent intervention with kin on the wife's than on the husband's side and the greater frequency of intervention in relationships with the wife's than with the husband's mother are in keeping with the structural hypotheses of caseworkers that the effect on the marital relationship of strong ties with the husband's kin is different from that of strong ties with the wife's kin. They highlight the observation of some caseworkers and supervisors, as our data show, that the strongest unbroken ties of kinship are likely to be on the wife's side; that both husbands and wives readily accept strong ties to the wife's family, whereas wives often resent their husband's ties to his kin. Thus the underlying implicit logic of intervening most frequently in ties with the wife's kin is to seek to alter the strongest ties of kinship.

The kin with whom intervention occurs in the cases in the Service to the Aged differ from those in the district offices. In almost all cases intervention was in relationships with descendants; it was never in relationships with members of the ascending generation and only very infrequently in relationships with members of the client's generation. However, these data clearly reflect the same processes from the point of view of those at a different stage in the life cycle.

The numbers are extremely small because the population contained only 33 cases, and there was not sufficient information for coding all of these. However, the patterns of intervention are similar to those found among the other clients. Here also restriction was more frequent than expansion, restriction occurring in six cases as compared with only two of expansion. Expansion occurred in efforts to increase children's obligations to assist in the support of aged parents. Again redefinition was the most frequent category, occurring in seven cases.

The underlying therapeutic assumptions about changes in relationships with kin were revealed in interviews with caseworkers and supervisors. Almost all of these changes entailed an alteration in the personality organization of the individual clients. For example, "restricting" interaction with the wife's mother implied helping the wife become more independent psychologically so that she might be better able to cope with her mother's interference.

In some instances, however, an effort was made early in treatment to make what may be considered direct "situational" alterations. Individuals were helped to accept these changes, but the situational changes preceded a more thorough "working through" of the psychological ramifications of the change. This type of intervention was true of some residence changes; for example, helping a family arrange for an aged parent to move to an institution, or making a decision to avoid having an elderly parent move in with them, or helping young couples decide to move out of a parental home.

The focus in many instances was to help clients alter their feelings toward kin, thus enabling them to function more independently. This direction was described as helping clients to feel less "guilty" toward parents and helping clients learn ways of "setting limits" on interaction with kin.

These forms of casework intervention imply the support of greater structural and functional independence of the nuclear family from its kin, leading to more independent action in authority, decision-making, child rearing, economic and financial arrangements. The norms that caseworkers implicitly or explicitly hold up as ideals to their clients indicate that it is healthy and normal for the nuclear family to function primarily as an independent unit. The right of kin outside the nuclear family to participate in nuclear family functions is minimized. Casework intervention therefore involves altering the kinship values of clients.

In some cases intervention entailed redefining priorities of obligations to the husband's and wife's kin. For example, in a conflict over the division of financial responsibilities of the husband and his siblings toward his parents, the wife felt her husband's siblings were not taking their share of the responsibilities. An effort was made to help the husband recognize his wife's feelings in order to equalize obligations of the siblings to their parents and reduce the priority given to the husband's parents over the wife's parents and the nuclear family. Such shifts of priority are difficult to separate from reducing involvement with the family of origin of both spouses because these alterations usually occur through reducing obligations to one side, not through increasing obligations to the other side.

The processes of alteration of the bonds of solidarity within the kinship system are remarkably similar whether the caseworker is dealing with regular clients or the Aged. It might be expected that the perspective of the caseworker would shift when dealing with older clients, that the goal would be to help them realize some of their hopes for continued involvement with their adult children. But the reverse is true. Intervention, whether classified as restriction or redefinition, most often involves helping the aged parents realize their children's right to independence in their new families. The processes of helping an aged client make this type of change may be somewhat different from helping younger clients become more independent of their parents, but the desired result is similar. Intervention of this sort with aged clients was described as helping them become more "independent" of their children, helping them to expect less of their children, and helping them to "interfere" less in their children's households. Sometimes substitute interests in nonkin activities were sought. In one case the caseworker tried to channel a client's energies into a Golden Age Club so that he would be "less a source of pressure on his children."

Statements of some of the caseworkers in the Service to the Aged illustrate this type of change: the goal in one case with an elderly woman was to "help her look at her dependency and effort to manipulate [her daughter]. [Help her see that] she has the strength to function without her husband. Help her use this [in separating from daughter]. Help her see what needs [presumably unhealthy] she wants satisfied by the daughter."

In one case a residential change was described as follows: "Help son and grandson to see that mother's self-determination must be honored, even though I can understand their concern, that she will have to come to the decision herself, with help, if it is necessary for her to enter a home."

In another case, the parents were helped "to become more independent and adequate, not so dependent on daughter." In one case the effort was "to help [the aged] mother see why her demands are unrealistic. Help [her] ventilate tremendous hostility she has toward daughter." In another case the [aged] mother was considered to be "dominant, controlling, controls family even from bed," and the goal was "to get her to express some of her negative feelings, see that family is overly dependent. [Aged] father supports her control, get him to see this." In another case the "relationship with daughter was most important to [the aged mother]. She can verbalize anger at daughter, and what she wants from her. Try to make her see that this is something she can't really get from her daughter."

In some cases the process of loosening parent-child ties is encouraged from both sides simultaneously. For example, a caseworker reported that she tried to "help the mother see the daughter isn't as incapacitated as the way she treats her would indicate, why she is so possessive. Help daughter look at her dependence, help mother look at the idea of home for the aged."

Thus whether the process is seen from the perspective of clients in the middle stages of life, or from that of older clients of the generation of clients' parents, the goals of therapeutic intervention in relationships with kin are similar. A major part of the process may be seen as realigning the bonds of solidarity, primarily through reducing bonds with members of the family of childhood, that is, parent-child and sibling bonds, and thereby aiming to strengthen marital bonds and the family of marriage.

CLIENT PERCEPTIONS
OF INTERVENTION

Clients' perceptions of intervention in relationships with kin are similar to those of caseworkers and supervisors. In interviews clients were not asked specifically about their perceptions of therapeutic intervention or how they viewed changes in relationships with kin occurring in the course of treatment. It was felt that to do so might confuse the interviewer's role with that of the therapist's and that an apparent evaluation of casework therapy in the research interviews might complicate the ongoing treatment relationships. Nevertheless, these changes were sometimes brought up spontaneously by clients, so that some clues about their perceptions are available. In addition, some items on clients' views about casework intervention in kin relationships were included in the client questionnaires sent to husbands and wives in each family in the sample.

Clients and caseworkers hold similar views about the forms of change in kin relationships that occur in treatment. Items from the questionnaires were classified according to the categories used for the caseworkers' statements: restriction, expansion, and redefinition. The client data do not correspond completely to the content of the categories from the caseworker interviews because only the checked answers to the questionnaire statement were obtained from the clients, whereas the caseworker data were from open-ended interviews. But the general criteria for classification were the same.

These findings parallel those from the caseworkers. The statements with the highest proportion of "Yes" answers fall in the redefinition category; a high proportion of "Yes" answers also fall in restriction. Most of the items in both redefinition and restriction received more "Yes" answers than those in expansion. Although fewer "expansion" items were included in the questionnaire than those in the other categories, the expansion items that were included did not receive a high proportion of "Yes" checks.

The two items that explicitly mentioned a shift from kinship bonds to marital bonds, "I feel I am less involved with them and closer to my husband [wife]," and "I feel my husband [wife] is less involved with them and closer to me than before," both received a high proportion of "Yes" answers (Table 14).

On the basis of these questionnaire data, the overall directions of casework intervention in relationships with kin that are most frequent as perceived by clients appear similar to those reported by caseworkers and supervisors. Moreover, it is clear from this table that many clients do perceive some sort of change in relationships with kin to be occurring as a result of casework treatment.

*Table 14.   Clients' Perceptions of Changes in Kin Relations
During Casework Treatment*[a]

	Per Cent of Clients Checking "Yes"[a]	
Restriction		
I feel I am less involved with them and closer to my husband [wife].	56	(317)
I feel my husband [wife] is less involved with them and closer to me than before.	43	(289)
I don't depend on them so much any more.	39	(317)
I confide in them less.	43	(284)
I see them less often than before.	23	(291)
I find I am less involved with family circle or cousins club than I was.	14	(254)
Expansion		
I see them more often than before.	12	(315)
I confide in them more.	9	(293)
Redefinition		
My husband [wife] and I feel freer to express our differences about relatives to each other.	67	(300)
I'm better able to accept them as they are.	61	(299)
My husband [wife] and I don't have as many fights about relatives as we used to.	55	(296)
I don't feel so guilty about them anymore.	38	(283)
I realized this relationship was taking too much out of me.	34	(268)
I've learned to accept their help without feeling so bad about it.	21	(266)
I realize I've made things harder for them than I had thought.	15	(278)

[a] The percentages indicate those who checked "yes" in response to the following question: "Have any of the following things changed in your relationship with relatives—including your relatives, your husband's [wife's] relatives, and your married children—as a result of coming to the agency? This was followed by the items listed in the table.

Clients sometimes see changes in treatment as learning appropriate norms from the caseworker, that is, what kinds of kin relationships they *should* have. Some feel that they were initially ignorant of proper kinship behavior which they had been taught through casework. One case in which the wife reduced her sibling ties in conjunction with trying to strengthen her marital relationship illustrates the clients' view that they are learning appropriate norms for kin relationships from the caseworker:

I used to be the one to call [my sisters], before I went to the Jewish Family Service. I voiced all my complaints and so on to them. I didn't have the opportunity, or let's say, the understanding that these things should be discussed with my husband, and he, by the same token, was resentful that I used to go to my sisters instead of discussing things with him. He felt that close relationships—in fact, all the brothers-in-law used to resent that—that we kept that close, that everything was discussed among ourselves, and they felt left out. Then we found out it wasn't a good thing, it wasn't right, it wasn't fair. So as soon as I started to get a different relationship with my husband, that's when the phone calls on my part left off.

Another client explained that, during treatment, he saw changes in the family's relationship with his wife's mother. As a result of casework, he and his wife became aware of the problem they had with the wife's mother, who lived in their household. For him one result of therapy was understanding a residence norm, that "two people who are married should live alone," of which he had not previously been aware. However, he did not see any way of achieving this ideal:

HUSBAND: I'll tell you, my mother-in-law is a problem to us. I mean it's a situation which we can't help. But we have, well . . . she's a nice woman. . . . But what else can you do with the situation? . . . It's more so since she's been ill, but . . . it seems like she's always been a problem, but we never realized it. We never looked at it as a problem, all these questions that they ask at the Jewish Family Service. . . . We began to realize, we realized that there are many things in a household, and two people who are married should live alone, and, well, when there's a third person, things are just never the same, and we never realized it. I knew there was something to it, but we never really thought of it 'til this, and, but this is a situation that can't be helped, so we just go along with it.

One change that clients perceived to be occurring as a result of casework was that kinship ties were being modified by substituting friendship ties. One client, for example, felt her caseworker emphatically supported this type of change:

Mrs. F. [caseworker] knows about these new-found friends of ours.

She's all for it. She thinks it's very good because, as I said, we didn't have friends before. We hardly had any visitors besides family, and, you know, family is sort of forced on you, you know? You can't choose them, they're there.

In some situations clients did not view the changes in kin relationships occurring during treatment as a result of explicit learning of norms but felt they gained the "strength" to make these changes through therapy. In one case, for example, the husband stopped working in business with his wife's father during the course of therapy. Although he claimed that leaving the business was not directly brought up with the caseworker and that the condition of the business itself was also a factor, both the husband and the wife agreed that treatment had been significant in enabling him to make the change:

WIFE: He [husband] went out [of business with my father] through being in therapy.

HUSBAND: During therapy. . . .

WIFE: I think so, yes. He wouldn't have had the strength to do it without it. Right?

HUSBAND: Well, I don't know. It's one of these things. Who knows?

WIFE: Well, I know a year or two before. . . .

HUSBAND: No, but I mean it's something like, if you have such and such, you know that you're cured. But I mean, the situation is ponderous. My father-in-law, as far as I was concerned, was desperate. I mean, it was just no, no place to go but out, and. . . .

WIFE: But you felt that way a couple of years prior to that, and you just thought. . . . I remember him [husband] being in a very depressed mood, sitting in the dark in a chair, saying, "How did I get into this?" He just felt he was at the mercy of my father whom he didn't respect, and he thought, "How did I get to be under his . . . and not standing up on my own two feet?" . . . terrible mood. But at that time he didn't get up and say, "I'm walking out. I'm going to work for myself." That's why I think it was through the therapy he got strength to do it.

HUSBAND: Well, that might be true. . . . I don't ever remember in therapy discussing leaving . . . as such . . . it was a big surprise to the worker [when I] came in and announced, "I left." But I, I mean to say, it was during the therapy, and, of course, the assumption jumps to the mind that it did that. I'm quite satisfied that that's the way it is.

This family also reported another change in relationships with kin that resulted from their treatment. Here they felt the change stemmed directly from having gained insight into the quality of certain relationships with kin so that they were not so "gratified" by them. The change was not a general reduction of all involvement with kin but a realignment of kin ties, cutting contacts with both the husband's and wife's parents and with a sister of the husband who lived with his parents, and strengthening ties to the other siblings who were less involved with the parents:

> WIFE: In general, I feel that my mother-in-law . . . tells me more than she would even her daughter. . . . In a way it's a compliment . . . [but now that] we're more aware of what's going on . . . [we are] not so gratified. . . .
>
> INTERVIEWER: What does she talk to you about?
>
> WIFE: The other children. She tries to complain about Marian or Helen [husband's sisters], but we've learned a little bit lately, that now we're closer to the other sisters [those not living with husband's parents]. . . .
>
> HUSBAND: We've spread our therapy around. . . .
>
> WIFE: . . . like we cut it from my parents, we also cut it from his parents, and realigned, had a little bit of a clearer picture of what was going on there too. . . . As you can see, living with the mother, there's such a lot of friction between them [husband's mother and husband's sister], and we hear from both sides, and we can't start to tell them what's wrong with them.

Both questionnaire and interview data therefore indicate that clients as well as caseworkers see changes that occur in relationships with kin as a result of casework intervention.

Caseworkers and supervisors, and clients, regardless of life-cycle stage, agree that therapeutic intervention often involves changes in the family's relationship with kin. Although these changes may be described in psychological terms, and brought about through psychological modifications that enable the individual to alter his kin relationships, research results reveal systematic regularities in the directions of this intervention from the perspective of a kinship system. Although caseworkers and supervisors had many significant hypotheses about kin relationships, the fact that systematic regularities exist in the directions of intervention was not evident prior to research. Most often intervention entails or aims to produce a realignment of kinship bonds, moving away from strong adult parent-child and adult sibling bonds toward strengthening ties within the nuclear family of marriage, particularly the marital bond.

Insofar as this general pattern holds true, casework is implicitly seeking to aid clients in moving toward the type of kinship structure that has been hypothesized as typical of the American middle class, in which independence of the nuclear family from kin is ideal. The effort to shift the kin relationships of clients also implies that the initial kin relationships diverge from those that have been considered representative of the middle classes in a western urban industrial society. In view of the immigrant background of these clients, and cultural differences between clients and those in their parental generation, the question arises whether this direction of intervention represents a part of the process of acculturation from Eastern European Jewish traditions.

Because all kinship systems require role changes during the individual's life cycle, it is also possible that casework intervention is enabling those who for some reason have special problems to make life-cycle transitions in their kin relationships and to shift from bonds in their family of childhood to those in their family of marriage.

The regularities in intervention have some interesting parallels with and differences from regularities in interaction and conflict. Intervention is generally most frequent with the categories of kin with whom there is most interaction. However, intervention does not occur most frequently where clients perceive most conflict. Perhaps some of these discrepancies and similarities are related in part to caseworkers' values about kinship and their own experience with kin. Therefore, we will now examine the comparative values and experiences of caseworkers and clients. In the last chapter we will reexamine the data on interaction, conflict, and intervention in light of these comparisons.

CHAPTER 8

Caseworkers and Clients:
Contrasting Kinship Values
and Experience

We have found that therapeutic intervention involving relationships with kin outside the nuclear family most often involves redefinition or restriction of interaction with kin; rarely does it mean expansion of kin contacts. It can therefore be assumed that caseworkers are attempting to alter the kinship system of the nuclear family in consistent directions.

Interviews with caseworkers and supervisors clearly revealed that implicit therapeutic assumptions exist about desirable forms of kinship structure. These include, for example, the notion that the "healthy," "mature" person will have the "strength" to set limits on interaction with kin. It is also assumed that it is most desirable for the nuclear family to reside alone, not in the same household with grandparents or other kin.

The source of these therapeutic assumptions, however, is not entirely clear. They might reflect objectively validated knowledge that one type of kinship system is more desirable than another because it is more likely to be associated with certain preferred forms of nuclear family relationships. At the same time, implicit cultural assumptions undoubtedly underlie these therapeutic ideas and the observed regularities in directions of intervention. The social and cultural background and experience of caseworkers inevitably enters to some degree into the therapeutic process. It is therefore important to know the ways in which caseworkers and their clients differ in background, kinship experience, and values.

Comparisons between caseworkers and their clients indicate that while caseworkers and clients are generally similar in background, certain significant differences exist. Caseworkers are younger and more frequently single. Because the research questionnaire was returned by a similar proportion of husbands and wives, the staff sample includes a higher proportion of women than is true of the clients; of the staff, three-fourths are women and only one-fourth men. A higher proportion of the staff were born in the United States than is true of clients. In addition, the parents of staff are somewhat more often native-born than clients, although the majority of the parents of both staff and clients were foreign-born. Educational achievement and occupational status are, of course, also different; all the staff had received graduate training beyond the bachelor degree, which was true of only a small proportion of clients and of virtually none of the client wives. The religious orientations of staff and clients also differ, 19 per cent of the staff being non-Jewish, whereas the clients included in the research sample were Jewish (the 2 per cent non-Jews being married to a Jewish partner). Although slightly over half of both clients and staff identify themselves as "just Jewish," more of the clients (40 per cent) identify themselves as either Orthodox or Conservative than is true of staff (14 per cent). Clients also more often indicated that they attended religious services either on High Holidays or regularly than did caseworkers. These data are summarized in Table 15.

The sample selected for research purposes, Jewish families primarily of Eastern European origin or descent, married and living in currently intact households, does not represent the entire agency caseload because it excludes single clients and those who are neither Jewish nor married to a Jew. In some respects this maximizes differences between caseworkers and clients; single clients might be somewhat more like the single caseworkers than would the married clients. Nevertheless, this group of married clients rep-

Table 15. Social Background of Caseworkers and Clients

	Per Cent of Caseworkers[a]	Per Cent of Clients[b]
Thirty-five years old or younger	50	22
Unmarried	35	0
Born in United States	86	78
Fathers born in United States	30	8
Mothers born in United States	33	13
Education beyond college	100	7
Orthodox[c]	5	14
Conservative	9	26
Reform	10	5
"Just Jewish"	56	53
Other	19	2
Attend religious services on High Holidays, other holidays, or regularly	45	62

[a] The caseworker sample contains 123 members of the professional staff.
[b] The client sample includes 420 individuals, 210 husbands and 210 wives. These percentages are based on those who answered the question in each instance.
[c] Includes Hassidic clients; there were no Hassidic staff.

resents the vast majority of agency cases. Therefore, the comparison between caseworkers and clients in the research sample is with those clients typifying most caseloads.

The kinship values of clients, as derived from both interview and questionnaire data, were discussed in Chapter 3. These client values will now be compared with comparable questionnaire material from caseworkers. Data are also included on the values of client in the Service to the Aged. The expressed values may be influenced by a variety of factors. Among the caseworkers, for example, kinship values may contain a melding of personal reactions and professional ideology. The values of both caseworkers and clients are influenced by such factors as age, marital status, birthplace of parents, religious orientations, and other social characteristics and experiences.

Whatever the source of the values of either clients or caseworkers may be, the fact of their similarity or difference is significant. The therapeutic process represents a melding of both personal and professional experience and knowledge, so that existing differences from any source have a potential significance for therapy. It is important, first, therefore, to determine what differences and similarities exist. The size of the staff does not permit extensive analysis of the factors such as age, sex, and professional experience that influence values, but after mapping out the comparisons of caseworkers and their clients it is at least possible to speculate on some of the factors that may underlie these differences.

COMPARISON OF KINSHIP VALUES

The Values Form, "Opinions About Family Life" presented to husbands and wives, was included in identical form in the questionnaire given to all members of the agency's professional staff.[1] For a discussion of the caseworker sample and the procedures of analysis in this part of the study, see the Appendix. The grouping of items here parallels that in Chapter 3 on the kinship values of client families.

Marriage

The procedures by which marriage partners are selected and the definitions of whom it is appropriate or permissible to marry are a keystone of the kinship system. Caseworkers and clients differed considerably in their views about the marriage process. The Aged differed from the caseworkers even more strongly than the other clients.

One question related to that of the role parents should take in the selection of marriage partners concerns whether children should reside at home until marriage, thus affording parents an opportunity to oversee the dating process. On this point caseworkers and clients differed greatly. To the statement, "Children should not leave home before they get married," 63 per cent of the clients agreed, whereas only 3 per cent of the caseworkers agreed. The Aged agreed even more often than other clients, in 72 per cent of the cases (Table 16). As we have seen, those clients who hold this view believe that there is a sanctity in the home, that parents must control their children's dating, and that a child who leaves home before marriage reflects adversely on the quality of the home. Caseworkers emphatically do not agree with this view. Here caseworkers had a lower proportion of no opinions than clients.

A related question concerns the type of break in family ties that is expected for men and women at marriage. As we have seen, kinship systems in which the young bride goes to live with or near her husband's kin are likely to impose a more radical transition at marriage for the bride, whereas in other cases it is the husband who must make the greatest break. We have also observed a repeated tendency in client kin relationships of skewing toward the wife's side. The traditional saying, "It is true that a daughter's a daughter all her life, a son's a son 'til he gets a wife," implying a greater continuity in the wife's than the husband's kin ties after marriage, was used to probe this issue. It was also a point on which caseworkers and clients differed significantly. Clients were fairly evenly split in responses to this item, agreeing and disagreeing in approximately the same proportion of cases. The Aged agreed somewhat more frequently than the other clients. Caseworkers, on the other hand, disagreed with this statement in 78 per cent of the cases. Insofar as this statement may represent a carryover of the Eastern European tradition of the *kest,* or support of the son-in-

Table 16.   *Values on Marriage*

Statement	Respondent	Agree	No Opinion	Dis-agree	
		PERCENTAGES			
Children should not	Aged	72	15	13	(39)
leave home before	Clients	63	9	28	(381)
they get married.	Caseworkers	3	4	93	(122)
(0.001 level)[a]					
It is true that	Aged	46	14	41	(37)
"A daughter's a	Clients	40	19	41	(381)
daughter all her life;	Caseworkers	8	14	78	(123)
a son's a son 'til					
he gets a wife."					
(0.001 level)					

[a] A "significant difference" simply means that the difference in responses between caseworkers and clients is not likely to be a result of pure chance fluctuations. If the difference is significant at the 0.001 level, a difference of the magnitude shown in the table would occur by chance alone no more than once in a thousand. A difference at the 0.05 level would occur by chance alone no more than five times in one hundred. Differences that might occur by chance more than five times in one hundred are labeled "not significant"; see Tables 17, 21, and 22. In each of these tables the reader may still wish to see the direction of the relationship.

law by the wife's family, for those who agree with it, this view is not held by most caseworkers. Clients who disagreed with the statement sometimes did so on the grounds that it was merely an old saying, and the same reasoning may apply to the caseworkers. Whatever their reasons may be, caseworkers are less prone than either clients or the Aged to see greater continuity in the daughter's than the son's ties to parents after marriage. In this sense caseworkers hold a more bilaterally symmetrical view of marriage than clients.

Residence

The marriage process implies questions about residence, or where it is appropriate to live in relation to kin at different stages of the life cycle. Following marriage the issue becomes whether one should live in the same household with or near the kin of either spouse, and if one should live with or near kin, which kin this should be. On these questions caseworkers and clients again differed considerably. However, on the issue of combined households, caseworkers, clients, and the Aged held similar views. In all three groups, combined households were generally seen as undesirable, although this was slightly less true of the Aged than of other clients. In views about residential proximity, and about which kin one should live near, however, caseworkers and clients differed. Again the Aged consistently differed from the caseworkers in the direction of the clients, but even more strongly.

To the statement, *"It is usually nice for a young married couple to live near their parents,"* 61 per cent of the Aged agreed, 40 per cent of the clients agreed, and only 14 per cent of the caseworkers agreed. Similarly, there were differences in views about whether "It is good for a young mother to have her mother close by to help her learn how to take care of her baby," with 67 per cent of the Aged agreeing, 48 per cent of the clients agreeing, and only 21 per cent of the caseworkers agreeing (Table 17). Thus clients are clearly more likely than caseworkers to favor residential proximity to kin, and the Aged are even more likely to favor it.

On the issue of which kin one should live close to, clients and caseworkers again differed. One question in this respect is whether a newly married couple should live closer to the wife's or the husband's kin. At a later stage in life, the question becomes whether a widow would prefer to live with a married son or a married daughter. Caseworkers and clients differed in the response to the idea that "*A widow would usually prefer living with a married daughter than with a married son.*" Living with a married daughter in preference to a married son implies a skewing that is comparable from another perspective to a preference to live near the wife's rather than the husband's kin after marriage. This statement was agreed to by 65 per cent of the clients. Whereas only 28 per cent of the caseworkers agreed, the Aged agreed slightly more frequently than the clients (Table 17).

Thus caseworkers and clients not only differ in their views about the desirability of living close to kin, but also in ideas about greater proximity toward the wife's than the husband's kin.

Table 17. Values on Residence

Statement	Respondent	Agree	No Opinion	Dis-agree	
		PERCENTAGES			
If a mother and married daughter live in the same household, there's usually trouble. (not significant)	Aged	66	18	16	(38)
	Clients	72	14	15	(379)
	Caseworkers	72	9	20	(123)
It is usually nice for a young married couple to live near their parents. (0.001 level)	Aged	61	24	16	(36)
	Clients	40	12	47	(380)
	Caseworkers	14	18	68	(123)
It is good for a young mother to have her own mother close by to help her learn how to take care of her baby. (0.001 level)	Aged	67	17	17	(36)
	Clients	48	11	41	(380)
	Caseworkers	21	25	54	(123)
A widow would usually prefer living with a married daughter than with a married son. (0.001 level)	Aged	68	24	8	(38)
	Clients	65	30	6	(376)
	Caseworkers	28	49	23	(122)

Obligations for Kin Interaction

On questions about general obligations to interact with kin, clients and caseworkers again differed significantly, and the Aged were consistently more kin-oriented than other clients.

One item dealt with attitudes about reducing interaction with kin: "It's selfish for someone to cut himself off from his relatives." To this, 76 per cent of the Aged agreed, 63 per cent of the clients agreed, and only 16 per cent of the caseworkers agreed; 66 per cent of the caseworkers disagreed, whereas only 3 per cent of the Aged disagreed. Another phrasing of the general question of obligations to interact with kin was: "*Regardless of what brothers or sisters have done, one should never stop talking to them.*" Even among the caseworkers nearly half tended to see a permanency in brother and sister ties as binding and unbreakable, but clients were significantly more kin-oriented than the caseworkers. Clients agreed with this statement in 72 per cent of the cases, as compared with 47 per cent of the caseworkers who agreed. Of the Aged 84 per cent agreed (Table 18).

In another item, "It is a thing of pride and joy to have a family circle or cousins club," the desirability of formal kin organizations, which necessarily entail an obligation to interact, was questioned. Here both caseworkers and clients had a fairly high proportion of "no opinion," but clients were significantly more likely to see formal kinship groups as desirable than were caseworkers; 71 per cent of the Aged agreed, 58 per cent of the clients agreed, while only 16 per cent of the caseworkers agreed. Thus through several different areas of kinship obligation, clients were significantly more kin-oriented than caseworkers.

Mobility

One important question about kinship is what implication ties of kinship have for social mobility; whether extensive obligations to kin interfere with occupational mobility when it requires geographic separation from kin. In this instance the responses of caseworkers and clients to the different items in the Values Form were not as obviously consistent in direction as in other areas, but again significant differences exist.

One item concerned the value of education: "No sacrifice is too great for the education of a son." If a high value on education

Table 18.   *Values on Obligations for Kin Interaction*

Statement	Respondent	Agree	No Opinion	Dis-agree	
		PERCENTAGES			
It's selfish for someone	Aged	76	22	3	(37)
to cut himself off from	Clients	63	15	21	(375)
his relatives.	Caseworkers	16	19	66	(122)
(0.001 level)					
Regardless of what	Aged	84	5	11	(37)
brothers or sisters	Clients	72	9	19	(380)
have done one should	Caseworkers	47	11	42	(123)
never stop talking to					
them.					
(0.001 level)					
It is a thing of pride	Aged	71	26	3	(38)
and joy to have a family	Clients	58	34	9	(375)
circle or cousins club.	Caseworkers	16	57	28	(122)
(0.001 level)					

is considered an indication of a more general value of social mobility, clients are in this respect more mobility-oriented than caseworkers. The Aged agreed in 70 per cent of the cases, clients in 52 per cent, and caseworkers in only 7 per cent (Table 19). Clients therefore place considerably more stress on the absolute value of education than caseworkers. The caseworkers may view other things as more important than educational success, or the term *sacrifice* may be one against which the caseworkers react, taking it to imply too great an educational striving at the expense of other values. It may also be that the urgency of educational values diminishes as education is actually achieved and can more or less be assumed; the Aged, who have the least formal education, value it most. Although both the Aged and the clients place greater value on education than the caseworkers in response to this item and are in this sense more mobility-oriented, the question of geographic separation from kin for the sake of mobility was not specifically raised in this question.

When the issue of ties to kin is explicitly introduced, clients are again significantly more kin-oriented than are caseworkers. To the statement, *"It is better to take a good job near your parents and relatives than to take a better job where you will have to move away from them,"* the responses of caseworkers and clients differed to a statistically significant extent. Clients more often agreed, in 24 per cent of the cases, with the idea that it was preferable to remain near kin than did caseworkers, of whom only 11 per cent agreed. Of the Aged, 51 per cent agreed. Both among caseworkers and clients, the majority disagree that it is better to remain near kin regardless of job consequences. On this item, however, clients are less likely than caseworkers to give occupational success priority over proximity to kin, despite the greater emphasis that clients, especially the Aged, place on the value of education. Clients value education more strongly than caseworkers, but at the same time they are less likely than caseworkers to give occupational success priority over ties of kinship.

Another statement used in this connection was: *"It should be enough satisfaction to parents if a son is a success even if he moves away from them."* In this instance caseworkers and clients again differed in their responses. The differences were significant at the 0.001 level. Here the direction of response appears different from that in the previous question. Both caseworkers and clients agree more frequently than they disagree with the idea that it should be enough satisfaction if a son is a success even if he moves away. Clients, however, agreed with this statement somewhat more frequently, in 81 per cent of the cases, than did caseworkers, who agreed in 67 per cent of the cases. The Aged also agreed in 81 per cent of the cases. In this case it would appear that the clients are placing slightly less stress on proximity to kin than are the caseworkers. The direction of difference between caseworkers and clients on this item and the previous item therefore appears to be inconsistent. In this statement, however, the stress is perhaps mainly on success and the satisfaction parents should have with this success, whereas the previous question poses more pointedly the problem of geographic mobility versus ties to kin.

Therefore, it appears that in some respects clients place more emphasis on educational achievement and occupational success than do caseworkers. But when posed specifically in terms of moving away from kin for the sake of success, clients remain more reluctant to give up proximity to kin than caseworkers.

Another question about kinship and mobility concerns ties to kin in different social positions. An item used to get at this issue was: *"Even if some relatives are better off than others, that shouldn't stop them from getting together as often as they can."* Here the question of reduction of kin ties because of status differences was phrased directly. Both clients and caseworkers agree that being better off should not be a reason for failing to get together with relatives. However, clients agree more frequently than caseworkers in 91 per cent of the cases, whereas caseworkers agreed in 76 per cent of the cases. Here clients and the Aged were almost the same, 89 per cent of the Aged agreeing. The differences were statistically significant at the 0.001 level.

Despite the apparent inconsistencies between some of the mobility items and the logical inconsistencies in client attitudes between emphasizing both education and proximity to kin, when the phrasing directly points to the key issue as that of proximity to kin, in this area, as elsewhere, clients are more kin-oriented than caseworkers.

Table 19. Values on Mobility

Statement	Respondent	Agree	No Opinion	Dis-agree	
		PERCENTAGES			
No sacrifice is too great for the education of a son. (0.001 level)	Aged	70	16	14	(37)
	Clients	52	12	36	(378)
	Caseworkers	7	9	84	(123)
It is better to take a good job near your parents and relatives than to take a good job where you will have to move away from them. (0.001 level)	Aged	51	31	17	(35)
	Clients	24	13	62	(378)
	Caseworkers	11	4	85	(123)
It should be enough satisfaction to parents if a son is a success even if he moves far away from them. (0.001 level)	Aged	81	16	3	(37)
	Clients	81	8	11	(379)
	Caseworkers	67	13	20	(122)
Even if some relatives are much better off than others, that shouldn't stop them from getting together as often as they can. (0.001 level)	Aged	89	8	3	(36)
	Clients	91	7	2	(381)
	Caseworkers	76	22	2	(122)

Kin and Nonkin Institutions

Another important issue concerns the range of social functions that are carried out on the basis of kinship. Here again differences exist between caseworkers and clients in their views about the extent to which the nuclear family should rely on kin as compared with other institutions, and in expectations about what economic dealings with kin will entail.

One item used to probe views about the desirability of carrying out economic activities with kin as compared with impersonal institutions was: *"If you have to borrow money, it is better to do it from a relative than from a bank."* The responses of caseworkers and clients differed to a statistically significant extent, but not in the direction one might expect in view of values in other areas. Clients, despite their greater emphasis on obligations toward kin, more frequently disagreed with the idea that it is better to borrow from a relative than from a bank; 67 per cent of the clients disagreed, whereas only 50 per cent of the caseworkers disagreed. The Aged disagreed about as often as the other clients but agreed much less frequently (Table 20). In light of the interview data from clients, it seems likely that this item reflects views about the problems inherent in economic dealings with kin, rather than directly reflecting views about obligations toward kin. Here, as compared with some other areas, nonkin institutions are readily available. The client's attitude that it is better to borrow from a bank than from a relative does not necessarily imply that economic obligations of kinship would not be strongly felt. If this is so, the caseworker's view may be taken to reflect a lesser degree of anticipation on conflict in economic dealings with kin.

A second item yields results that are consistent in this respect: *"When relatives go into business together they are likely to end up enemies."* Here the question does not pose an alternative between kin and nonkin institutions, but rather concentrates specifically on the likelihood of conflicts in business dealings with kin. Here again the responses of caseworkers and clients are significantly different. The Aged agreed that the kin would be likely to end up enemies in 53 per cent of the cases, the clients agreed in 48 per cent of the cases, and the caseworkers agreed in only 19 per cent. In one sense this response might be considered to represent a lesser degree of pro-kin orientation on the part of clients, but from the interview data, it would seem that the clients, and particularly the Aged, although generally more geared toward maintaining interaction and obligations toward kin, also are more likely to expect conflict in kin relationships.

When the question was posed more specifically in terms of the safety of trusting a relative as compared with an outsider in business dealings, the Aged were most likely to feel it safer to trust a kin, the clients next most likely, and the caseworkers least likely to feel a kin safer than an outsider. With the statement, *"In business dealings it is usually safer to trust a relative than an outsider,"* 47 per cent of the Aged agreed, 41 per cent of the clients, and only 22 per cent of the caseworkers. Thus when statements are phrased in terms of the possibilities of trusting nonkin, clients are definitely more kin-oriented than caseworkers.

Two other questions posed the issue of the comparative reliance that can be placed on kin and nonkin, specifically friends. On both of these questions the clients were more kin-oriented than the caseworkers, and the Aged were most kin-oriented of all. To the statement, *"Friends can't give you the love you can get from relatives,"* there was agreement from 63 per cent of the Aged, from 32 per cent of the clients, and from only 7 per cent of the caseworkers. In response to the statement, *"One usually has more in common with relatives than friends,"* the values of caseworkers and clients were again different, to a statistically significant extent, and in the direction of greater reliance on kin by clients. Of the Aged, 47 per cent agreed; of the clients, 29 per cent agreed; and of the caseworkers, only 7 per cent agreed. Here again, therefore, the clients are more kin-oriented than the caseworkers, and the Aged most kin-oriented of all.

Values about reliance on kin and nonkin institutions and expectations about economic relationships with kin fit the picture that has emerged in most areas. The fact that clients, and particularly the Aged, are more likely than caseworkers to anticipate conflicts in economic relations with kin is not really inconsistent with their greater general involvement with kin. Perhaps in part because of more frequent economic dealings with kin, clients are more likely to see these relationships as potentially difficult, but this awareness does not necessarily reduce the degree of involvement with kin. In a sense, clients, and particularly the Aged, see less basis for trusting generally; they are less likely to trust out-

siders than are caseworkers, but they also see less reason to trust
kin. Nevertheless, when questions are posed in terms of comparative reliance on kin as compared with friends and other impersonal
institutions, clients are more kin-oriented than caseworkers.

Table 20. Values on Kin and Nonkin Institutions

Statement	Respondent	Agree	No Opinion	Dis-agree	
		PERCENTAGES			
If you have to borrow	Aged	3	32	65	(34)
money, it is better to	Clients	22	11	67	(380)
do it from a relative	Caseworkers	23	27	50	(123)
than from a bank.					
(0.001 level)					
When relatives go into	Aged	53	28	19	(36)
business together they	Clients	48	25	28	(378)
are likely to end up	Caseworkers	19	36	46	(123)
enemies.					
(0.001 level)					
In business dealings it	Aged	47	29	24	(34)
is usually safer to trust	Clients	41	25	34	(380)
a relative than an	Caseworkers	22	32	46	(121)
outsider.					
(0.001 level)					
Friends can't give you	Aged	63	16	21	(38)
the love you can get	Clients	32	13	55	(378)
from relatives.	Caseworkers	7	3	89	(121)
(0.001 level)					
One usually has more in	Aged	47	25	28	(36)
common with relatives	Clients	29	12	59	(374)
than friends.	Caseworkers	7	7	86	(122)
(0.001 level)					

Husband-Wife versus Parent-Child Bonds

The relative priority that different kinds of kinship systems accord the marital, as compared with the parent-child, bond at different stages of the life cycle varies greatly. A number of questions
were used to elicit values concerning the priority of parent-child
and marital bonds. Although, particularly when phrased as an

open choice of loyalty, more clients gave priority to the marital than to the parent-child bond, the proportion of clients giving priority to the marital bond was generally lower than the proportion of caseworkers who gave such priority. The Aged more frequently gave priority to the parent-child bond than the other groups.

To one question the responses of caseworkers, clients, and the Aged were almost exactly the same. This question posed a definite issue of an overt choice of a woman between her husband and her mother in a disagreement. With the statement, *"A woman should take her husband's side even if her mother doesn't think he is right,"* the majority in all the groups agreed, and the proportion of agreements for all three groups was almost the same (Table 21).

When the issue was phrased in terms of where the woman could get most warmth and understanding, from her husband or her mother, but not in terms of a specific choice between the two, significant differences were found between caseworkers and clients, although even here the majority of clients gave priority to the marital bond. To the statement, *"A woman can often get more warmth and understanding from her mother than from her husband,"* only 9 per cent of the caseworkers agreed, whereas 23 per cent of the clients agreed, and the Aged agreed even more frequently in 36 per cent of the cases.

The issue of priority between the marital and the parent-child bond was also raised in another item that approaches the situation from the perspective of the mother in terms of the comparative pleasure that she derives from her children and her husband. With this statement, *"It is natural for a mother to get more pleasure from her children than from her husband,"* caseworkers and clients again differed to a statistically significant extent. Caseworkers virtually never accorded the mother-child bond priority, agreeing in only 2 per cent of the cases, as compared with 20 per cent of the clients and 34 per cent of the Aged. Here again a majority, even among the clients, gave priority to the marital bond, but clients were significantly more likely to emphasize the mother-child bond and the Aged were the most likely of all to do so.

Another values statement posed the issue from a man's point of view in terms of his tie to his own mother: *"A man can often get more warmth and understanding from his mother than from his wife."* Here again the responses of caseworkers and clients were significantly different. The majority both among clients and caseworkers gave priority to the marital bond; but more clients, 16 per cent, than caseworkers, 8 per cent, agreed that the man could get more warmth from his mother than from his wife. The Aged agreed most frequently, in 27 per cent of the cases. The clients agreed with the item about the mother-son tie somewhat less frequently than with the one about the mother-daughter tie, reflecting the lateral skewing evident in so many areas of interaction, but in both cases they placed more priority on the parent-child bond than did the caseworkers.

The responses to questions about the priority given to specific kinship ties as compared with others therefore yield quite consistent differences between caseworkers and clients. Both clients and caseworkers give priority to the marital bond when an open choice of alliance of a woman between her husband and her mother is raised. But when the issue is the general strength of the parent-child, as compared with the marital bond and not one of overt alliance, clients consistently give more emphasis to the parent-child bond and caseworkers give more emphasis to the marital bond. The Aged consistently give most emphasis of all to the parent-child bond.

Differentiation of the Nuclear Family from Kin

Related to the question of the relative priority accorded marital and parent-child bonds is the question of the roles that various kin take within the nuclear family. Even though clients as well as caseworkers are most likely to give priority to the marital bond, the more frequent emphasis on the strength of the mother-child bond by clients, and particularly the Aged, implies that clients will be likely to expect the mother to have an active role in the household of her married daughter. A strong mother-daughter bond that is seen as natural and desirable implies some active involvement of the mother in her married daughter's household, even if this bond is not given priority over the marital bond.

One item designed to measure the scope of the mother's role in her married daughter's household was: "*A woman can usually get better advice about child rearing from books than from her mother.*" In this case the responses of caseworkers and clients were significantly different, but with the clients less frequently seeing the mother's advice as superior to books. Of the clients 46 per cent

Table 21.   Values on Husband-Wife Versus Parent-Child Bonds

Statement	Respondent	Agree	No Opinion	Dis-agree	
		PERCENTAGES			
A woman should take her husband's side even if her mother doesn't think he is right. (not significant)	Aged	70	19	11	(37)
	Clients	73	16	11	(374)
	Caseworkers	67	21	12	(121)
A woman can often get more warmth and understanding from her mother than from her husband. (0.001 level)	Aged	36	45	18	(33)
	Clients	23	20	58	(379)
	Caseworkers	9	12	79	(121)
It is natural for a mother to get more pleasure from her children than from her husband. (0.001 level)	Aged	34	24	42	(38)
	Clients	20	18	63	(377)
	Caseworkers	2	7	92	(123)
A man can often get more warmth and understanding from his mother than from his wife. (0.05 level)	Aged	27	30	43	(37)
	Clients	16	18	66	(377)
	Caseworkers	8	15	77	(123)

agreed that better advice usually came from books, whereas only 31 per cent of the caseworkers agreed with this (Table 22). The Aged agreed in almost exactly the same percentages as the other clients on this item. In this instance it would appear that clients are more prone to rely on a nonkin source than are caseworkers. However, this item specifically questions the relative quality of the advice from a mother and from books, not whether the mother's advice would be offered or expected. From interviews it appears that clients are likely to question the quality of the mother's advice on grounds of generational differences and feelings that her advice may not be up-to-date, but that they still expect the mother to be advising. On this item caseworkers had a high proportion of no opinions, and those who did answer one way or the other agreed as often as they disagreed. Although clients are more likely to grant an active role of the mother in her daughter's household, they are also more likely to expect that the best child-rearing advice will come from a source other than the mother. This response may be somewhat parallel to the reactions to questions about business dealings with kin, in which clients are more likely to expect active economic interaction with kin but also more likely to see this involvement as a source of conflict.

Another question about the scope of a mother's role in the household of her married daughter was: *"A mother has reason to be hurt if her daughter doesn't listen to her advice about taking care of the house and children."* Caseworkers and clients again differed significantly in their responses. Although both clients and caseworkers most frequently disagreed with the idea that a mother has reason to be hurt, caseworkers disagreed with this more frequently than clients. Caseworkers disagreed in 91 per cent of the cases, whereas clients disagreed in 71 per cent of the cases. Of the Aged only 53 per cent disagreed. Both clients and the Aged more frequently agreed that a mother had reason to be hurt than did caseworkers. Thus when viewed in terms of expectations of the role that a mother should take in the household of her daughter, both clients and caseworkers believed that ideally she should not expect to intrude in advising her daughter about child rearing and house care. Nevertheless, clients were more ready than caseworkers to see that the mother might have reason to be hurt if her advice was not heeded. At least from the point of view of the mother, there are implied legitimate expectations of a fairly active role in the household of her married daughter.

Inherent in questions about the scope of the mother's role is the more general question of the degree to which the nuclear family is expected to operate as an independent unit. Moreover, extensive separation of the nuclear family from kin implies a priority of the marital bond. A statement used to obtain information on this general question was: *"Parents should make all the decisions about child rearing even if grandparents don't approve."* This item clearly poses the issue of the role of the grandparents and the extent to which child-rearing functions should be carried out by the family of marriage. On this item caseworkers and clients did not differ significantly, and the views of the Aged were similar to the others. Both caseworkers and clients agreed in a large ma-

Table 22.   Values on Differentiation of Nuclear Family from Kin

Statement	Respondent	Agree	No Opinion	Dis-agree	
		PERCENTAGES			
A woman can usually get better advice about child rearing from books than from her mother. (0.001 level)	Aged	47	21	32	(34)
	Clients	46	22	31	(370)
	Caseworkers	31	39	31	(121)
A mother has reason to be hurt if her daughter doesn't listen to her advice about taking care of the house and children. (0.001 level)	Aged	19	28	53	(36)
	Clients	16	13	71	(378)
	Caseworkers	6	3	91	(123)
Parents should make all the decisions about child rearing even if grandparents don't approve. (not significant)	Aged	84	5	11	(37)
	Clients	93	2	4	(380)
	Caseworkers	89	7	4	(123)
Even a nonobservant couple should keep a kosher house for the sake of more observant parents if it means a lot to the parents. (0.001 level)	Aged	68	16	16	(38)
	Clients	51	15	34	(377)
	Caseworkers	11	20	69	(120)

jority of the cases, 93 per cent of the clients and 89 per cent of the caseworkers, that parents should make all decisions about child rearing. Of the Aged, 84 per cent agreed. Thus when stated in extreme terms of a choice between grandparental and parental influence in child bearing, caseworkers, clients, and the Aged all agreed on independent functioning of the nuclear family.

Another item designed to elicit the valued areas of independent functioning of the nuclear family raised the question of whether or not the nuclear family should alter its religious observance for the sake of parents. To the statement, *"Even a nonobservant couple should keep a kosher house for the sake of more observant parents if it means a lot to the parents,"* caseworkers and clients again differed significantly. Clients agreed more often than did caseworkers that a couple should keep a kosher house for the sake of parents, agreeing in 51 per cent of the cases, whereas only 11 per cent of the caseworkers agreed. The Aged agreed most frequently of all, in 68 per cent of the cases. Thus although caseworkers, clients, and the Aged all agreed that ideally parents should make independent decisions about child rearing regardless of the reactions of grandparents, clients were more ready than caseworkers to allow for other areas of alteration of the nuclear family's activities through the influence of kin.

Although in child rearing, perhaps the most critical area of family functioning, the ideal is independence from kin for both caseworkers and clients, clients are more prone to see the likelihood of parental involvement in child rearing than are caseworkers, and more willing to see kin involvement in the affairs of the nuclear family in other respects.

Obligations Toward Aged Parents

The extent to which the nuclear family is differentiated from kin is affected by obligations toward aged parents. Obligations toward the aged vary greatly in different kinds of kinship systems. Caseworkers and clients tended to differ in their views, with clients being more likely to stress obligations toward the aged, the respondents in the Service to the Aged being most likely of all to stress these obligations, and caseworkers giving them least emphasis.

A potential conflict exists in the allocation of resources between aged parents and children. An item used to measure this was: "*A family should be willing to sacrifice some of the things they want for their children in order to help support their aged parents.*" To this statement the responses of caseworkers and clients differed significantly. Clients agreed more often than caseworkers that responsibilities toward aged parents might even take priority over those to children; of the clients 74 per cent agreed, whereas of the caseworkers only 54 per cent agreed. The Aged agreed most frequently of all, in 84 per cent of the cases (Table 23).

One basic question about obligations toward aged parents concerns the way in which these responsibilities are distributed among siblings, another point at which kinship systems differ greatly. When an eldest son receives the main inheritance, for ex-

Table 23. Values on Obligations Toward Aged Parents

Statement	Respondent	Agree	No Opinion	Dis-agree	
		PERCENTAGES			
A family should be willing to sacrifice some of the things they want for their children in order to help support their aged parents. (0.001 level)	Aged	84	8	8	(38)
	Clients	73	13	13	(379)
	Caseworkers	54	21	25	(123)
If you have more money than your brothers and sisters, you should be willing to contribute more to the support of your aged parents. (0.05 level)	Aged	92	8	–	(37)
	Clients	89	7	4	(378)
	Caseworkers	81	12	7	(123)
It is humiliating for parents to be supported by their children in later life. (0.001 level)	Aged	59	14	27	(37)
	Clients	38	13	49	(375)
	Caseworkers	18	13	69	(122)
Parents are entitled to some return for all the sacrifices they have made for their children. (0.01 level)	Aged	63	16	21	(38)
	Clients	48	13	39	(380)
	Caseworkers	33	9	58	(120)

ample, he is also likely to be given the major responsibilities for the parents. It was assumed that in the absence of major formal distinctions in inheritance among siblings on the basis of either sex or birth order, a critical issue in distributing financial responsibilities for parents would hinge on the comparative financial means of siblings. The item used for this was: *"If you have more money than your brothers and sisters, you should be willing to contribute more to the support of your aged parents."* Here there was general agreement, on the part of the Aged, 92 per cent, clients, 89 per cent, and caseworkers, 81 per cent, that those who are better off should be willing to take more responsibility. The clients were somewhat more likely than the caseworkers to see financial advantage as a basis for added responsibility and the Aged were most likely to take this view. This item, however, deals with the allocation of responsibility, not with whether responsibility for parents exists.

A related question concerns whether parents should feel ready to accept financial assistance from their children. On this issue the responses of caseworkers and clients again differed significantly, but with the Aged, the least willing to accept financial assistance from children. To the statement, "*It is humiliating for parents to be supported by their children in later life,*" only 18 per cent of the caseworkers agreed, whereas 38 per cent of the clients and 59 per cent of the Aged agreed. From interview data it is evident that financial assistance is not the ideal form of support for parents. Because of Social Security and other nonkin forms of aid in financing old age, the ideal is clearly not to be supported by one's children. However, a central obligation to parents revolves around giving them a chance to have joy in their children's successes, implying continuing interaction. Thus the ideal of financial independence in old age does not mean social independence. Caseworkers were perhaps least willing to accept the notion of humiliation if financial assistance were necessary, but this does not imply a generally stronger sense of overall obligation to aged parents.

When the question was phrased not in terms of finances but rather as an issue of parents getting "some return" in their old age, caseworkers and clients again differed significantly, but the clients were more willing to grant the parents the right of such a return. To the statement, "*Parents are entitled to some return for all the sacrifices they have made for their children,*" 48 per cent of the clients agreed, whereas only 33 per cent of the caseworkers agreed. The Aged agreed most frequently of all, in 63 per cent of the cases. In this instance caseworkers and some of the clients may have reacted against the notion of sacrifice. Nevertheless, when phrased in terms of some general, not necessarily financial, obligation toward parents, clients are again more oriented toward kinship responsibilities than caseworkers.

Thus when the issue is one of the distribution of responsibility, caseworkers and clients do not differ; and when it specifically concerns finances, caseworkers are less willing to see financial support as humiliating. But when the issue is phrased generally as one of overall obligations toward parents in old age, clients are again more oriented to kinship obligations than are caseworkers.

Contrasts Between Caseworkers and Clients

Consistent differences exist between caseworkers' and clients' values pertaining to different areas of kinship. Caseworkers and clients do not differ in their views about all aspects of kinship, but they do have differences in many areas which are consistent in direction, with the clients more kin-oriented than the caseworkers. The values of the Aged, although not compared with tests of statistical significance, were also consistently different in the direction of being more kin-oriented than the caseworkers, and even more strongly so than the other clients.[1]

When phrased in extreme terms, both clients and caseworkers, and even the Aged, believed that the nuclear family should function as an independent unit in child rearing, and that in case of open differences a wife's primary loyalty should be to her husband not her mother. Moreover, there was general agreement that combined households were not the ideal. Thus caseworkers, clients, and the Aged all emphasize a good measure of independent functioning of the nuclear family, more than might be the case in some kinds of kinship systems. However, clients and especially the Aged consistently gave more leeway for involvement with kin than the caseworkers.

In all the areas of kin relationships examined, there were significant differences between caseworkers and clients, despite a basic core of agreement about separate households and the importance of the marital bond. Clients are more likely to accord parents a right to oversee their children's dating through residence at home until marriage. Clients are more likely than caseworkers to see residential proximity to kin, short of combined households, as desirable. Clients are more likely to stress obligations to maintain interaction with kin. Although clients are somewhat more likely to stress the importance of educational and occupational advancement, they are also less willing than caseworkers to give up ties to kin for the sake of success. Although clients were more likely than caseworkers to anticipate conflicts in economic dealings with kin, they were also more likely to stress reliance on kin than on nonkin sources. Despite the core of agreement about the marital bond, moreover, caseworkers and clients differed consistently in the degree to which they stressed the parent-child as compared with husband-wife ties. They also differed in their allowance for the involvement of parents in the affairs of the nuclear family.

Finally, although clients do not see financial support in old age as desirable, they are more likely than caseworkers to stress the right of aged parents to some form of return from their children.

From responses to the Values Form, therefore, caseworkers and clients appear to hold consistently different views about the most desirable form of relationships with kin. These contrasts are between caseworkers and clients as groups. Of course, views of all caseworkers are not different from those of all clients. The views of a given individual in different areas are also not necessarily consistent. In a specific therapeutic relationship the caseworker may be generally more kin-oriented than the client or more kin-oriented on a specific point. Moreover, the sampling of caseworkers is different from that of clients. The caseworkers represent almost the entire professional staff of the agency at the time. The client sample is of married clients, and although these constitute the vast majority of cases in the family agency, in values young single clients might be more like caseworkers. In addition, almost all the caseworkers responded to every question on the Values Form, whereas some of the clients, particularly husbands, did not answer the values questions. However, there seems little reason to suppose that those clients who did not answer the values questions would be more likely to be similar to the caseworkers than different. Thus one can conclude that the observed value differences between caseworkers and clients are sufficiently representative of the two groups that they are likely to occur in a fair proportion of actual therapeutic relationships. Moreover, insofar as the Aged are similar to the parents of at least some clients, it is likely that the clients are in a value position between that of their parents and their caseworkers.

These differing notions about desirable kinds of relationships with kin may stem from a variety of sources. Differences in their age, marital status, birthplace, and the birthplace of parents all undoubtedly contribute to these differences. Also differences in the degree to which caseworkers have moved away from a social background not totally dissimilar to that of clients, through education and changes in other areas of belief, for example, religious orientations, may contribute. Value differences undoubtedly also reflect professional points of view that caseworkers have come to adopt through their specific training. They may also stem from the particular kinds of problems that clients have faced. In this respect it is significant, however, that three-quarters of the caseworkers have had some sort of therapeutic treatment. This treatment may have been in part related to training, but caseworkers and their clients are not sharply separated by the experience of having sought professional help with problems.

It is impossible completely to sort out the various factors that contribute to these value differences. The source of a values difference undoubtedly has implications for practice; differences that stem from professional training may have different consequences from differences in early background. However, regardless of the source, one can assume that to some degree there is a melding of individual and professional experience in a therapeutic relationship, so that the fact of a difference, from whatever source, will have implications for the treatment relationship.

COMPARISON OF KIN RELATIONSHIPS

Caseworkers and clients differ not only in kinship values but also in the kinds of interaction they have with their kin. In a great many areas caseworkers are less involved with their kin than are clients. At some points caseworkers and clients have similar patterns of kin interaction and in a few respects caseworkers are more involved with kin than clients, but by and large the differences are in the direction of greater involvement on the part of clients. No comparison between values and action is attempted for specific items of behavior because the data in the two areas are not always exactly comparable. But the broad differences between caseworkers and clients in values are paralleled in the direction of differences in actual behavior. Interaction with kin, however, is a product of the characteristics of the kin as well as those of caseworkers or clients, so that comparisons of behavior go beyond the individual in a way not equally true of values. For example, although social interaction influences values, views about the desirability of living near kin may be held by caseworkers regardless of what their kin think, but actual residential proximity to kin depends on a choice of the kin as well as on a choice of the caseworkers. Thus the way social factors impinge upon values and actions is somewhat different. Nevertheless, caseworkers and clients differ in values and actions in a broadly consistent direction.

As we have seen, differences between caseworkers and clients may be due to a variety of factors. But even though at a later stage caseworkers might be involved with their kin in a way similar to that in which clients are at present, the fact that they have not yet reached the same life-cycle stage may have implications for the therapeutic relationship, for example, affecting their evaluation of their client's kin contacts. Regardless of their source, differences that exist imply that to some extent caseworkers and clients inhabit different social worlds.

We will compare highlights of kin interaction of caseworkers and clients but we cannot make a comparison in all the details with which the kin relationships of clients have been studied. Although comparable questionnaire data exist, no personal interviews were conducted with caseworkers about their kin relationships. The purpose is not to do a full-scale comparative study of the kin relationships of caseworkers and clients, but simply to determine whether there is evidence of consistent differences in a variety of areas, sufficient evidence so that one may presume that differences of actual experience as well as differences of values enter into the therapeutic process. In view of the complexity of the analysis of kin interaction, the data from the Aged have not been included in this portion of the analysis. For the same reason tests of significance have not been employed here. The analysis at this point rests on consistency of a number of differences rather than the statistical significance in a particular instance.

Geographic Proximity to Kin

Differences in values about the desirability of living near kin are reflected in actual residential behavior. In terms of several measures, clients exhibit greater residential proximity to kin than do caseworkers. Although very few client families are presently living with kin, a fairly large proportion have actually done so in the past, despite views that combined households cause problems. Caseworkers have lived in the home of relatives since their marriage less often than clients. Moreover, those clients who have stayed in the home of relatives are more likely to have stayed for a longer period of time than have caseworkers; very few of the caseworkers who have lived with kin since their marriage have done so for longer than a year (Table 24).

Both caseworkers and clients are more likely to have lived in the home of relatives than to have had relatives living with them, but again clients have more frequently had kin in their household than is true of caseworkers. Moreover, when kin have moved into the respondent's home, the duration of their stay has been longer for clients than for caseworkers. The form of combined households reflects the stage in the life cycle; young couples most often move into the home of their parents, whereas aged kin are more likely to move into the household of their children. But both of these types of combined households have been more frequent, and of longer duration, among clients than among caseworkers. We are comparing clients only with married caseworkers, who are more likely to be similar to clients, but even here differences exist.

The reasons for combined households with kin differ somewhat between caseworkers and clients. The most frequent reason given by clients for moving into the home of kin was "lack of housing," while the most frequent reason given by caseworkers was a "geographic move"; 42 per cent of the clients mentioned lack of housing, while only 11 per cent of the caseworkers mentioned it; and 35 per cent of the caseworkers mentioned a geographic move, while only 1 per cent of the clients gave this as the reason. The emphasis on lack of housing on the part of clients may reflect

Table 24.   Proximity to Kin

Form of Proximity	Per Cent of Caseworkers		Per Cent of Clients	
Lived in the home of kin at some time in the past since marriage.	37	(76)[a]	48	(203)
Residence in the home of kin lasted longer than one year.	16	(28)	43	(88)
Kin lived in respondent's home at some time in the past since respondent's marriage.	24	(79)	31	(203)
Residence of kin in respondent's home lasted longer than one year.	33	(15)	52	(50)
Lived in a town or city where no relatives resided.	72	(117)	22	(201)

[a] In the statements on the duration of joint residence with kin, the figures in parentheses refer to the percentage of cases that resided with kin for more than a year, not of the total number of those that responded to the questionnaire. The last item refers to the experience of client wives only. The other items refer to the family unit.

their stage of the life cycle and the specific historical period when many of them married. The reasons given for having kin move in with the family differ less for caseworkers and clients than those for going to the home of a kin, the largest single category in both cases being illness or pregnancy. Again, however, caseworkers more frequently mention the reason for the stay being a "geographic move" than do clients, and clients mention "old age" as a reason for a kin moving in more often than caseworkers. Thus there is evidence that caseworkers and clients differ both in the amount of combined residence with kin and in the reasons for it.

On another dimension of geographic proximity to kin, caseworkers and clients differ considerably. Of the caseworkers, 72 per cent have lived in a town or city where none of their relatives lived, whereas of the client wives only 22 per cent have ever lived in a city where no kin resided. This question was not asked of client husbands. They may have spent more time owing to military service away from kin than wives. But, in any event, the difference between caseworkers and client wives is striking. In general, one may conclude that most clients have experienced a far greater degree of geographic proximity to kin than is typical of caseworkers.

Communication, Social Contacts, and Assistance

When involvement with kin through communication, face-to-face contacts, and assistance is compared for caseworkers and clients, differences are again apparent. Although caseworkers are by no means cut off from their kin, differences that appear are most often in the direction of less involvement on the part of caseworkers than clients. Thus the differences in values are paralleled in action.

When questioned about what may be considered the minimum essentials of kin contacts, caseworkers and clients were similar in some respects; caseworkers as well as clients most often maintain some form of telephone contact with kin. In this, caseworkers are more like client wives than client husbands, who indicate maintaining telephone contact less frequently than caseworkers. However, when the question shifts from whether any telephone contact is maintained to the intensity of telephone involvement, caseworkers show a lesser degree of telephone involvement with kin than do client wives. Here again client wives and husbands differ. When asked if they talked to at least one relative once a day, only 10 per cent of the caseworkers and 11 per cent of the client husbands indicated that they did, whereas 44 per cent of the client wives reported daily telephone contacts with kin. Respondents were not only asked to list the frequency with which they had telephone contact with specific kin, but also to indicate who called whom. For some kin both "I call" and "they call" were checked. Such instances were considered a "mutual" phone relationship. The existence of mutual phone relationships is similar for all groups. Those who maintain phone relationships with kin are likely to have mutual ones.

Thus both caseworkers and clients have some degree of telephone communication with kin. Sex differences in telephone behavior apparently exist, with client wives maintaining most intensive telephone contacts. Differences between male and female caseworkers were not examined, but the very low percentage of caseworkers who talk to kin once a day implies that caseworkers, whether male or female, are less likely than client wives to have continuous phone contacts with kin.

Another dimension along which the intensity of kin involvement can be measured concerns whether kin have easy, informal access to the family's home. On two questions in this area clients indicated more kin involvement than caseworkers. Of the clients 46 per cent indicated that kin had a key to their apartment, whereas this was true for only 27 per cent of the caseworkers. Similarly, 66 per cent of the clients indicated that kin drop in unannounced, whereas this was true of only 29 per cent of the caseworkers. (Here, as at a number of other points where the data refer to activities of the nuclear family as a unit rather than the actions of an individual family member, information was collected from the wife only.)

Another basic question about kin relationships centers on the comparative involvement of an individual or family with kin and nonkin in various areas. On two questions indicating the comparative involvement with kin and friends, caseworkers were less kin-oriented than either client husbands or client wives. Here, in fact, client husbands indicated a proportionately greater degree of involvement with kin as compared with friends than was true for client wives, client husbands possibly having less time available for contacts with individuals they consider "friends" than client wives. In any event, caseworkers indicate proportionately least involvement with kin as compared with friends.

Although differences that exist were most often in the direction of lesser kin involvement on the part of caseworkers, there were some areas of social involvement with kin where caseworkers and clients were similar. Clients and caseworkers were similar in the proportion indicating that they had taken a trip or spent a vacation with kin. Possibly, however, the factor of having the financial means to take a trip or spend a vacation away from home is relevant. Of all the trips taken, caseworkers indicated a lower proportion was with kin compared with friends than is true of clients, 97 per cent of client trips and vacations having been with kin, whereas this was true for only 53 per cent of the caseworkers trips and vacations. Thus although a similar proportion of caseworkers and clients have been involved with kin through trips and vacations, caseworkers are again comparatively more involved with nonkin than is true of clients. Clients and married caseworkers were similar in the proportion indicating that their children visit the children of relatives and stay overnight alone. Undoubtedly children form an additional link to kin, so that married caseworkers with children may have more similarity to clients than other caseworkers. Thus caseworkers are also not isolated from their kin, but in a number of areas they are less kin-involved than clients.

A similar picture emerges when assistance is examined. The great majority of both caseworkers and clients report having received some service or monetary assistance from kin, 95 per cent of the clients and 88 per cent of the caseworkers. Thus caseworkers, like clients, are enmeshed in reciprocity with kin. However, there are apparently differences in the extent to which assistance has been received from kin. A number of specific kinds of assistance, for example, baby sitting, shopping and errands, financial help, were included in the questionnaire. The kinds of assistance given and received are, of course, colored by life-cycle and economic status. Some of the assistance items, such as baby sitting, would not apply to single caseworkers. It is not surprising, therefore, that caseworkers report having received fewer different kinds of assistance from kin than is true of clients. Of the caseworkers, only 37 per cent checked three or more of the assistance items, whereas 55 per cent of the clients did so. Regardless of whether this is due to the inapplicability of some assistance items to single caseworkers, and whether or not young caseworkers will become more like clients in the future, differences exist at present; and again they are in the direction of less extensive kin involvement on the part of caseworkers.

In terms of assistance *given*, both caseworkers and clients are again anything but isolated from their kin. Of the clients, 94 per cent and of the caseworkers, 93 per cent report having given some kind of assistance to kin. Moreover, caseworkers and clients gave almost the same number of different kinds of assistance.

On certain other areas that may be considered basic kinds of kin ties, caseworkers and clients are again similar. They are similar in the proportion reporting having received help from a relative during an illness. To the hypothetical question about whom you would want to take care of your children if they should be orphaned, the vast majority of both caseworkers and clients said kin rather than nonkin. Although caseworkers indicated kin slightly less frequently than clients, they were nonetheless kin-oriented when asked about critical areas of obligation.

In one area of assistance caseworkers were notably more kin-involved than clients, giving child-rearing advice. Of the clients only 36 per cent indicated that they had been asked for advice on child rearing by kin, whereas of the caseworkers 63 per cent made this claim. The special professional role of caseworkers is undoubtedly relevant, and implies that although professional values and education may tend to reduce certain kinds of kin involvement, when a kind of expert status is achieved it may substitute for other kinds of kin obligations, that is, instead of talking to kin on the telephone everyday or giving them a key to one's apartment, the caseworker gives expert advice. The expert status may substitute for a more generalized type of intimacy in kin relationships, but it implies that expertise is used to discharge basic minimum obligations of kinship, which are still accepted. Consistently caseworkers less frequently ask their kin for child-rearing advice than do clients. Of course, many do not have children, but again whatever the source, the difference exists. Moreover, the professional expertise aspect of the caseworker's role in child-rearing advice is highlighted by the fact that even though many do not have children and few, only 8 per cent, ask for child-rearing advice, 63 per cent have given it (Table 25).

When the comparative involvement in kin and nonkin in assistance is examined, caseworkers and clients are again different. As in the case of face-to-face contacts, caseworkers are likely to be more involved with nonkin institutions than are clients. Certain basic obligations exist for both caseworker and clients in the areas where kin are conceived as a main source of assistance—help during illness and obligations toward children in the event of a family tragedy. Moreover, there are some areas such as cooking and housecleaning where caseworkers and clients are similar in relying on kin only to a limited extent. However, for some kinds of assistance clients turn most frequently to kin, whereas caseworkers turn most frequently either to friends or nonkin institutions such as hired help. For example, while both caseworkers and clients have relied upon the help of kin when making a move, caseworkers have turned to friends or neighbors for such help more often, in 22 per cent of the cases, than have clients—only 2 per cent of whom have done so. Similarly, 34 per cent of the caseworkers have relied on hired help in child rearing, as against only 15 per cent of the clients; and 29 per cent of the caseworkers have used hired help for cooking and housework, as against only 9 per cent of the clients. Thus in some areas the proportions of clients and caseworkers who rely on kin are similar but caseworkers are more likely to turn to nonkin sources, whereas clients are more likely to manage alone. In other areas clients turn more frequently to kin, and less frequently to nonkin than do caseworkers; of those caseworkers who have been given household furnishings 57 per cent received them from kin and 72 per cent of the clients received them from kin, but 43 per cent of the caseworkers received such items from friends or neighbors, whereas only 28 per cent of the clients did so. Thus although there are some basic similarities in relationships of assistance with kin, differences that exist almost always show less kin involvement, and comparatively more nonkin involvement on the part of caseworkers. The one exception is the caseworkers' special area of "expert" assistance in child-rearing advice.

From the standpoint of communication, social contacts, and assistance, therefore, caseworkers as well as clients are not "isolated" from their kin; certain minimum obligations are accepted and carried out by both, and professional knowledge may even be the basis for special involvement with kin as a role of expert. But

Table 25. Communication, Social Contacts, and Assistance

	Per Cent of Husbands		Per Cent of Wives		Per Cent of Caseworkers	
Telephone Communication						
Maintain some form of telephone contact with kin.	78	(179)	96	(209)	93	(120)
Talk to one or more relatives at least once a day.	11	(140)	44	(201)	10	(116)
Have some mutual phone relationship with kin.	64	(151)	60	(201)	59	(113)
Face-to-Face Contacts						
Kin have a key to apartment.	a		46	(200)	27	(121)
Kin drop in unannounced.	a		66	(203)	29	(118)
Kin know more than friends about the family's life.	72	(159)	52	(197)	32	(117)
Have more in common with relatives than friends.	44	(156)	28	(197)	12	(119)
Have had more trips and vacations with kin than friends.	a		97	(186)	53	(118)
Have taken a trip or spent a vacation with relatives.	a		59	(189)	63	(116)
Children have visited relatives' children.	a		54	(179)	50	(28)
Assistance						
Family has *received* some service or monetary assistance from kin.	a		95	(209)	88	(121)
Family has *given* some service or monetary assistance to kin.	a		94	(210)	93	(118)
Relatives have helped during an illness.	a		64	(202)	54	(117)
If children were orphaned, would want kin rather than nonkin to take care of them.	97	(102)	91	(129)	83	(40)
Have asked kin for child-rearing advice.	a		32	(197)	8	(44)
Have been asked child-rearing advice by kin.	a		36	(201)	63	(113)
Household furnishings have come more from kin than friends.	a		72	(83)	57	(68)

a Data on this item were collected from the wife only. She was taken as representative of the nuclear family where activities refer to the family as a unit.

when the intensity and informality of kin ties are considered, caseworkers generally show less kin involvement than clients, and at a number of points caseworkers show comparatively more non-kin involvement than do clients. Thus differences are consistent with value differences and differences in geographic proximity between caseworkers and clients.

Kin Groups and Assemblages

When examining kin groups and assemblages, the unit of analysis shifts from the nuclear family or individual to the kin group itself. In order to understand which kin attend a Thanksgiving gathering, for example, it was necessary to shift the point of reference from the client who provided the data to the sponsor of the gathering, that is, the person at whose house the event was held because the sponsor generally has a more direct influence on attendance than other participants. The sponsor was sometimes but not always the client. But to understand the gatherings in which clients participate it was necessary to focus directly on the social events because the characteristics of these gatherings are determined by many individuals, not just by the clients. Thus when comparing the kin gatherings and formal kin groups in which clients and caseworkers participate, one is not merely comparing individual or family characteristics of caseworkers and clients, but rather characteristics of the kin networks in which they participate.

The existence of a family circle or cousins club in the kin network of an individual, regardless of whether the individual is a member, is a clear example of a characteristic of the network itself. In this respect clients and caseworkers differ only slightly. Of the 238 families in the total client sample, 31 per cent had one or more family circles or cousins clubs within their kin network to which they were eligible to belong. Most families had only one organization with which they could affiliate, but some had more than one. Although a slightly lower proportion of caseworkers, 25 per cent, had one or more organizations with which they could affiliate, the difference is not striking (Table 26). Moreover, the places where descent groups are found within the kin network of caseworkers is very similar to the patterns observed for clients. Kin groups are distributed almost equally between the caseworkers' father's and

Table 26. *Kin Groups and Assemblages*[a]

	Per Cent of Clients		Per Cent of Caseworkers	
Have one or more family circles or cousins clubs in kin network at present.	31	(238)	25	(123)
Kin group is five years old or younger.	41	(76)	41	(34)
Had family circles or cousins clubs in network in past that no longer exist.	15	(381)	10	(113)
Kin on respondent's side of network see kin on spouse's side:				
When respondent's family is present	42	(410)	46	(63)
When respondent's family is not present	14	(410)	27	(63)
Spent last Thanksgiving with kin.	57	(238)	71	(121)

[a] For the analysis of kin groups and assemblages, where the unit was the kin group, not the respondent's family, data from all clients, including those in the Service to the Aged, were combined.

mother's sides of the network; the same is true for clients. Most caseworkers having formal kin groups report only one, but, similar to clients, some have more than one, 6 out of the 30 caseworkers who had such organizations reported that more than one existed within their own or their spouse's kin network. In addition, the ages of the organizations that caseworkers report are similar to those of client descent groups. Caseworkers, like clients, report that new organizations are starting within their networks; of the 34 organizations reported by caseworkers 41 per cent were five years old or younger, and of the 76 organizations reported by clients 41 per cent were five years old or younger. Thus in the networks of caseworkers as well as in those of clients one may assume that such organizations have continuing, vital functions at present; although a particular organization may cease to exist, new ones are being formed all the time. The network characteristics of clients and caseworkers also do not appear to have differed greatly in the past. Of the client husbands and wives 15 per cent reported that they had had one or more family circles or cousins clubs in their kin networks in the past that no longer exist; this was true for 10 per cent of the caseworkers. Thus although a slightly lower proportion of caseworkers report having or having had a descent group within their network, the differences are only slight, and less striking than the similarities between caseworkers and clients in the location and age distribution of descent groups.

Another characteristic of a family's kin network concerns the extent to which kin within the network interact with each other. A question about this interaction was whether kin on the respondent's side of the family see kin on the spouse's side. The behavior of the nuclear family is important; a family may, for example, invite the husband's kin to gatherings with the wife's kin. But it also depends on the kin, particularly when the kin of a family see each other when the family is not present. Clients and married caseworkers report with almost exactly the same frequency, 42 per cent of the clients and 46 per cent of the caseworkers, that kin on the husband's side and kin on the wife's side see each other in the presence of the nuclear family. On the other hand, caseworkers more frequently report that their kin see each other independently, apart from the nuclear family, 14 per cent of the clients as compared with 27 per cent of the caseworkers.

In terms of one specific kind of ad hoc kin gathering, Thanksgiving, caseworkers report more frequent celebrations with kin than is true of clients; of the client families 57 per cent said they celebrated last Thanksgiving with kin, whereas 71 per cent of the caseworkers had done so. In view of indications that celebration of Thanksgiving is less familiar among older, less "Americanized" families, and, for example, that the sponsors are generally of the client's rather than their parent's generation, it is not surprising that caseworkers whose parents were somewhat more often American-born than those of clients would more frequently celebrate Thanksgiving with kin. This finding may therefore reflect the specific cultural connotations of Thanksgiving rather than modes of kin assemblage in general. But it is an example of one area in which gatherings within a kin network are evidently increased rather than reduced with acculturation. Spending Thanksgiving with kin is more specifically a characteristic of the individual or family than is true of the existence of a formal kin group in the network, but it also depends on characteristics of kin in the network. These differences, therefore, do not indicate that caseworkers come from networks in which social interaction among kin is less extensive than in the kin networks of clients.

COMPARISON OF CONFLICTS WITH KIN

Caseworkers talk about their conflicts with kin in terms somewhat different from those employed by most clients. Under certain therapeutic circumstances, clients, of course, are likely to pick up the professional vocabulary and assumptions of their caseworkers. But the habit of looking at life in terms of "dynamic" psychological constructs is undoubtedly more firmly engrained in caseworkers.

The Language of Conflict

No formal content analysis was made of answers to the write-in questions about conflict with kin posed in the questionnaire. But certain phrases recur in the caseworker's replies that do not typify the client answers. Caseworkers describe their feelings about conflicts with kin in such terms as "conflicted," "guilty," "ambivalent," "hypersensitive," "resolved." They are sensitive to the impact of the conflict on their own feelings; for example, it "heightened my own guilt over my sense of responsibility," and "I had a guilty feeling but did not express my anger." The behavior and attitudes of others in the conflict are described in terms such as "reacted with anger," "overreacted," "immature," "retaliative," "controlling," provocative," "destructive," "martyrlike." In some instances diagnostic labels or evaluations are employed; for example, an "unhealthy psychological influence," "obsessive," "paranoid." But more typically the personality patterns of other parties to the conflict are described and interpreted in terms of what are presumed to be their "true" motivations and personality problems; for example, needing to "separate her feelings," "denying problems," not being able to "understand the meaning of behavior," "colored by his own anxiety," having "feelings blocked," showing signs of "withdrawal" and "projection," revealing "insecurity in her relationship with me," having "rigid standards," and not being able to "carry the role."

Different levels of feeling are distinguished, as implied in the term "their basic feelings," or "on a deeper level they were conflicted." This professionally phrased approach to kin conflicts is exemplified in one man's description of his sister-in-law as "slightly paranoid which, combined with her narcissism, makes her someone it is not easy to want to see too often." The importance of expression of feelings is frequently explicit. "Not avoiding differences," for example, was good, as was having "expressed my feelings." Related to this expression is a high value placed on self-assertion. One female caseworker, describing a conflict with her mother in terms of the need for self-assertion, said, "I wanted the right to be stepped on and didn't want to stand up for my rights just because she wanted me to." At the same time descriptions of how feelings were expressed during conflicts are likely to be fairly abstract, for example, "angry verbalization," "verbally," "a great deal of verbalization—no action," "silent resistance," or through "diminished contact."

A notion of the possibility of healthy development, almost therapeutic in tone, through conflict experience and resolution is sometimes stated. A conflict was said to have "helped us to better understand what our relationships are," another resulted in an "emotionally meaningful change," or conflict may entail learning to "handle" a problem or "understand the factors involved." Sometimes the caseworker seems to have deliberately taken an almost therapeutic role in a conflict, such as one who "planted a thought I knew they would work on." Reports of the therapeutic gains of kin in a conflict are sometimes noted, such as the parents of one caseworker who, as a result of a conflict, "gained some insight into the basis of their original reluctance" to accept help from their children. Sometimes it is the caseworker who experiences "growth," as with one for whom the conflict described was a "lifelong repetitious pattern, I now handle differently." Other times growth is simply reported as having "learned to live with it."

A few clients talk of their conflicts with kin in terms that closely approximate the professionally phrased vocabulary and concepts with which caseworkers describe their own kin conflicts. One client specifically reports a learning experience from treatment as follows: "Counselor helped me understand my displacement of anger. . . . I have learned how important it is to recognize one's anger for what it really is, and to be able to discuss subjects with persons directly motivating, if possible." In a similar vein another client reports that a conflict with kin "helped to bring buried hostile feelings to the surface so that they could be understood."

But phrasing of this sort is rare in client descriptions of kin conflicts. Clients almost never employ psychological diagnositc labels in describing their kin, except when reporting a specific diagnosis made by a therapist. They rarely make elaborate distinctions of levels of underlying feeling or motivation. Even when the emotional problems of kin are invoked to account for their behavior, the usual wording diverges somewhat from that of caseworkers. A caseworker might speak of "her need to separate her feelings," but clients typically use more global terms for emotional distress; for example, a "disturbed man," "emotionally upset," an "emotional upheaval," "the man is emotionally sick," "going through a difficult period," "in a very disturbed state at the time," a "peculiar personality."

Client descriptions of the attitudes and behavior of those in a conflict are likely to be more concrete than those of caseworkers. Sometimes the difference appears merely a subtle one of wording: when a caseworker speaks of "immaturity," a client says, "childishness," when a caseworker mentions "overreacting" a client says, "The reaction was out of proportion to the situation." But these differences also go beyond wording and hinge upon the level of conceptualization. When a caseworker speaks of "displacement," a client says, "She can't blame him, so she puts the blame on me." When a caseworker describes kin as "controlling," "provocative," or "destructive," a client uses such terms as "headstrong," "nagging," "interfering," and statements such as: "she bosses me," "makes accusations," "passes nasty remarks," "as per usual used vile language and behaved disgustingly."

Although caseworkers by no means express approval of all the actions of their kin, they sometimes employ psychological interpretations of the behavior of others in lieu of moral judgment. Clients on the other hand are highly judgmental in many of their reports. For example, "She should not interfere as she does"; "An injustice has been done to me"; "He treated my mother shabbily"; "They are selfish and mistaken; "He should not put me through the paces"; "She made unreasonable arguments and demands";

"He used improper epithets"; "It was an uncalled-for remark"; "They are ignorant to doing the right thing"; "My wife was one hundred per cent right and my sister was a loudmouth."

In describing their own feelings in conflicts with kin, clients generally use more concrete everyday terms than caseworkers. When a caseworker speaks of feeling "conflicted," "guilty," or "ambivalent," a client reports such states as "remorse" and "regret" or feeling "annoyed," "upset and angry," "bad," "disgusted," "fed up," very hurt and terribly disappointed," "sick," "exasperated," "very hurt inside," "let down," "surprised," "terribly unhappy," "completely rejected," "unloved and unprotected," "abused," "infuriated," "fatalistic," "rotten." When a caseworker speaks of "learning to recognize my anger," a client says, "I feel like murdering the woman—can't stand her—never could. Tart, cold, brittle, tactless, unfeeling bitch!" A caseworker speaks of the "right" to assert oneself when a client says, "My husband was a doormat"; "I can't have the wool pulled over my eyes"; "He sits back and lets others take arguments for him."

Although caseworkers place great value on recognition and expression of "true" feelings, they often use generalized, neutral terms in reporting how people expressed their feelings during conflicts where clients give more definite descriptions. When a caseworker speaks of "angry verbalization," a client speaks of "emotional outpourings," "animosity," "giving it to them," "disparaging remarks," "slights," "accusing me of lying," "deliberately inflicting hardships," "accusations of who did most good deeds and favors."

Although caseworkers are sensitive to the impact of a conflict on the "underlying" emotional states of those involved, clients seem to assume the emotional impact of one person on another and describe it in dramatic terms. A recurrent report is that someone was made "sick" by the use and abuse that another person inflicted. As one man claimed, my wife felt "my mother is responsible for all her emotional trouble."

Caseworkers and clients also talk of the solution or termination of conflicts in different terms. Clients rarely talk of "growth," "emotionally meaningful change," or insight, but rather of more concrete developments such as having "my wife and my father make an effort to refrain from antagonizing each other" or deciding "the whole thing was ridiculous." When a caseworker talks of "handling a lifelong repetitious pattern" differently, a client reports being on "guard against a repetition" or trying to "get out of a rut." Some clients simply invoke the bonds of kinship to cut across differences, as one woman said of her mother-in-law, "She's a selfish woman, but she's his mother."

In short, a distinct professional vocabulary of emotion and interpersonal relationships may be detected. The exact frequency with which this vocabulary is employed by caseworkers and clients in describing kin conflicts has not been determined. There is overlap; some caseworkers use concrete everyday terms in reporting kin conflicts, and a few clients employ distinctly professional concepts. Moreover, the vocabulary of even a single individual is not always uniform in the extent to which professional terms are employed. But this particular vocabulary of emotion is specifically related to the caseworker's professional training and is undoubtedly much more frequent among caseworkers than among clients. In other words, caseworkers do apply the terms of their profession in thinking about their own experiences of conflict with kin.

In view of their professional training, and the fact that 75 per cent of the staff report having had some psychoanalytic or psychotherapeutic treatment (although no staff member reports having received treatment from a caseworker), it is not surprising that caseworkers should look at their own kin conflicts in terms that reflect their training and experience. But what does this mean about the way in which conflicts with kin are conducted? Does the insertion of professionally phrased thinking alter the form, frequency, or resolution of kin conflicts?

The Structuring of Kin Conflicts

For the clients, regularities in kin conflicts mirror regularities in other kinds of kin interaction; interaction is most frequent with the wife's kin, but kin conflicts where marital discord is also present are most frequent with the husband's kin. Thus the focal points at which conflicts erupt are related to the general structuring of kinship bonds.

When one examines the kin with whom conflicts most frequently occur for the caseworkers, the results are strikingly similar to those for the clients. Moreover, the mirror-image relationship of conflict and other areas of interaction is also found among caseworkers.

For married caseworkers as well as clients, ties in many areas are more extensive to the wife's than to the husband's family. Only married caseworkers can be compared with clients in this respect. In the case of both married caseworkers and clients, when kin lived with the respondent's family, or when the respondent's family lived with kin, it most often involved the wife's kin (Table 27.) The lateral skewing toward the wife's side is also evident in a number of other areas, such as baby sitting and household assistance, where contacts are more frequent with the wife's than the husband's kin for both caseworkers and clients. Thus the lateral emphasis in kin relationships is similar for caseworkers and clients.

Table 27.   Laterality and Conflict

		Per Cent of Husband's Kin		Per Cent of Wife's Kin	
Laterality and Interaction					
Kin family lived with	Clients	30	(98)	61	(98)ᵃ
	Caseworkers	26	(27)	59	(27)ᵃ
Kin that lived with	Clients	32	(70)	54	(70)ᵃ
family	Caseworkers	26	(19)	53	(19)ᵃ
Laterality and Conflct					
Kin in conflicts *not*	Clients	55	(306)	45	(306)
involving *marital*	Caseworkers	51	(82)	49	(82)
discord					
Kin in conflicts	Clients	62	(373)	38	(373)
involving *marital*	Caseworkers	67	(63)	33	(63)
discord					

ᵃ These percentages do not add up to 100 because the remaining cases, where both the husband's and the wife's kin resided with the respondents, have been omitted from this table for simplicity of presentation. The figures in parentheses represent the number of units, families or kin, on which the percentage is based, that is, household units for residence and specific kin for conflict.

Caseworkers and clients are also similar in terms of which kin are most frequently parties to conflicts. Here also the comparison is of necessity only between married caseworkers and clients. Kin conflicts that do not entail marital discord are distributed fairly equally between the husband's and the wife's kin for both case-workers and clients. But those conflicts with kin that also entail marital strain are most often with the husband's kin both for case-workers and clients; for caseworkers 67 per cent and for clients 65 per cent of the kin involved in such conflicts were on the husband's side. Moreover, the specific kin most often mentioned by both caseworkers and clients is the husband's mother. She is mentioned by both caseworkers and clients almost twice as frequently as the wife's mother, who ranks second in both cases. Therefore, both the lateral skewing toward the wife's side in interaction generally, and the lateral skewing of conflicts toward the husband's side are similar for clients and married caseworkers.

Thus caseworkers and clients may employ a different vocabulary in talking about their conflicts with kin, but the more formal structuring of these conflicts is strikingly similar, at least for married caseworkers and clients. Similarities appear in other respects for both married and unmarried caseworkers and clients.

Because caseworkers differ from clients in values, and yet have kin networks that are similar in many respects, one might conclude that caseworkers stand in a different position in relation to their kin from that of clients. Because of their special position, one might expect caseworkers to have more kin conflicts. On the other hand, their lesser involvement with kin might diminish the sources of friction to offset some of the tension stemming from having moved away from kin in values.

There is no indication, however, that caseworkers and clients differ in the frequency of their kin conflicts. Questionnaire respondents were asked to check a series of items to indicate whether these had been a source of conflict. These items included: children's behavior, keeping kosher, ways of housekeeping trips or vacations, borrowing money, what kind of wedding or bar mitzvah to have, politics, gifts, invitations to family gatherings, financial support of a relative, living arrangements for a relative. Some of these items, for example, children's behavior, do not apply to single caseworkers and, therefore, the caseworkers as a whole had slightly less chance of reporting several topics of conflict than did clients. The rank order of the frequency with which various topics are checked is somewhat different for the two groups; invitations ranked high for both groups, but children's behavior was checked less frequently and politics more often by caseworkers.

Despite these differences the two groups are similar in the proportion checking different numbers of items as a source of conflict. Of those who answered the question, 33 per cent of the clients and 33 per cent of the caseworkers indicated that *none* of these particular topics had been a source of conflict, 23 per cent of the clients and 18 per cent of the caseworkers indicated that *one* of these items had been a source of conflict, and 44 per cent of the clients and 49 per cent of the caseworkers indicated that *two or more* of the items had been a source of conflict. Thus clients and caseworkers, both single and married, are similar in the frequency with which they indicate that several topics have been a source of conflict with kin.

It proved extremely difficult to categorize conflicts in terms of whether they had been resolved. Various levels of resolution may be distinguished in reports, with one often shading into another. Sometimes the conflict simply seems to have receded from prominence, as when "time was the healer." Sometimes the overt event of conflict ends without any basic change in the differing positions of those involved, for example, "The event is over, but basic differences are unchanged." In such cases it is often expected that the source of conflict will arise "again and again." Other times the undercurrent of friction remains nearer the surface, despite some lessening of open tension, for example, when "feelings have simmered down," but have not been "resolved." Sometimes an overt conflict seems to have produced some salutory release of tension without a basic change, for example, "no resolution, but we all felt better afterward." Sometimes resolution consists of one party coming closer to the position of the other through "compromise," "overriding," "coming through," "both sides yielding," or even "total agreement." Thus a modification of the position of the parties involved may occur mutually and equally, or with one party shifting position more than the other. But in all of these cases there is some perception of a positive solution and continuity of the relationship. Bolstering the relationship may also occur without a basic shift of position simply when the parties "agree to disagree." Other times resolution may entail termination of the conflict-producing relationship through slight "estrangement" or even a permanent rupture, for example, it "terminated a rather distasteful contact with finality." Because of such complex shadings it did not prove feasible to code and count the comparative frequency with which conflicts of caseworkers and clients were resolved. Again vocabulary differences were evident; caseworkers were inclined to talk in terms of "resolution," further complicating the comparisons on this particular point. It is impossible to say, therefore, whether the professional experience and training of the caseworkers aids them in making more frequent resolutions of their conflicts with kin than is true of clients, but for caseworkers as well as clients resolution also depends on the kin.

In terms of one measure of conflict resolution, however, the temporal duration of the conflict, caseworkers and clients do not differ greatly. Here again the coding is complex, because the reported duration sometimes refers to the overt dispute and sometimes to the duration of underlying tensions. But in terms of stated duration the two groups do not differ very much. Reports of the duration of conflicts range from "minutes" to years, and some statement of indefinite conflict such as "continuously," "constantly," "forever." Such continuous conflicts were categorized with those lasting more than a year. Caseworkers reported a slightly greater proportion of very short conflicts than did clients. Of the caseworkers 32 per cent reported that the conflict described lasted "minutes," "hours," or "days," while 20 per cent of the client conflicts were of this duration. On the other hand, caseworkers and clients were very similar in the proportion of their conflicts that lasted over a year, 35 per cent of the caseworker conflicts, and 33 per cent of the client conflicts. Thus the formal dimensions of the conflicts described do not differ greatly for caseworkers and clients. The comparison on this point is between clients and all caseworkers, both married and unmarried.

Despite these similarities in the formal structuring of the kin conflicts of caseworkers and clients, there are indications that caseworkers are likely to take a different position in relation to their kin than is true of clients.

The issues of caseworker kin conflict are often very similar to those of client kin conflicts, but caseworkers take a different stand. One value item, for example, on which caseworkers and clients diverged radically concerned the right of an unmarried child to reside away from home before marriage. Clients most often felt that "children should not leave home before they get married," whereas almost no caseworkers believed this. However, some caseworkers report that this is a real issue between themselves and their kin. One caseworker, a single woman, reports such a conflict as follows:

> [The conflict was] between myself and parents re question of my establishing my own home. Question revolved around fact that I was not married and their negative feelings regarding this in view of the fact that I would be living in same city. [Feelings were expressed] rather heatedly. [It was resolved] by my taking own apartment—parents finally acquiesced. . . . It seemed a natural phenomenon—I expected this conflict to take place and have been pleased by the way it was resolved and subsequently, better relationship.

Thus in some instances the beliefs that caseworkers react against in their conflicts with kin may be very similar to the values held by clients. The differences between caseworkers and clients may therefore sometimes parallel the differences between caseworkers and some of their own kin.

THERAPEUTIC RELATIONSHIPS AND KINSHIP DIFFERENCES

The observed differences between caseworkers and their clients in kinship values and experience are of definite relevance for treatment relationships. The two groups differ markedly in many respects, and these differences are largely consistent in direction, with clients showing more pronounced kinship orientation in both values and interaction than their caseworkers.

On certain value points, specifically those concerning minimum independent functioning of the nuclear family, both groups see separate residence as the ideal and emphasize the marital bond as primary over ties to kin outside the immediate family. But beyond this core of agreement clients allow more leeway for involvement with kin, even at the expense of the marital tie, and lay greater stress on obligations of kinship than is true of their caseworkers. The Aged, moreover, are consistently even more strongly kin-oriented than other clients.

These differences in values are also paralleled in actual experience with kin. The relationship between belief and action in each specific area was not determined, for instance, whether those respondents who believe it desirable to live near kin actually do so more frequently than others. But comparing the two groups, the differences between caseworkers and clients in experience are consistent with differences in values. Clients have experienced more geographic proximity to kin, more informal daily communication, and more informal social interaction with kin. Caseworkers, however, are by no means isolated from their kin; they also accept and carry out many acts of reciprocity with kin. They may even discharge some of these obligations through use of their professional skills in the role of an expert adviser. But, generally, caseworkers show less informal involvement with kin, and comparatively more involvement with nonkin.

Certain features of the kin networks of caseworkers and clients are, however, very similar, despite some differences in age, marital status, and social backgrounds of the two groups. The existence of kin groups within the network and interaction among kin in the network, whether or not the respondent participates, are similar for caseworkers and clients. Thus the broader setting of kin interaction may be quite similar for the two groups.

Conflicts with kin reflect these points of similarity and difference. The vocabulary of emotion used by caseworkers in describing conflicts and that of clients appear to differ considerably. But the formal structuring of conflicts, in terms of the kin with whom they are most likely to erupt, is very similar. Moreover, in both groups the locus of most frequent conflict reverses the point of most frequent interaction; conflicts that also entail strain in the marital relationship are more frequent with the husband's kin whereas interaction is more frequent with the wife's kin. The kin conflicts of caseworkers and clients also do not differ greatly in frequency or duration. Thus the differences between caseworkers and clients in kinship values, and the differences in the extent of kin involvement, do not appear to derive from major differences in their kin networks, or to result in different forms of kin conflict. Although professional training and experience alter ways of talking about kin conflicts, they do not appear to have much effect upon the locus or form of conflicts.

Although no direct data are available from the kin of either caseworkers or clients, one may speculate about the position that members of each group have in relation to the values of their kin. It seems likely that the values of the caseworkers' kin, at least their parental kin, are often similar to the values of the clients; and the values of the clients' kin, at least those in their parents' generation, may be similar to the values of the Aged. Both caseworkers and clients have probably experienced value differences between themselves and their kin, and each has undoubtedly dealt with relatives who place even greater emphasis on ties of kinship than they do themselves. In some cases the value differences between caseworkers and clients may be the very points at issue between caseworkers and their own kin. Insofar as clients are similar to real individuals in the lives of caseworkers, the differences between the two groups that arise in therapeutic relationships may be of special significance. The kinship values of caseworkers may be similar to those of the grown children of clients, thus adding another potential emotional element in the therapeutic relationship.

These kinship values and experiences are part of the social and emotional equipment with which therapist as well as client enters the therapeutic relationship. Kinship is only one specific area in which the experiences of caseworker and client are relevant for their relationships. Although no observational data were obtained on therapeutic interaction itself, we can point again to the data indicating that certain types of changes in kin relationships are sought by caseworkers in treatment. The direction of change in kin relationships that is sought in treatment, that is, more frequent reduction than expansion of kin involvement, is consistent with the value and experience differences between caseworkers and their clients; caseworkers, therefore, are in effect attempting to change clients' kin relationships to accord more completely with their own kinship values and experience.

The differences that have been observed are between caseworkers and clients as groups. They may or may not arise in any particular treatment situation. We are not able to demonstrate that those caseworkers who are least kin-oriented are most likely to steer their clients toward reduction of kin involvement. The observed directions of intervention are for a sample of cases and have not been analyzed for specific caseworkers. But the differences between the groups imply that in many instances value and experience differences will arise between a particular caseworker and client.

It is impossible for present purposes to consider the determinants of these differences. In addition to differences in social background, such as the frequency with which parents are native-born or foreign-born, age and marital status are undoubtedly relevant. As noted above, although the married clients in the research sample typify the agency caseload, single clients may be more like single caseworkers. It is entirely possible that when they have experienced the kinship-binding effects of marriage and children, single caseworkers may come to be more like most clients than they are at present. Moreover, the analysis of kin interaction was complicated because certain comparisons could be made only between married caseworkers and clients, for example, whether interaction and conflict center on the husband's or the wife's side. At some of these points, moreover, married caseworkers and clients are similar. However, the value differences between caseworkers and clients do *not* disappear when only married caseworkers are compared with clients; married as well as single caseworkers have values that are different from those of clients. The source of a particular value or experience may make a difference in terms of its meaning to the individual. But whatever the source of differences in values and experience between caseworkers and clients, whether they stem from age, marital status, social background, or professional training, these differences are potentially relevant for their relationship in treatment. The possible implications of these differences in the specific treatment combinations in which they actually do arise clearly merit consideration.

One may distinguish two major dimensions of the treatment relationship that may hypothetically be influenced by the congruence of kinship values and experience between caseworker and client. The first, communication and rapport, includes:

For the caseworker:
    Liking of client
    Ease of communication with client
    Ease of training client in therapeutic role
For the client:
    Liking of caseworker
    Ease of communication with caseworker
    Ease of learning client role

The second dimension, diagnosis and evaluation, includes:

For the caseworker:
    Evaluation of symptomatology
    Evaluation of motivation

Evaluation of change
For the client:
Evaluation of the problem
Evaluation of caseworker's skills
Evaluation of benefit from treatment

Communication and Rapport

The determinants of ease of communication and rapport in any social relationship are obviously complex. One may presume that a minimum degree of common symbolism is a prerequisite for meaningful communication.[2] But greater similarity of values and experience does not necessarily produce easier understanding. The grasp of another person's experience probably requires more involved presentation and explanation when it is dissimilar to one's own. But as those who specialize in working with dissimilar cultures have noted, the process of transcending such differences may itself be highly illuminating, leading to special levels of understanding that do not ordinarily become as explicit between those of similar background.[3] The norms of certain kinds of therapeutic relationship, in fact, specifically preclude the intrusion of personal preferences based on such things as similarity of background, views, and experience.[4]

Some data from the caseworker questionnaire, however, indicate that congruence of values and experience may contribute to the caseworker's feeling of ease in working with a client. Caseworkers were asked to indicate the type of client they find it easiest to work with in terms of a number of dimensions of social background and interaction style, including education, religion, nativity, ethnicity, income, fee payments, age, and verbal and expressive style. On all of these dimensions, except age and verbal and expressive style, the majority indicated that the characteristic made "no difference" in the ease of working with the client. The caseworkers thus in a sense expressed a therapeutic norm against preferences based on social background.[5] Even on the two dimensions that may be considered essential components of a verbally based treatment relationship, verbal fluency and expressiveness, some indicated that it made no difference. However, those who did express an opinion that it was easier to work with one kind of client than another consistently selected clients who were similar in background to the caseworkers as a group. Thirty-eight per cent found it easier to work with well-educated" clients, but only 1 per cent preferred "poorly educated"; 18 per cent selected "not religious" clients as easiest to work with, but no one selected "religious"; 14 per cent indicated "native-born" were easiest, but no one indicated "foreign-born"; 15 per cent checked "Jewish," but only 1 per cent checked "non-Jewish"; 17 per cent selected "middle income," but only 1 per cent "high income" and 10 per cent "low income"; 9 per cent found "fee clients" easiest, but, 3 per cent found "nonfee clients" easier. The main preference in age was for young adults, with adolescents and middle aged next, and elderly and young children being selected by practically no one. Thus where differences are indicated, the clients considered easiest to work with are those who happen to be similar to the social background of the majority of caseworkers (Table 28).

From the data presented here one may presume that the specific differences in kinship values and experience that have been observed do in some instances contribute to the caseworkers' feeling of experiential rapport with a client and hence the ease of the working relationship. But it is also significant that in most cases an effort is probably made to avoid letting such factors make a difference in the relationship.

The degree to which the client perceives the therapist's experience and values to be congruent with his own may also affect the client's sense of ease of communication, liking for the therapist, as well as evaluation of the therapist's skills. But again differences as well as similarities may be a basis for establishing rapport; for example, the client may see the caseworker as a model of a different but attractive way of life. The ease with which the client comes to learn the norms of the therapeutic relationship is undoubtedly also affected by initial similarity of outlook of therapist and client. These data are also paralled by the work of others showing the difficulties of traversing class differences in expectations about roles in therapy.[6]

Diagnosis and Evaluation

The congruence of values between caseworker and client is also relevant for the process of diagnosing the client's problems and evaluating motivation and change. In any diagnostic process

*Table 28.   Caseworkers' Perceptions of the Ease of Working with
Various Types of Clients*

**"Which of the following types of clients
do you find it easier to work with?"**

	Per Cent			Per Cent	
Well-educated	38		Fee clients	9	
Poorly educated	1		Nonfee clients	3	
No difference	61		No difference	88	
	100	(119)		100	(119)
Religious	0		Young children	2	
Not religious	18		Adolescents	15	
No difference	82		Young adults	38	
	100	(120)	Middle aged	10	
			Elderly	1	
Foreign-born	0		No difference	34	
Native-born	14			100	(109)
No difference	86				
	100	(121)	Verbally fluent	79	
			Inarticulate	0	
Jewish	15		No difference	21	
Non-Jewish	1			100	(119)
No difference	84				
	100	(118)	Expressive	82	
			Placid	0	
High income	1		No difference	18	
Middle income	17			100	(118)
Low income	10				
No difference	72				
	100	(119)			

that which would be pathological with the therapist's culture must
be distinguished from that which appears pathological but is actually typical and normal within another cultural group. As others
have pointed out, this distinction has complex ramifications and
is often hard to make.[7] Errors may be made in two ways; that which
is atypical of the therapist's culture may be judged as pathological
when it merely represents the normal way of another culture; or a
pathological act may be assumed normal on grounds of cultural
relativity when this is not actually the case.[8] In the specific area
of kinship, a caseworker may evaluate a client's sense of obligation
and ties to kin as a form of immaturity and dependency when, in

fact, these ties are common among the client's kin and hence do not have the pathological significance that might be ascribed by those whose values are less kin-oriented.

The client's initial presentation and understanding of the problem will also be set within the framework of value assumptions about what is normal in family and kin relationships. If caseworkers and clients diverge in values they may, at least initially, have very different views about the problem. The purpose in seeking help is, of course, to obtain a new perspective on one's problems, but this process does not necessarily mean taking on the values of the therapist. If the caseworker reacts to that which is culturally normal for the client as if it were pathological, the development of understanding on the part of the client may be impeded. There has been a good deal of consideration in the casework field of the role of value differences in the treatment relationship: when it is important to respect the values of the client, and when to act as an agent of acculturation in helping a client to change values.[9] Here the notion of "self-determination" in the solution of problems is relevant.

Perhaps the most critical factor is the extent to which value differences are explicitly recognized. It is extremely difficult to be aware of one's own values because they are built into omnipresent cultural assumptions. Although it may be relatively easy to perceive cultural assumptions when confronted with dramatic differences between widely disparate cultures, it is much more difficult to be aware of socially derived assumptions when working within a more subtle range of variation. Insight into personal values may help the caseworker clarify his role in treatment just as other self-knowledge helps in understanding one's relationships with others. But acquiring cultural self-knowledge also requires systematic effort.

A critical question is the way in which implicit cultural assumptions enter into professional thinking. The finding that caseworkers and their clients differ in their experience and views about obligations toward kin poses questions of why restriction of kinship contact was so frequently sought in casework treatment. Is this a product of cultural assumptions or of scientific knowledge? Is it known that one form of kinship structure is preferable in given respects; for example, that it is more likely than another to reinforce desired forms of marital and parent-child relationships?

Even if there is no proof that one form of kinship organization is better than another, it may still be reasonable to attempt to change relationships with relatives. It may be useful for caseworkers to act as agents of one value position in society, and help clients move from the ways of life of one subgroup to those of another. But it is important to be able to distinguish professional thinking that embodies implicit cultural assumptions and that based on objectively validated knowledge.

Because of the difficulties of becoming aware of personal implicit cultural assumptions as well as those embodied in professional thinking, it is useful to have concepts and research that serve as guides, indicating areas of possible difference. Caseworkers usually look at relationships with kin through psychological rather than sociocultural concepts, making it difficult to see regularities in the ways they are modifying systems of interpersonal relationships. The findings discussed in Chapter 7 on systematic patterns of changes that casework treatment helps to produce in relationships with kin are therefore useful in pointing out regularities that might otherwise not be observed. The concept of kinship structure, derived from anthropology and sociology, helps to map out certain areas of behavior where differences between societies have been observed. It points to the existence of cultural values and differences in social behavior in a number of areas, including whom it is considered appropriate to marry, household composition and where one lives in relation to kin, rights and obligations of kinship, economic relationships with kin, and expectations about which kin one should have the most intimate ties with at different stages in the life cycle. Examining differences in values and experience in the specific area of kinship moreover adds a new perspective on the general question of social background differences and similarities between therapist and client.

It is probably not the degree of congruence in kinship values and experience but the extent to which the caseworker has knowledge and understanding of the client's position that is most significant in treatment. If a caseworker is able to predict the client's values and reactions, differences may not be a barrier to the treatment process. However, such understanding when differences do exist, can undoubtedly be furthered by greater knowledge of the cultural background of these differences.

NOTES TO CHAPTER 8

1. As a result of an expression of interest in participating in the research by several members of the agency board, a form of the questionnaire comparable to that given to caseworkers was developed and sent to them. Their responses are of considerable interest since they represent another segment of the agency; the issue of value similarities and differences between agency board and staff generally is clearly one that has significance for agency functioning. Space precludes detailed presentation of the board results. However, it is interesting that, in general, the kinship values of board members were closer to those of caseworkers than they were to those of clients. The exceptions were mainly on items having to do with economic obligations toward kin. Here again there were too few cases to allow comparisons in terms of statistical significance.

2. For a general theory of social systems, including discussion of the basic prerequisites for social interaction, see Parsons, Talcott, *The Social System,* The Free Press, Glencoe, Ill., 1951.

3. Descriptions of the types of understanding that may be reached between those of different cultures may be found in a recent collection of articles by anthropologists about relationships with particular informants with whom they have worked. Casagrande, Joseph B., editor, *In the Company of Man: Twenty Portraits by Anthropologists,* Harper and Row, New York, 1960.

4. Fromm-Reichmann, Frieda, *Principles of Intensive Psychotherapy.* University of Chicago Press, Chicago, 1950. See especially Chapter 3, The Psychiatrist's Attitude Toward Cultural and Ethnical Values in Its Relatedness to the Goals of Psychotherapy, and Chapter 4, Considerations of the Psychiatrist in the Establishment of the Treatment Situation.

5. In Parsons' terms, this may be called "universalism."

6. Hollingshead, August B., and Fredrick C. Redlich, *Social Class and Mental Illness.* John Wiley and Sons, New York, 1958.

7. Devereaux, George, "Normal and Abnormal: The Key Problem of Psychiatric Anthropology" in *Some Uses of Anthropology: Theoretical and Applied,* The Anthropological Society of Washington, Washington, 1956, pp. 23–48. Also see Hallowell, A. Irving, "Fear and Anxiety as Cultural and Individual Variables in a Primitive Society" in *Culture and Mental Health,* edited by Marvin K. Opler, Macmillan Co., New York, 1959, pp. 41–62.

8. Devereaux, George, *op. cit.*

9. Recent discussions of this issue include: Hellenbrand, Shirley C., "Client Value Orientations: Implications for Diagnosis and Treatment," *Social Casework,* vol. 42, April, 1961, pp. 163–169; Weisman, Irving, and Jacob Chwast, "Control and Values in Social Work Treatment," *Social Casework,* vol. 41, November, 1960, pp. 451–456; Taylor, Robert K., "The Social Control Function in Casework," *Social Casework,* vol. 39, January, 1958, pp. 17–21; Blum, Arthur, "Values and Aspirations as a Focus for Treatment," *Social Work Practice, 1963,* Selected Papers, 90th Annual Forum, National Conference on Social Welfare, Columbia University Press, New York, 1964.

CHAPTER 9

The Dynamics of
Change in Kinship Systems:
Implications for Casework

We began our analysis by examining the kin relationships of client families through looking at their kinship values and at a variety of areas of kin interaction. Certain regularities in the relationships of clients with their kin were observed, both in the forms of interaction with kin and in patterns of conflict: conflicts are particularly likely to arise in the relationships between those in certain kin categories. We have also presented data indicating that in many instances casework intervention entails an attempt to change relationships with kin. Finally, we have seen that caseworkers and clients differ in their values about kinship and to some extent in their experiences with kin. We will now reexamine these findings and consider their implications for casework practice.

INTERVENTION, INTERACTION, AND CONFLICT

Regularities

Systematic regularities in casework intervention in the relationships with kin come into sharper focus when they are viewed together with the findings on kin interaction among client families. In some respects intervention is similar to the direction of the involvement of clients with their kin, but in other respects it is strikingly different. Intervention of all forms, particularly restriction of involvement with kin, is more frequent with members of the parental generation than with kin in the client's own generation. In terms of absolute numbers more areas exist in which interaction is most frequent with members of the client's own generation than with the parental generation. But when the proportion of living kin in the two generations is considered, it becomes evident that a special priority is attached to interaction with parents. Thus intervention is most frequent where the bonds of relationships with kin are strongest, that is, with kin in the parental generation. Both kin interaction and intervention are more frequent with female than with male kin. The side of the family of the kin most often involved in different areas of interaction varies from one activity to another; activities that are usually male, notably family business, most frequently involve the husband with his kin. But in most other areas, interaction is more frequent with the wife's than with the husband's kin, so that the total interaction of a nuclear family is larger for the wife's than for the husband's kin. Intervention is more often with kin on the wife's side than on the husband's, just as is kin interaction. Thus intervention is most frequent with the categories of kin with whom most interaction or greatest strength of involvement arises.

Intervention, however, does not entirely parallel conflicts with kin. Conflicts most often arise with female rather than male kin, which is parallel to the directions of intervention. Conflicts are also more frequent with kin in the older than the client's own generation, and this direction again is parallel. However, a striking difference in the direction of intervention and the categories of kin with whom there is most conflict arises with respect to laterality. Intervention is more frequent with the wife's than with the husband's kin, the wife's mother being the kin on whom intervention most frequently focuses; but the husband's mother is the kin with whom there is conflict considerably more frequently than is true of the wife's mother.

Of all conflicts reported by husbands and wives, more involve the husband's kin than the wife's kin. Both husbands and wives report having more conflicts with their own kin. But skewing toward the husband's side is evident when the perspectives of husbands and wives are examined separately; wives report an almost equal number of conflicts with their own and their husband's kin, but husbands report considerably more conflicts with their own than with their wife's kin. Moreover, when those conflicts with kin that also involve marital discord are examined, the husband's kin are mentioned more frequently than the wife's kin by both husbands and wives. Thus it is conflicts with the husband's, not the wife's kin, that most often either cause or reflect strain in the marital relationship as seen by clients. This pattern coexists with the direction of interaction in which the husband is more frequently involved with the wife's kin than the wife is with the husband's kin; the husband is more readily accepted into his wife's family than she is into his family.

Intervention, however, most frequently seeks to restrict or redefine the ties to the wife's family and therefore does not focus on those kin relationships that are associated with greatest marital conflict as recognized by clients. One is reminded of the statement of the supervisor that husbands often do not have the resentment caseworkers expect them to have about the wife's ties with her kin. What caseworkers call the "strong, unbroken" ties are most often the focus of intervention, not ties that clients most often associate with marital conflict.

Regularities in the direction of most frequent interaction, most frequent conflict, and most frequent caseworker intervention are shown in Table 29.

Table 29.   Comparison of Kin in Client-Kin Interaction,[a] Conflict, and Casework Intervention

	Sex	Generation	Laterality
Most frequent interaction	Female	Sibling	Wife's kin
Most frequent conflict	Female	Parental	Husband's kin
Most frequent intervention	Female	Parental	Wife's kin

[a] Conflict is, of course, also a form of interaction but the term "interaction" is used here for areas of interaction other than those directly described as the subject of conflict in questions about conflict.

If the locus of conflict reflects points of strain in kin relationships, why is it then that intervention does not most typically focus on these points? A number of answers may be suggested. First, it is possible that clients are unable to recognize the areas of conflict that most seriously disrupt the marital relationship; that the conflicts they report are symptomatic of difficulties in other relationships but not the true "underlying" conflicts. It is possible that the objects of conflict are not those which initially produced the hostility; the wife may, for example, select her mother-in-law as a target for feelings that were initially generated in the relationship with her own mother; that is, she may "scapegoat" her mother-in-law. This transfer of objects may apply especially to conflicts about kin in which the kin themselves are not involved. However, as we have argued above, when the kin are involved directly in the conflict it must be seen as a phenomenon of interaction; the frequent conflicts between certain kin statuses cannot be considered to derive entirely from the motivations and emotions of one individual. One can assume that something in the relationship between the husband's kin, particularly the husband's mother, and the wife makes this relationship a frequent focus of conflict.

It is also possible that conflicts with kin as reported by clients do not represent "problems." It is conceivable that some of these conflicts may be a form of disputation that clients do not consider a problem but a normal situation that is preferable to withdrawal. Conflicts stemming from differences in values and attitudes, or differences of interest in the allocation of time and attention could be seen as a healthy manifestation of the ability to express differences openly. In this sense conflict may be a process of interaction whereby changes are produced and differences resolved. If it is true that conflicts are a way of resolving differences, it would follow that those relationships in which there is greatest conflict might be those in which resolutions were already being worked out, and therefore least in need of casework attention.

One may assume that in order to alter ties with kin in the process of life-cycle development, a certain degree of open conflict is essential to assert independence and alter the childhood role relationships. The conflicts of adolescents with parents, for example, may be regarded in part as this type of role-change conflict. However, one might ask whether such maturational conflicts with the family of childhood would also lead to conflict in the marital relationship. On the contrary, it seems that conflicts that were part of a healthy process of role change and separation from the family of childhood would tend to support the solidarity of the marital relationship rather than lead to conflict in it.

It is also possible that the most frequent kin categories in casework intervention reflect the wife's rather than the husband's perspective. Although both husbands and wives may be seen by caseworkers, and are sometimes seen jointly, the fact remains that more wives see caseworkers for more interviews than do husbands. However, even from the wife's perspective, the conflicts with kin that most often also entail marital conflict are with the husband's kin rather than with her own kin. Thus in emphasizing the relationship of the wife to her own kin in casework intervention, the focus is not on those areas of conflict with kin that most often also entail marital conflicts as seen by wives.

It is also possible that the focus of kin intervention derives in part from the value assumptions of caseworkers, either implicit or explicit, personal or professional. Thus the emphasis on intervention at the point of "strong, unbroken" ties, rather than at the points of maximum conflict with kin is consistent with values that emphasize the importance of reducing and breaking from more traditional types of kin relationships.

It is important that the direction of intervention not only parallels value differences between caseworkers and clients, but also parallels differences between clients and the Aged, who may be assumed to be somewhat similar to the client's own parents. Clients hold an in-between position; they are less kin-oriented than the Aged but more kin-oriented than caseworkers. Moreover, some of the conflicts with kin may reflect the process of evolving new role definitions in the course of acculturative or social class changes between generations. Thus the support that caseworkers offer for less kin-oriented values and behavior, consistent with their own kinship values, may also represent a support for a process of acculturation that is under way between generations, apart from intervention. Because intervention focuses on the kin with whom there is most frequent interaction or greatest involvement, it must also affect the values that support this distribution of contacts. Thus caseworkers may further foster acculturative changes by attempting, implicitly, to change the clients' norms of kin relationships; however, acculturative changes cannot account entirely for the lateral skewing of conflict. Although slight differences of age of parents and proportion of parents currently living exist between husbands and wives, differences in birthplace and background do not appear sufficient to warrant the assumption that cultural differences between husband's kin and the nuclear family are greater than those between the wife's kin and the nuclear family. Thus if conflicts were primarily acculturative disputes over role definition, they would be distributed equally between the husband's and the wife's kin.

It is also important that the reduction of kin involvement in intervention generally parallels changes that occur in the life cycle. One could, in fact, assume that just as individual therapy may represent an attempt to help the individual move beyond stages in his development at which he has become inappropriately fixed, intervention in relationships with kin represents an effort to help the family members move through the stages of kinship organization and role change which are usual in that group. Clients may have become fixed in roles representing earlier stages of the developmental cycle, and it is these kin relationships that have the most serious consequences for the marital relationship and the health of the nuclear family, and hence the greatest need for therapeutic intervention.

In this case, the greater involvement of the wife with her kin may represent a more arrested kinship development than the husband's relationship with his kin. Lateral skewing toward the wife's family may derive in part from the Eastern European Jewish tradition of the *kest*. Thus marriage itself may represent a sharper break in the life of the husband than of the wife so that if separation from the family of childhood is to be desired, the husband's kin ties may be less in need of further change. From the traditional point of view the developmental norms for the family would not be exactly the same for husbands and wives. The idea, implicit in casework intervention, that at marriage husbands and wives should go through an equal emancipation from the childhood families represents a view of a kinship system with less skewing toward the wife's side than was apparently the case for the traditional Eastern European Jewish family in the *shtetl*. Therefore, in emphasizing equal emancipation of husbands and wives from their families of childhood, caseworkers may be implicitly engaged in helping clients shift from one type of kinship system to another.

Casework intervention most often seeks to restrict or redefine rather than to expand relationships with kin, particularly those with parents; this pattern corresponds to the developmental processes of a kinship system in which primary ties and allegiance to the family of childhood shift to those of the family of marriage. The lateral emphasis on intervention in relationships with the wife's kin also corresponds to this pattern because the greatest involvement is found in this area. Thus the directions of casework intervention correspond to value and experiential differences between caseworkers and clients, to acculturative process, and also to life-cycle changes.

Implications of Structural Perspectives

One may ask: Is this direction of casework intervention in relationships with kin appropriate? First of all, it is necessary to note that this analysis is based on caseworkers' reports of what they hope to do and what they had actually done, but it is not based on any external measure of whether these sought-after changes actually occurred. Insofar as the perceptions that clients have of casework goals and changes correspond with those of caseworkers, one may assume that these directions of change occur in many instances. However, the data do not permit firm conclusions about which types of change resulting from treatment are most frequent and are most readily and lastingly sustained after treatment. Nevertheless, the regularities in the goals of treatment are striking enough to be highly suggestive.

Intervention that supports life-cycle developmental processes in kin relationships, which have for some reason been momentarily blocked, may be entirely appropriate; it may parallel efforts to help an individual move from one developmental stage to another. Intervention that supports acculturative changes, that is, changes over time and between generations, working toward a new style of kinship organization for the younger generation, may also be highly appropriate. Both of these levels of intervention may support or stimulate "normal" processes of change, which have not moved sufficiently smoothly.

However, if casework is in part supporting life-cycle and acculturative changes in kinship organization, this support should be recognized explicitly. Our interviews with caseworkers indicate that at present these changes are not generally seen as changes in family and kinship organization. Even if the direction of change is usually appropriate, it is likely that it stems in part from unrecognized value assumptions made in the treatment profession. The directions of intervention may not be based on explicit goals that rest on knowledge of the developmental stages or consequences of different types of family kinship structure. Rather, caseworkers view the changes sought in treatment most often in terms of concepts of individual psychological development. Although individual reorganization is, of course, also involved, it is only part of the picture.

If changes in kin relationships are seen only as individual psychological processes, the social world of the family becomes an undifferentiated blur. But if the caseworker considers concepts of social structure as well in arriving at a diagnosis, he should be better able to observe and evaluate differentiating aspects of the family's social relationships, including sources of both strength and difficulty. Although at best it is hard to distinguish between abnormality and a cultural pattern different from that of the observer, it is impossible to make this distinction if the cultural pattern is unknown. The more frequent intervention in ties with the wife's than with the husband's kin, for example, raises questions about the significance of relationships with different kin for the family. The difference between ties to the husband's as compared with the wife's kin can be more fully understood in terms of a pattern that the husband and wife and their kin all consider socially valuable. A knowledge of the frequency of ties between female kin within various social groups and under varying social conditions provides a better basis for evaluating whether a particular client conforms to the modal pattern. Moreover, if an attempt is made to change the relationship between the wife and her kin, the outcome can best be estimated if considered from the perspective of more than one individual, so that all the factors that facilitate or inhibit change in each individual are taken into account. It is useful, for example, in considering the crisis of achieving independence for the newly married wife, to consider also the crisis of relinquishment for her parents.

Despite the general preponderance of ties to the wife's kin, ties of the husband to his male kin prevail in areas of specifically male activity. This difference raises the question of the extent to which the ties of the wife to her female kin stem from the division of labor by sex within an industrial society; the wife's ties to her female kin may in some cases derive as much from common interests and activity as from individual dependency.[1] This kind of tie also can be judged best in a specific case if the common social patterns are recognized. The dependence of a particular family on its kin for assistance is better understood as part of a pattern of reciprocity that is supported by the kin. Extensive communication of a family with its kin can better be evaluated in terms of the views of both the family and its kin about the rights of kin to initiative and access in communication. The meaning for a family of participation in a family circle as compared with a cousins club can be better understood if the differences between the two types of organization, which derive from their different generational composition, are recognized.

Casework intervention should also benefit from a more thorough understanding of the interconnections within the family and the kinship systems. If these connections are known, the probable effects of changes in one area on other areas may be estimated more accurately. However, the degree to which one area is linked with another may vary. Again implicit therapeutic assumptions are inevitable. It is commonly assumed that a change in the marital relationship will affect the children. It is often implicitly assumed that reduction of dependence of a husband and wife on their parents will strengthen the marital bond. Greater knowledge and more careful scrutiny of assumptions about how one area of kinship and family affects another should help the caseworker estimate the outcome of changes.

It would be useful, for example, to have greater knowledge of which kinds of kin involvement disrupt and which kinds support the marital relationship. In attempting to alter the "strong, unbroken" ties of the wife to her family, the caseworker may be trying to assist in a developmental process that presumably leads from parent-child attachments to marital ties. However, some kinds of parent-child attachments may not constitute an interference; they may instead actively support the marital tie. For example, the acceptance of a husband into the wife's family may help to define the marriage as a socially accepted and significant bond and thus to support it in much the same way in which the ritual and economic involvement of the two families to a marriage did in some traditional peasant kinship systems. Insofar as the client picture of those kin relationships that most frequently strain the marital tie is accurate, it suggests that the extensive involvement of the wife with her kin, particularly mother-daughter and sister-sister ties, does not place strains upon the marital relationship in quite the same way as do ties of the husband to his kin, particularly his mother. The caseworker should be better able to estimate whether reducing ties between a wife and her female kin will, in fact, strengthen the marital relationship if the way in which these ties are viewed by the family and its kin is known.

Some kinds of kin relationships, which may on some level appear to represent a change from an early stage of attachment to the childhood family to one of emancipation and a more mature relationship, may not produce this effect because of the clash with kin. For example, points of battle between the wife and the husband's family and the husband and his own family may not represent movement to a more independent nuclear family, but rather a continuing dispute over the validity of the marriage.

The effects of other kinds of kinship ties on the marital bond also need careful scrutiny. It is clear, for example, that family circles and cousins clubs differ from many types of descent groups because the spouse is incorporated as a member of the group. Thus the groups do not produce conflicting loyalties or serve to pull the marital partners in opposite directions, as often happens in societies where husbands and wives belong to different descent groups. Moreover, ties to kin of the parental and the client's own generation do not appear to have the same kind of implication for the marital relationship. Business contacts between the husband and his male kin do not have the same consequences either for the husband or for the marital relationship as contacts that involve the husband as a subordinate of his wife's father. Thus various types of activity with kin must be differentiated before concluding that extensive kin involvement places a strain on the marital relationship. For some clients it may be inappropriate to apply the more general cultural assumption that it is desirable to work toward a "close" marital bond; for example, a kinship system that stresses the mother-daughter tie may be most congenial for some.

In estimating the outcome of changes sought in treatment, the caseworker will also be aided by looking for links of change within the kinship system. Differences in values between client families and their kin, for example, are undoubtedly a source of change in relationships. A client may be receiving differing sanctions from various sources for the way in which he plays kinship roles. For example, cousins clubs, organized on a single-generation basis, may support changes and movement away from the ties to parents and the traditional values of parents, whereas this may not be equally true of family circles, which are organized on a cross-generational basis. Moreover, the sanctions of kin and the sanctions of caseworkers for the same behavior may diverge radically. In order to understand the impact of these various sanctions, that is, the effect that interaction in one area will have in producing changes in another area, one must be able to examine and weigh the balance of the various forces both within and outside the family, both within and outside the individual, which are impinging upon kinship behavior.

In planning changes it is important for the caseworker to be able to evaluate both the positive and negative functions of relationships with kin for the family. If this task is not clearly set, the built-in emphasis on acculturative and life-cycle changes, as well as the different social perspectives and values of caseworkers and clients, may lead caseworkers to cut off some relationships that may, in fact, support the very changes they are seeking to assist. As we have seen, cousins clubs may very well have the function of supporting the younger generation in working out a new set of values and models for family life while still retaining strong ties of kinship.

Cousins club membership may therefore support the changes in relationships with parents that caseworkers also seek to support. However, if cousins club membership is considered to be an undifferentiated form of immature dependence on kin, parallel to some forms of dependence on parents, the caseworker may unwittingly cut off valuable allies.

Kin may provide many positive functions for the nuclear family: emotional support and assistance, a significant reference group and aid for occupational mobility, assistance in child rearing, augmentation of the role models available to children, and support in defining the marital relationship as an important bond.

Kin groups may be an arena of joint participation for family members, ritual recognition of life-cycle transitions, and support for the process of social mobility and acculturation. These positive functions of kinship need to be weighed against the problems of conflict, interference, and overinvolvement with kin arising in specific cases. In attempting to reduce the negative aspects of kin relationships, one should not lose sight of the positive functions. Although the possible consequences of a change in one area cannot be precisely predicted on the basis of present knowledge, they should at least be seriously considered lest an ameliorative change in one area undo a valuable support for family life.

SOCIETY AND INTERVENTION IN KIN RELATIONSHIPS

Kinship in Urban Industrial Society

The findings of this research have a number of significant implications for theories of kinship and society. However, the modifications that these findings imply for both anthropological and sociological theory will not be presented in detail in this volume. Here we will regard the theoretical implications of these findings only as issues about kinship and society have bearing on casework intervention.

These data on the kin relationships of client families indicate that extensive involvement with kin is typical of many. The frequency of daily contact, the extent of geographic proximity, the participation with kin on ritual occasions and in formal kinship organizations, the reliance on kin for various kinds of assistance, the sense of obligation to assist kin, all present a picture unlike that of an "isolate" nuclear family living independently from its kin. Some previous models have posited that the kinship system of the urban middle classes in an industrial society is based on a nuclear family that is structurally and functionally independent of its kin. It is clear that both the values and the actual behavior of clients diverge from these models.

The reasons for this divergence may be several. It is possible that a client group has special problems in acculturation and life-cycle transitions in kin relationships, resulting in greater involvement with kin than might characterize a nonclient group of similar background and socioeconomic status. It is also possible that the picture of client kinship is characteristic of Jewish groups of Eastern European origin or descent. At a number of points the kin relationships of client families show similarities to Eastern European traditions; for example, the lateral skewing of ties toward the wife's family, although not unique to Eastern European Jewish tradition, is characteristic of it. The particular type of formal kinship organization and religious practices that bring kin together or keep them apart, that is, keeping kosher, are special to the Jewish group. However, the findings on client kinship may not apply to Jews of other occupational and educational levels. The caseworkers cannot be taken as representatives of a social level different from the clients because they are drawn from only one occupational group. The comparison of the values and kin interaction of caseworkers and clients was made for purposes of examining implications for their relationships with each other in treatment. Nevertheless, it suggests that within the Jewish group those of higher educational and occupational status may be less wedded to traditional kinship values, although behavior and values may not always correspond. The extent of kin involvement found in this group may also typify those at the middle stages of the life cycle, when the need for assistance in such matters as baby sitting is at its height, and when parents as well as siblings are often still living. The Aged who were studied are mainly immigrants; in this group age and Eastern European background are blended and it is possible that when the clients themselves are older they may not be as kin-oriented as the present group of Aged. However, even those who postulate that the aging process entails disengagement from social roles do not extend this to relationships with kin. On the contrary, persistent close bonds toward intimate kin, particularly children, have been shown to remain intact until the end of life, although they may shift in quality with age.[2] It is also possible that this degree of kin involvement characterizes those segments of the population in an industrial society who live in large metropolitan areas where occupational advancement does not necessarily depend upon geographic moves, thus permitting a high degree of proximity to kin that does not interfere with occupational advancement.

It is impossible to say which of these various factors is the most influential determinant of the forms of kin relationship that have been observed for this group. Whatever the most significant determinants of client kin relationships may be, these findings add additional evidence to the growing body of data indicating that various kinds of interaction with kin outside the nuclear family are not as infrequent as previously assumed.

Other studies have shown that extensive interaction with kin occurs in urban industrialized societies. Elaborate kin involvement with various forms of service and assistance has also been documented for other ethnic groups within urban industrial societies, including Italians in England and the United States, French Canadians, and Negroes and Puerto Ricans in the United States. These studies have shown that kinship may play an important part in the life of a nuclear family, and that the family itself may diverge from a nuclear family model. The finding of extensive involvement with kin in the client group is, therefore, not unprecedented. In fact, client kinship may be typified by a greater degree of segregation, both ideally and actually, of the nuclear family as a functional unit than is probably true in some other instances. In any event, our findings add to growing evidence that supports the conclusion that extensive involvement with kin can occur in an urban industrial society.[3]

Interaction with kin within a network, however, is different from formal kinship organizations. Extended kin groups that have a structure persisting through time and a formal organization of authority and decision-making among families living in an urban industrial society add a new dimension to previous observations. Large groupings with a formal organization have been observed elsewhere, for example, in African cities, but the special types of organization and criteria for membership that allows the inclusion of spouses in each other's kin groups is seemingly unparalleled, although they may eventually be documented elsewhere.

It has been argued that descent groups tend to break down with industrialization; that the economic activity of descent groups is disrupted when the society offers individual members opportunities for profit and thereby undermines the economic control of the kin group. However, family circles and cousins clubs do not appear to be declining, and, in fact, many new organizations, particularly new cousins clubs, are being formed.

These organizations do not maintain their power by control over strategic economic resources. Although they are technically corporate because they hold some common property and have a structure that allows for group authority, decision-making, and continuity through time, their activities are primarily social and recreational. Thus they may not constitute an exception to the view that large kinship organizations tend to break down with changes that undermine their economic power, but they do indicate that certain kinds of large, corporate kin groups can maintain vitality in an urban industrial society.

Some models of kinship in urban industrial society have stressed the limited scope of kinship in organizing economic activity under these conditions.[4] Family businesses with kin, however, constitute a definite overlap between kinship and economic activities. Many of these businesses are fraught with problems, although some are successful. It is impossible to determine from the present data whether these problems derive specifically from their kinship organization or from the general economic position of small business. But certain problems of authority, decision-making, and organizational flexibility do appear to stem from the difficulty of disentangling kinship and business ties. The small size and general informality of many of the businesses studied may contribute to the difficulties of concomitantly maintaining "objective" contractual relations and kinship obligations.[5]

These small family-kin businesses are not the basis for organizing large-scale economic activities. They are often shortlived, so that their kinship foundation does not usually serve as a way of building up a community reputation and an organization that transcends the lifetime of the founding individuals.[6] However, their existence points to the importance of considering the role of kinship in small-scale as well as large and more powerful businesses. Although their existence is precarious and their future uncertain, these businesses do constitute an instance in which kinship is a basis for organizing economic activity in an industrial society. Moreover, these businesses are another area of vital kin contact for the families involved.

Although these data do not lead to any overall conclusions concerning the relations between kinship and society, they do add additional weight to questions about whether extensive involvement with kin is really incompatible with an urban industrial society. In light of findings on other groups one cannot conclude that the present results are unique to a client group, even though they may have special qualities related to the Eastern European Jewish traditions and the special problems of those who have sought casework help. This analysis should therefore lead to an examination of implicit assumptions about the forms of kin relationship that are most appropriate under given conditions.

Questions about the connection between forms of kinship and societal conditions have direct bearing on casework practice because changes in relationships with kin are sought in treatment. Assumptions about "healthy" or "normal" kinds of kin relationship are inevitably made. Such assumptions are necessary, but they should at least be clear, and they should be based on the best knowledge available of the range and variability of kinship forms. Even educated speculation about the probable future forms of kinship is better than unrecognized assumptions that any one form is necessarily either normal or a direct expression of the client's problems. Even when if it is recognized that differences between generations and acculturative changes contribute to the problems with which caseworkers are working and even if the caseworker directly supports or assists acculturative changes, assumptions regarding the direction in which these changes are moving still need careful examination. Although generational differences are a point of strain in the kin relationships of clients and such strains may be presumed to be part of an acculturative process, it is by no means clear that the only viable alternative mode of kinship organization toward which acculturation may be heading is that represented by previous models of the nuclear family "isolated" from its kin, or by the kinship values that typify caseworkers. Despite points of strain in kin relationships in the course of acculturation, viable forms of involvement with kin may be possible.

Questions of the connection between kinship and society also have important policy implications in areas where family organization must be taken into account, such as housing, urban renewal, poverty programs, public health planning, aftercare programs. Those concerned with social planning necessarily make assumptions about the present and future forms of family and kinship that are associated with various social conditions.[7] Knowledge that adds to or checks these assumptions is thus of concern to them.

Life-Cycle, Acculturative, and Social Changes in Kinship

An understanding of the way in which societal conditions affect kinship is also of immediate importance for casework because changes occurring in treatment take place in a moving field, not against a static background. Sources of change other than treatment, however, are sometimes not as explicit as those presumed to stem directly from the treatment process. No matter how "stuck" a client may be in a particular stage of development, no matter how "locked" in conflicted role systems, change on some level is always present; life-cycle and social changes are inescapable. When one focuses squarely on family organization, stages of change in family roles throughout the family life cycle are immediately obvious, if for no other reason, than that family composition shifts continually; the roles of parents and children who have married and moved out of the home are necessarily different from those of parents and children still in the home. Thus explicit examination of stages and processes of family development, and the various social, psychological, and cultural pressures for change should accompany consideration of therapeutic changes in family roles.

In this respect it is important to distinguish life-cycle changes from acculturative changes and from changes stemming from other sorts of social changes. Even for the more kin-oriented clients, the ideal is some degree of independent functioning of the nuclear family, and the emphasis is on the marital bond as the primary kinship bond of the adult. The transition at marriage from childhood kinship ties to those of adulthood must occur and is to some degree abrupt. Efforts to aid the transition from childhood kinship ties to those of marriage, however, should not be based on assumptions that confuse life-cycle and acculturative changes, presuming that the ultimate form of the family toward which acculturative changes are moving is that which can be derived from an extension of a model of a "mature," "independent" individual.

Changes in relationships with kin may stem from various sources. A schematic outline of some sources of change other than therapy is presented in Table 30. Changes stemming from movement from one society to another and from one social position or class level to another within a society are grouped under "acculturative" changes for purposes of schematic simplicity, although there are undoubtedly differences in the ways in which these different kinds of changes occur. The distinction between kinship changes deriving from social class mobility and those stemming from movement from one society to another clearly needs further study.

Table 30.   Some Sources of Change in Family-Kin Relationships

Life-Cycle Changes	Acculturative Changes	Social Changes
Changes resulting from shifts in the life-cycle stage of family members	*Changes stemming from movement of family members from one society to another or from one social position to another*	*Changes stemming from shifting social and economic conditions within the present society*
1. Changes in family roles with individual development	1. Changes over time in the kinship values and expectations of family members adapting to the new society or to new social positions within the society	1. Changes in kinship values and roles resulting from technological, economic, and other societal changes, e.g., new means of communication and transportation, urban expansion, suburban development, economic growth and decline, depression and war
2. Shifts of family composition with addition and departure of family members	2. Differences between family members, especially between age and generation groups, in kinship values and expectations resulting from different life experiences and different degrees of assimilation of the surrounding culture	

The changes that stem from some of these sources are fairly clear, and their recurrent forms may be predicted with reasonable certainty. The change during the course of the life cycle from the family of childhood to that of marriage is clear and reasonably predictable for most individuals. The change from an Eastern European form of kinship to a more "Americanized" form is less clear because neither the Eastern European baseline nor the Americanized form toward which acculturation is moving is entirely clear. The probable changes in kin relationships that may derive from more readily accessible communication and transportation facilities, or from movement from urban to suburban areas, or from social class mobility are at best speculative. But it is indisputable that these various sources of change can influence the same relationships that caseworkers are seeking to alter.

The caseworker will have added strategic tools if the larger social changes, of which casework is but one part, are known and if the casework process itself can be analyzed and viewed as one of the many factors inducing changes in the family's kin relationships.

THERAPEUTIC STRATEGIES

Therapeutic strategies are part of the social and cultural setting in which they exist.[8] The current concern with family diagnosis and family treatment is itself a product of particular social and cultural conditions. The emphasis on the individual as part of a family group probably reflects changes away from a period of more pronounced individualism. At the same time, the emphasis on the marital relationship as the keystone of the family, and on successful sexual and other areas of marital relations as critical determinants of parent-child relationships and the family's functioning in general, is also a cultural product. In another society the problem of being "unfilial" might be the counterpart of "immaturity" in our own professional thinking, and the goal might be to strengthen the parent-child rather than the marital bond. Thus the emphasis on the marital bond in much present-day family diagnosis and treatment is itself a reflection of one kind of kinship system. An alternative emphasis is not necessarily desirable, but further understanding of present forms of family diagnosis and treatment may be gained by viewing them in light of other kinds of kinship systems. This comparison is of immediate practical relevance in family diagnosis and treatment of diversified subcultural groups. Particularly in working with these groups in which the marital bond is not given central priority, the kinship assump-

tions of family diagnosis and treatment may need careful scrutiny
and possible modification.[9]

The Unit of Diagnosis

A central premise of this analysis has been that the unit of
diagnosis cannot effectively end with the nuclear family. The family needs must be examined in relation to other external systems.
The transactions between systems, the inputs and outputs between the family and its environment, are an essential part of understanding what goes on within the family. The argument that
an understanding of kin relationships is essential for family diagnosis rests in part on the observed fact that casework intervention
often does seek to change kin relationships.

But the reasons for understanding the quality and extent of kin
involvement apply to any family, whether or not they are deeply
involved with their kin. When these findings on the kin relationships of client families are placed in the broader framework of
environmental diagnosis of the family, the extent of interaction
with kin and the ways in which kin impinge upon the nuclear family clearly demonstrate the importance of understanding transactions between the family and other systems. This demonstration
in the kinship field should point the way to a comparable trans-
actional focus on other areas of the family's environment, such as
friendship, occupation, and schools.

It has not been possible to develop any complete diagnostic
scheme, either of the type or extent of kin involvement, or of the
connections between one area of kinship and another. However,
certain concepts that have been used throughout this analysis
should aid the caseworker in understanding a particular family.

One basic idea is that social interaction, specifically relationships with kin, may be regarded as a system that exhibits systematic regularities, reflective of the broader society, even if the system cannot be correlated with specific societal conditions in
exactly predictable detail. Another concept is that behavior toward
kin is guided by kinship values, that is, beliefs about the ways in
which individuals in particular kinship positions ought to act. Related to this concept is the idea that actions of individuals in particular kinship roles are connected to values by the reactions of

others; that is, the sanctions others exert in an attempt to influence behavior to conform to their expectations. The idea that different kinds of kinship systems stress different kinship bonds in varying degrees, and that kinship systems vary in their lateral emphasis, should serve as guides to the examination of critical dimensions along which one kinship system may vary from those of another. Finally, the notion that strain in interpersonal relationships derives not only from the personal characteristics of the individuals involved but also from the ways in which their relationships are socially structured should have immediate use for practice.

Because social work deals with interpersonal relationships, concepts about culture and social interaction must ultimately be part of the framework of its practitioners. Although present knowledge is incomplete and no consistent and clearcut conceptual scheme exists, the ultimate necessity of systematic understanding of social interaction should not be obscured. This analysis presents many complexities, perhaps more than can conveniently be grappled with in casework decision-making. Nevertheless, we believe it offers a more important statement about the kind of subtleties of human relationships that must ultimately be brought systematically into the framework of clinical practice than would a prematurely definitive scheme that leaves out many of the intricacies of social reality.

We have argued that family diagnosis must not end with the nuclear family, because the family is no more a closed equilibrium system than is an individual. The nuclear family is but one of the groups in which family members spend time and have an emotional investment; for husbands it is often second to occupational pursuits, at least in time spent. The family is emotionally intimate, and its historical duration for the individual is often greater than other groups; it is expected, in our society, to be the locus of emotional expression and emotional support for adults as well as for children. But as a determinant of individual behavior, other groups may be of equal or even greater importance than the family; the logic of family diagnosis thus applies equally well to diagnosis of the interpersonal relations of the individual in all his social encounters. A change in the behavior of an individual will be met by reaction of others, both within and outside the family, particularly when they are directly affected by the change; and their reactions will be crucial for the outcome of this change. For example, when the marital bond is strengthened by reduction of "dependency" on a parent, the parent will unquestionably react to this shift. It is true that a similar process of change may be undertaken when a parent is not actually present but is merely an internalized image; but when parents and other kin are part of a family's present life their reactions must be seen as part of the social reality, and as the source of meaningful sanctions.

Knowledge of the relationships between the family and its external environment are vital for an understanding of the individual and the family, and for an estimation of sanctions that are likely to support or contradict changes sought in treatment; this knowledge applies to kin, to occupationsl associates, to friends and other nonfamilial relationships. When embarking upon a program of change in any of these areas, it would be desirable to calculate the likely reactions to this change, both adverse and favorable.

Individual and family problems have their source outside as well as inside the individual and family. Conflicts in marital relationships may be as much a function of current interaction with parents as of internalized feelings about the marital partner. An accurate estimation of the sources of problems requires a theoretical base broad enough to scan the many influencing factors.

We have documented the morally binding quality of relationships with kin. Family members may be locked in roles with their kin that are a product of the total constellation of the family and its kinship system. Moreover, because the kinship system is itself interconnected, changes in one area may produce changes in another area, for example, reduction in interaction with kin may lessen dependency and strengthen the marital bond, but it may at the same time reduce contacts with reference groups that contribute significant models for occupational achievement.

If the interconnections between the family and its environment are not estimated, and the connections within this environment not taken into account, the outcome of change cannot be accurately anticipated. It is clear that the understanding of the family and planning for changes within it must systematically take account of the family's environment. The complexities are infinite, and the list of variables that may be relevant in a particular case are long. But systematically weighing the possible effects of the environment, is in the end less costly than embarking on changes that may be aborted by unconsidered factors in the family's environment. The logic is the same as in the argument that changes in individual treatment may not be efficient if they fail to take account of the ways in which the individual's problems are maintained by certain types of family relationships.

The relevance of the kinship system is incontrovertible. It may not be of the same importance in each family, but it is always relevant to examine what effects it actually has in a particular case. The problem of extending diagnostic thinking is relatively simple; it is essentially one of training.

The Unit of Treatment

The problem of the unit of treatment is more difficult. Those concerned with treatment of the family as a unit are constantly faced with questions about the conditions under which the entire family or various segments of the family are the most appropriate unit of treatment. When family members are interacting with each other in ways that maintain the problem for which help is sought, their interaction itself must be altered if a change is to be effective. The nuclear family or household group is relatively accessible to treatment, because it is sufficiently intimate so that the problems of one individual are seen by participants to reflect upon other members. Motivation for change as a group, or change in interpersonal relationships, is relatively common; although in actual practice husbands are still much less frequently involved in treatment than are wives. Moreover, compared with other social systems, the family does not have a highly institutionalized structure. The single family does not persist in time beyond the life cycle of its members; it does not have a formal table of organization with codified positions and job descriptions, and it is relatively small. As compared with some other social groupings, it is more accessible to treatment as a unit.

Many have pointed out that the community and the entire society are the source of individual, family, and social problems. In a broad sense the family is radically altered by large-scale social changes, possibly even more than it can be by casework intervention. Urban renewal, housing policies, technological development, and economic changes all have widespread and lasting effects on the family and its relationships with kin. In the long run intervention strategies of all sorts may be modified in relation to other social changes. The boundaries between welfare institutions and the entire strategy of existing treatment facilities are products of our present social organization that can undoubtedly be modified in beneficial directions, and will themselves be changed by changing social conditions, including changes in the kinship system.[10] But this does not necessarily alter the immediate strategies of casework therapy.

The strategies by which social units can be treated with any likelihood of influence are limited. The family is amenable to change as a unit, as may be some occupational situations; for example, casework may alter the organization of a family business. Therapists of various types have been employed in industry to assist in fostering personal adjustment to produce behavior desired for the occupational system. But given the present organization of social welfare institutions, casework most often deals with occupational problems by altering the individual, not the system. The most basic changes in individual personality and family relationships go along with the connections of the family and the occupational system: the role of husband and wife in the home, the amount of joint participation of family members, the overlap of membership groups of individuals in the family are all affected by the degree of segregation or overlap of the occupational and the family world. At present large-scale social changes in the occupational system may be beyond the scope of casework, although ultimately casework may find it necessary to become more closely allied with those concerned with implementing broader social changes.

The kinship system is intermediate between the nuclear family and the occupational system in its degree of accessibility to modification by casework intervention. Some parts of the kinship system are more amenable to change than others—its interconnections are not all equally tight. An individual may receive significant gratification and ego support from participation in a family circle or cousins club, or the organization may support ties to siblings and parents that impede independent functioning of the nuclear family. The caseworker may tackle the individual's participation in the kinship organization, but it would be extremely difficult to alter the organization itself or even the client's role in the organization through changing the organization, given present definitions of the casework role. The caseworker should be aware of the diagnostic importance of the organization and its relevance for the family members and their other areas of kin interaction. Perhaps a group of kin could even be an effective unit of group treatment. This unit would differ radically in some of the characteristics of externally impersonal relationships that pertain in group therapy as most often practiced today. But it has been shown that groups in which individuals are actually related to each other in outside life, such as husband-wife groups, can be highly effective.[11] A group of kin might be an effective unit of treatment precisely because they are interrelated, and changes in one would have actual relevance for changes in the others. But the treatment unit should not necessarily be a wide segment of the kin network wherever changes in kin relationships are desired. However, the possibility that this unit might be effective in some instances is no more far-fetched than the notion that the family rather than the individual is sometimes the appropriate unit of treatment.

The three-generation family is sometimes involved in treatment, for example, when it is a household unit. But this unit is not common at present. Parents generally are more likely to be brought in than adult siblings of the husband and wife. It may well be that changes in adult parent-child relationships can be more effectively accomplished by treatment of a three-generation family unit. But problems in the social definitions of therapy and its social and symbolic significance may make this difficult. Husbands are less readily involved in casework treatment of families than wives, in part because of social as well as therapeutic expectations that define the family's emotional problems as the sphere of the wife's activity and responsibility (not only in the sense of responsibility for "causing" problems).

Given the present social definitions and symbolic connotations of casework, clients' parents are likely to be even more difficult to bring into treatment than are husbands. Social differences have been shown to exist between caseworkers and their clients in critical areas such as kinship values. Others have shown that social differences can complicate therapeutic relationships between psychiatrists and their patients,[12] and the same applies to casework therapy, although such differences can also be used as levers for change.[13] Differences between the caseworkers and those in the clients' parental generation are likely to be even greater than those between caseworkers and clients, as indicated by the data on the Aged, who are themselves clients and thus may be less distant than the actual parents of many clients would be. Techniques can be developed for bridging gaps in values and experience, but these may be complicated if the older generation represents a way of life from which the caseworkers themselves are also moving. Greater knowledge of the subtleties of culturally influenced role expectations may assist in bridging differences with clients as well as in facilitating treatment of the three-generation unit when it is considered appropriate.

It should be clear from knowledge of kinship that even the "family" unit is not necessarily the nuclear family. Is it the household unit? Is it the nuclear family but not the entire household unit? Is it the nuclear family and a parent living in the same building or within walking distance? Is it the nuclear family and the family of a sibling with whom the husband is in business or the family of a sister with whom the wife shares many household activities, including child rearing? The most meaningful social boundary of the family is not automatically that of the nuclear family.[14] But because of cultural assumptions that the nuclear family is the normal household unit, it is often assumed that this is *the* family. Systematic questioning about the most appropriate composition of the unit of "family" treatment is always in order. Questions of this sort are not logically different from considerations about treatment of the family as a group. The notion that under some conditions it might be beneficial to treat more extended segments of the kin network sounds removed from present thinking, but is a possibility that should not be arbitrarily excluded. In any event, a thorough review of the social and cultural assumptions underlying the drawing of family boundaries for therapeutic purposes should help to avert unrecognized biases and arbitrary exclusion of factors that have a significant effect upon the nuclear family's life.

The importance for casework of kinship and other external systems in which family members currently participate does not rest alone on the feasibility of including them in the unit of treatment, any more than the importance of the family for the individual's problems rests on whether or not the family can be treated as a group. Regardless of the strategies of treatment in a particular case, an understanding of the family relationships of an individual is always essential to understanding the individual's problems. Whether kin have a great or negligible effect upon the problems of a particular family, and whether there is any possibility of treating a unit more extensive than the nuclear family, an understanding of the family's relationships with kin is always of diagnostic relevance.

Just as it may be essential in medical practice to have a broad repertoire of knowledge of systems that may possibly be significant in a particular illness, the caseworker should be helped, even at the risk of greater uncertainty, by a conceptual scheme that permits a broad coverage of a great many potentially significant factors. In any particular case, only some of these many dimensions may be of immediate concern. But unless the practitioner's framework is broad enough to encompass most of the areas that are likely to affect the family, and to require at least cursory examination and elimination in any particular instance, critical conditions may be overlooked.

The caseworker faces the challenge and responsibility of understanding, diagnosing, and treating a particular family. This research has been designed to contribute not answers to specific problems but a broad framework of concepts, which should provide a more comprehensive and effective base from which to make decisions.

NOTES TO CHAPTER 9

1. Sweetser, Dorrian Apple, "Mother-Daughter Ties Between Generations in Industrial Societies," paper read at the 34th Annual Meeting of the Eastern Sociological Society, Boston, April, 1964; also Young, Michael, and Peter Willmott, "Mothers and Daughters" in *Family and Kinship in East London*, The Free Press, Glencoe, Ill., 1957, p. 43; Dore, Ronald P., *City Life in Japan: A Study of a Tokyo Ward*, University of California Press, Berkeley and Los Angeles, 1958, p. 133.

2. Cumming, Elaine, and William E. Henry, *Growing Old: The Process of Disengagement*. Basic Books, New York, 1961, pp. 51–63. Similar findings have also been reported by others. See, for example, Sussman, Marvin B., "Family Continuity: Selective Factors Which Affect Relationships Between Families at Generational Levels," *Marriage and Family Living*, vol. 16, May, 1954, pp. 112–120.

3. For further reading references, see Bibliography.

4. Bennett, John W., and Leo A. Despres, "Kinship and Instrumental Activities: A Theoretical Inquiry," *American Anthropologist*, vol. 62, April, 1960, pp. 254–267; Parsons, Talcott, "Some Principal Characteristics of Industrial Societies" in *Structure and Process in Modern Societies*, The Free Press, Glencoe, Ill., 1959, pp. 132–168; Abegglen, James G., *The Japanese Factory*, The Free Press, Glencoe, Ill., 1958.

5. Despres, Leo A., "A Function of Bilateral Kinship Patterns in a New England Industry," *Human Organization*, vol. 17, Summer, 1958, pp. 15–22.

6. Parsons, Talcott, *op. cit.*, pp. 132–168.

7. For a discussion of certain policy implications of kinship, see Marris, Peter, *Family and Social Change in an African City: A Study of Rehousing in Lagos*, Routledge and Kegan Paul, London, 1961; also Mogey, J. M., *Family and Neighborhood: Two Studies in Oxford*, Oxford University Press, London, 1956; Townsend, Peter, *The Family Life of Old People*, The Free Press, Glencoe, Ill., 1957; Gans, Herbert J., *The Urban Villagers: Group and Class Life of Italian-Americans*, The Free Press of Glencoe, New York, 1962.

8. Wallace, Anthony F. C., "Institutionalization of Cathartic and Control Strategies in Iroquois Religious Psychotherapy," in Opler, Marvin K., *Culture and Mental Health*. Macmillan Co., New York, 1959, pp. 63–96.

9. For a description of a group in which the marital bond is de-emphasized compared with ties to kin of the same sex, in which, for example, men talk things over with brothers, and women with sisters and mothers, see Gans, Herbert J., *op. cit.*

10. For one discussion of this point, see Kahn, Alfred J., "The Social Scene and the Planning of Services for Children," *Social Work*, vol. 7, July, 1962, pp. 4–14; also see Wilensky, Harold L., and Charles N. Lebeaux, *Industrial Society and Social Welfare*, Russell Sage Foundation, New York, 1958.

11. This point has been demonstrated in the group treatment program of the Jewish Family Service. For relevant reports, see Sherman, Sanford N., "Group Counseling" in *Neurotic Interaction in Marriage*, edited by Victor W. Eisenstein, Basic Books, New York, 1956, pp. 296–301; Leichter, Elsa, "Scope and Versatility of Group Counseling in Family Casework," *The Use of Group Techniques in the Family Agency*, Family Service Association of America, 1959; Waltuck, Murray, "Group Counseling of Marital Partners by Joint Therapists," *Journal of Jewish Communal Service*, vol. 37, Winter, 1960, pp. 228–235; Leichter, Elsa, "Group Psychotherapy of Married Couples' Groups: Some Characteristic Treatment Dynamics," *International Journal of Group Psychotherapy*, vol. 12, April, 1962, pp. 154–163; Sherman, Sanford N., "The Choice of Group Therapy for Casework Clients," *Social Work Practice, 1962*, Columbia University Press, New York, 1963, pp. 174–186.

12. Hollingshead, August B., and Fredrick C. Redlich, *Social Class and Mental Illness*. John Wiley and Sons, New York, 1958.

13. Kadushin, Charles, "Social Distance Between Client and Professional," *American Journal of Sociology*, vol. 67, March, 1962, pp. 517–531.

14. For another statement of this point, see Leichter, Hope J., "Boundaries of the Family as an Empirical and Theoretical Unit" in *Exploring*

the Base for Family Therapy, edited by Nathan W. Ackerman, Frances L. Beatman, and Sanford N. Sherman. Family Service Association of America, New York, 1961, pp. 140–145.

A Note on the Process
and Application of Research
in a Practice Setting

Now that the storms of this interprofessional collaboration have subsided it is difficult to reconstruct the reasons for the intense emotion that surrounded some of them. Yet here, as in many interdisciplinary undertakings, collaboration had its trying as well as its rewarding moments. Since others are continuing efforts of this sort, it may be useful, in the spirit of the traditional epilogue, to look back at a few of the issues that arose and to consider their resolution. Basic to most of these issues is the question of how to establish a workable division of labor between professions.

Because this study was conducted in a family casework agency with a research staff comprised mainly of social scientists, collaboration between casework and social science occurred in two respects: between clinician and researcher, and between those working primarily with psychological and those with sociocultural concepts. Although the research undertaking, was jointly sponsored by Russell Sage Foundation and the Jewish Family Service, the research staff was physically located at the agency and its mem-

293

bers were therefore outside professionals within the bureaucratic organization of another profession. Moreover, the agency's case-workers were engaged in treatment with the families to be studied.

Within this context several issues about collaboration arose that we will consider briefly here: (1) who should formulate the research problem, (2) who should collect the research data, and (3) when and how the research results are to be applied to practice. More specific aspects of procedures—sampling, research instruments, and data analysis—are discussed in the Appendix.

WHO FORMULATES
THE RESEARCH PROBLEM

Issues about who is to formulate the problem often arise in collaborative research, particularly when it has a bearing on an area of practice. Those responsible for having research conducted in an agency must ultimately decide what is significant for the purposes of their organization. Executives must assume a responsibility in presenting the research undertaking to those who watch over the agency's activities. They may frequently be called upon to justify the existence of research as well as its specific content. In addition, a researcher may be seen as someone who brings to the task a set of technical skills, but the *content* of the researcher's training and interests may be largely overlooked. In this case the research staff was initially seen more as researchers than as social scientists. Under these circumstances it is not surprising that the task of formulating the research problem may not be seen as belonging to the researcher.

Yet in our experience the major responsibility for the formulation of a research problem inevitably lies with the researchers. This is true because a research problem is not fully formulated at the beginning of research.

Problem formulation is a continuing part of the research process. At each stage new information appears; new clues are discovered; new avenues suggested, explored, and either dropped or pursued further. In this case the problem on which the research finally focused was not the same as that initially proposed; it emerged from several stages of inquiry and preliminary data collection. This step-by-step reformulation of the problem is a necessary, although seldom reported, aspect of inquiry in any relatively unknown area. It requires sufficient flexibility to allow for the incorporation of new leads. Because this reformulation is continuous, it is likely that only those who are actively engaged in the research will have sufficient time to participate in its transformations. Researchers may have problems in communicating these shifts to those not involved in the research on a daily basis. Indeed, one source of inflexibility may derive from overcommitment to an early formulation of the problem because it has been presented publicly.

In this case the issue was complex because the researchers not only brought in technical research skills but also sociocultural concepts and theories about human behavior that entailed perspectives different from the psychological formulations with which the caseworkers were more familiar. If the researchers and the caseworkers had begun with more similar theoretical perspectives, some of the issues about problem formulation might have evolved differently. Yet we feel the basic question of the necessity for continuous reformulation of the problem would remain.

The significance of this continuing process of problem reformulation was not, however, clear to any of those involved in the research at the beginning. The researchers themselves sought the participation of the agency staff in the selection of the problem for study. Throughout the research process there were discussions between the researchers and the agency executives. In addition, a research committee consisting of executives, supervisors, caseworkers as well as members of the research staff met regularly in the early stages to consider what the research problem should be.

In collaboration between professions two related tendencies can frequently be observed. On the one hand, each profession is likely to be concerned with establishing and holding on to those areas that constitute its unique competence. Related to this desire to mark out areas of special jurisdiction a sort of misplaced deference may ensue, with each profession hesitating to step into those activties where an overlap of competence exists. These tendencies were evident in early attempts to formulate the research problem.

The initial assumption was that the problem was to be formulated from an agency viewpoint in terms of concern with family diagnosis and family treatment. However, in the early meetings with the research committee it proved difficult for caseworkers to formulate researchable questions, that is, questions framed so that they could be examined through the collecting of research data. Although committed to research in princple, it was difficult for the committee members to point to specific areas where their own knowledge could be enhanced through research. The researchers for their part were hesitant about formulating problems in their own terms because they wished to respect agency needs and to make use of the caseworker's special competence. Also the researchers were handicapped initially by lack of familiarity with the client population and with casework theory and practice. But it was not until the researchers themselves took the first step at problem formulation that the casework staff was able to participate effectively with the researchers by reacting to possible research problems.

A first attempt at problem formulation consisted in looking at various life-cycle changes to determine the family's ability to adapt to "normal" developmental transitions. The social science researchers conducted an initial series of interviews in which an attempt was made to examine the factors that contribute to the family's ability to make life-cycle adaptations. These initial interviews revealed the frequency and emotional intensity of contacts with kin, and it became clear that it was difficult to understand the family's adaptations to life-cycle changes without knowledge of external factors. The significance of contacts with kin was highlighted for the social scientists by theories about kinship and society. This step led to further questioning of the significance of kin for casework practice. These questions were examined from data in initial interviews and, in turn, required further data.

At this stage the agency staff entered the process of problem formulation in another way. The research staff interviewed supervisors to obtain specific hypotheses on relationships with kin and how these come up in casework treatment. At this time the research inquiry shifted from general questions of what kinds of knowledge can contribute to understanding the family as a system to specific questions about the family's relationships with kin. When questions, developed out of the researcher's own interviews with clients, were put to members of the agency staff, it proved easier for them to state hypotheses and formulate further questions, many of which proved invaluable. Thus the agency staff participated directly in the formulation of the research problem, but not simply by specifying it in advance. The major task of problem formulation was carried out by the researchers.

WHO COLLECTS RESEARCH DATA

In a casework agency, where the staff consists of highly trained interviewers, it might seem appropriate to rely on caseworkers to conduct research interviews. Yet in this instance interviewing was an area in which both the caseworkers and the researchers had special competence.

The social scientists did not hesitate to assert their claim to interviewing skills. As researchers they felt it was essential to conduct interviews themselves. This stand related in part to the process of problem formulation in a relatively new area of inquiry. Although researchers vary greatly in preferences about data collection, many find that they can work best if they have collected some of their data themselves, feeling there is no substitute for the ideas that come from first-hand contact.

Moreover, when open-ended interviews are used in the formulative stages of research, the data obtained depend on the built-in conceptual scheme of the interviewer. In early interviews in clients' homes, for example, the researchers had a chance to observe contacts with kin who telephoned or dropped in unannounced. These contacts were given special notice by the researchers, because of their familiarity with studies of kinship. Without these concepts the significance of kin would probably have gone unnoticed as it had in previous casework interviews. It would have been difficult, moreover, to translate these concepts to caseworkers because the researchers themselves were not aware of the special significance of kinship in the client population prior to initial data collection.

Yet while the interviewers were firm in asserting the importance of conducting their own interviews and their competence in doing so, the difference in the data obtained by researchers and caseworkers because of their differing conceptual schemes remained a source of underlying uneasiness for some members of the casework staff. It is easy for each profession to assume that the data collected through its particular concepts have some special order of "reality" that other data do not have. The researchers did collect much of their data through their own interviews, being convinced that they could not obtain adequate data on kinship as a form of social organization from interviews conducted with reference to psychological concepts. Although these interviews were transcribed verbatim and compared in detail with the data obtained on the same family in casework interviews, members of the agency staff continued to feel that social science interviewers were going to miss the "true" psychodynamic factors. Ultimately psychiatrists were brought in to interview some of these families in order to determine if significant data had been missed in either the social science or the casework interviews. But the psychiatric interviews did not substantially alter the picture, since the purpose of the research was to describe the social organization of relationships with kin, not the psychodynamics of the individuals involved. Moreover, the psychiatrists were interviewing as researchers specifically instructed to interview about relationships with kin; they were not engaged in treatment relationships with the families. Under these circumstances it was perhaps naive on the part of those involved to assume that the mere label of "psychiatrist" would produce some special order of data.

Questions as to who can best collect what kinds of data can be decided only with respect to the purposes of a particular investigation. The frame of reference of the interviewer will influence the material obtained in open-ended interviews in at least two ways: first, the concepts of the interviewer and the expectancies conveyed to the person being interviewed will influence the data that emerge; second, the interviewer's concepts will be applied to the data already obtained and this will influence interpretation of these data as well as the kinds of data that emerge subsequently. For research purposes this implies that interviewers should be intimately familiar with the conceptual framework that is to be examined in the research. In our case some issues that were discussed as questions of interviewing skill were actually more questions of conceptual preference. The purpose was to expand the sociocultural concepts that would be useful to casework, not to examine kinship from the standpoint of its intrapsychic meaning. For this purpose interviews by the social scientists were essential. Perhaps the goal of a future project should be to examine kinship both from an intrapsychic and from an interpersonal perspective. Interviews by caseworkers or psychiatrists would be necessary.

In any event, if a researcher works best through collecting his own data, then this preference should be honored wherever possible.

Connected with the issue of who should interview was an assumption on the part of some members of the casework staff that sociocultural data would not be emotionally meaningful. It should be clear from the interviews presented in this volume that this assumption was unwarranted. We have chosen to examine this material in terms of interpersonal rather than psychodynamic concepts, but emotional import is abundantly evident. Emotions are not the domain of psychodynamic concepts alone; such concepts are merely one way of looking at emotions.

A related assumption of the casework staff was that a treatment relationship is necessary for the revelation of significant emotions. Undoubtedly certain orders of material are revealed more easily in a therapeutic relationship than in one set up for research purposes. But in both cases the data obtained probably depend in good measure on the expectancies conveyed by the interviewer. Moreover, the needs of research for the pursuit of a particular area of inquiry may not coincide with the flow of topics that is most beneficial for a treatment relationship. The research interviews, for example, tended to contain more discussion of things that were not problems than was true of the casework interviews. Thus it may be easier to obtain many kinds of data in interviews specifically set up for research purposes than in those set up for treatment. In addition, material from the caseworkers' treatment interviews was available to the researchers, so that this issue was resolved with the decision to have special research interviews.

This decision, however, raised another concern, that of the possible effects of research interviews on the clients and on the therapeutic relationship with the caseworker. Research interviews were set up initially through a series of cautious trials. The first families to be interviewed were selected through extensive consultation with caseworkers and supervisors as to the suitability of a family for research participation. Although more cases were suggested by caseworkers than actually used, the research staff relied heavily on casework judgments in deciding which cases to include. The suggestions tended toward families of somewhat longer than average agency contact, reflecting confidence in the therapeutic relationship in these cases. The research interviews were clearly distinguished from therapeutic interviews in explanations given to families, and it proved feasible to maintain this distinction. The interview material was discussed in detail with the caseworkers and it was concluded with full confidence that the research interviews did not interfere with treatment relationships. This conclusion was so firm that at a later stage families were selected for research interviews from a random sample, in terms of research criteria. Caseworkers were asked whether they had reservations about the family's participation in the research, but in almost all instances the caseworker considered the family selected by the research staff to be suitable. Again, there were no indications that research interviews interfered with treatment.

Questionnaires were also used in collecting data directly from clients. Here also there was some consideration as to whether the questionnaires should be administered by the caseworkers, but it was decided to separate the questionnaires entirely from the treatment relationship by mailing them to clients directly from the research department. Again there were no indications that the questionnaires were detrimental to the treatment relationships.

At this juncture, after a successful demonstration of the feasibility of conducting separate research interviews with families in treatment, it is hard to imagine why the idea should initially have seemed so unusual. But at the time it was new. However, it is now clear from our experience there was nothing in the research interviews per se that was harmful. Moreover, life is not suspended during most forms of treatment; other experiences continue. If properly set up, even when conducted at the same agency where one is in treatment, research participation can simply be regarded as another experience.[1]

WHEN AND HOW RESEARCH IS APPLIED TO PRACTICE

Although a number of the findings of this research have been presented in this volume, the purpose has been to consider the ideas that emerged in the research rather than either findings or methods. This form of presentation rests on certain assumptions about the process by which research findings are applied to practice.

The Application of Concepts versus the Application of Findings

A basic assumption is that it is not the concrete findings of a particular study that have application to practice, but the concepts deriving from these findings. In any research on social relationships the results of a single investigation, whether experimental or descriptive, can never stand alone; they must add to or modify a conceptual framework.

How many of the details of a research operation should be incorporated into the conceptual framework of the practitioner? From the researcher's point of view, the evidence in a particular investigation must be made accessible to future investigators. But the clinician is probably less concerned with the details of mustering evidence than with the general conclusions that derive from the research, and some notion of the degree to which these formulations are supported. Thus it may be unnecessary for the practitioner to become acquainted with many of the details of an investigation.

Moreover, the scope of any single investigation is necessarily limited, compared with the knowledge needs of the practitioner. As a result, the necessity of rigorous specification of the area of observation in any empirical research undertaking may seem unnecessarily circumscribed to the clinician. In some respects the goal of rigorous scientific testing of concepts conflicts with the urgent clinical need for developing ways of understanding the family.

One possible contribution of research is to make predictions and test their accuracy. The researcher may say to the practitoner, "If you want to achieve A, you are likely or unlikely to achieve it by doing B." But another important contribution of the researcher is to say, "Wait a minute, perhaps you know less than you think; perhaps you are making assumptions of which you are unaware." No practitioner can be too pleased with an admonition to "wait," but the caution may alert the practitioner to find new knowledge from his practice experience. For a practitioner "tentativeness" may arouse anxiety, since he needs to believe that his knowledge is relatively complete and certain. But the tentativeness of research and the fact that it may point to areas where knowledge is uncertain, in the long run, may be more helpful to practitioners in making a more perceptive and meaningful diagnosis of the family than more simplified and complete conceptual formulations that have so-called "universal validity." A system that oversimplifies may ultimately prove more detrimental to the understanding of the family than the uncertainties required in recognizing incomplete knowledge as such.

From the casework point of view, part of the initial interest in our research related to developing typologies for use in family diagnosis. There are many levels on which contributions to diagnosis of the family may be made. The development of typologies for diagnosing family process and types of family disturbance is only one such level. A typology is, on the one hand, a scheme of classification and as such does not require empirical research. On the other hand, a typology is an implicit statement of correlation. The ability to predict the outcomes of changes in one area of family relationships requires extensive knowledge of the empirical clusterings of areas of family behavior. As the complexity of the area of family relationships under examination became apparent, the possibility of developing a classification of manageable simplicity became more remote. It is worth noting that even those who have attempted to outline the dimensions that should be examined in a family diagnosis have developed schemes of such length that they are exceedingly time-consuming and cumbersome to apply. And we have extended the problem further by pointing to factors outside the nuclear family that need to be considered. Perhaps, in fact, classification is not the most urgent goal in understanding the family for treatment purposes.

In any event, this book does not offer a complete scheme for family diagnosis, or even a complete scheme for the analysis of kin relationships. It does point to dimensions where significant variations in family relationships exist and to forms that such variations may take. It should give the caseworker increased understanding of one of the areas of relationships that ultimately should be included in any system for diagnosing the family.

Throughout the analysis we have indicated the ways in which this research is relevant to practice. We have noted, for example, that certain general concepts such as that of kinship system and values apply to examining problems in relationships with kin and more broadly to the understanding of all the social relationships with which the social worker is concerned. We have pointed to the utility of distinguishing life-cycle from acculturative changes in a family's relationships with its kin. We have noted the utility of considering the form of family-kinship organization that is likely to be compatible with various kinds of economic and ecological conditions, and the importance of examining assumptions about optimal forms of the family in light of expanding scientific investigation of kinship organization. Finally, we have pointed to the practice issues that stem from differences in kinship values and experience on the part of caseworkers and their clients. These questions have relevance for the particular population studied and others as well. The question of whether one's own concepts about family composition represent an optimum to strive for in other groups is one that arises in treatment with families of many kinds of background. It would apply, for example, with equal pertinence to family therapy with a matriarchal family in which the basic unit is one of mother-daughter rather than husband-wife. Should an attempt be made in such a case to alter the basic family organization by bringing the "husband" into treatment?

When the conceptual framework of the research is itself novel to the practitioner, one level of application consists in communicating new concepts to the practitioner, although these may not have been formulated as a result of the particular investigation but rather constitute a framework in terms of which questions were initially posed. In this research, the communication of social science concepts and assumptions was in itself one application of research ideas to practice.

Feedback to Practice During Research

It is frequently assumed that application of research occurs only after its completion. Yet significant forms of feedback may occur during the course of research itself. Indeed, new models for thinking about application of research are needed in this respect. Many segments of the agency's professional staff were involved in one way or another in research participation. Their participation included serving as members of the research committee, contributing hypotheses and ideas in interviews where the research staff asked the caseworker about clients, comparing casework and research information on the families interviewed, arranging and explaining the purposes of research interviews to clients, as well as participation through filling out the research questionnaire.

Contacts with the researchers and with the research process often served to communicate research ideas to the agency staff, as well as making a contribution to the research. When research involved fairly widespread participation in this way, the feedback in the course of research may be one of its most direct sources of impact on an agency, possibly even greater than at the final stage of reporting research where the participation of agency staff is likely to be less inclusive.

Examples of this kind of feedback included the discussions between caseworkers and researchers about the families interviewed. The information obtained through the research process, in a role different from that of therapist, with the guidance of concepts different from those usually employed by the caseworkers, often proved useful to the caseworker. Such discussions stimulated new areas of questioning about more healthy areas of family relationships and the perspective of another discipline.

Data from questionnaires also proved useful to caseworkers in giving background information on the client, sometimes being obtained more readily than it could be in casework interviews. One by-product of the research was, in fact, the institution of the routine questionnaire procedure for collecting information on all clients entering continuing treatment. In the course of research collaboration the utility of information of this sort for both casework and administrative purposes, as well as the feasibility of collecting it, came to be recognized. At one point an effort was made to develop procedures for examining the data from the routine agency questionnaire in terms of certain social science concepts. A guide for analysis, termed the "Social Sanction, Value-Orientation, and Reference Group Chart," was developed for examination of questionnaire data. Although this chart proved too complex to become a routine agency procedure, its development and the discussions of it served further to introduce ideas from the research to members of the agency staff.

Another example of feedback during research was a Social Science Seminar for agency executives, and later one for supervisors, that grew out of early discussions with executives and members of the research committee. This Seminar included joint social science casework interviews with individuals from another culture, Thailand, which facilitated examination of the relevance of cultural material and comparisons of the strategic usefulness of social science and psychological concepts.

Feedback from research to practice also occurred when staff

members filled out the questionnaire, thus becoming more familiar with the research purposes and ideas.

Feedback through direct reporting of research results to staff, at meetings of the entire staff and in various groups, was also important. It is significant that feedback of research does not have to wait until research has been completed, but is instead a constant concomitant of the research process itself.

The Task of Applying Research

A great deal has been written about who should conduct practice-based research, how problems should be formulated, who should gather data. Much less has been said about how research findings are applied to practice. Often an implicit assumption is made that "findings" will automatically be applied merely by their existence. But such an assumption overlooks the question of the channels by which findings of research are communicated to those who are to apply them in practice. Ultimately application of knowledge to practice depends on integration of that knowledge into the conceptual framework of those actually carrying out treatment. But this does not happen automatically because findings exist or even because they are presented in verbal or published form.

As we have seen, feedback of research to practice can occur during the research through various forms of collaborative contact between practitioner and researcher. Communication of ideas deriving from the research occurred in this case through contacts with a variety of segments of the agency staff. Although the researchers asserted the importance of conducting interviews themselves, the practitioners were to some degree participants in the research at a number of points, either through contributing data or ideas. In this way the more general research questions took on meaning for them. It may not often be feasible for the practitioner to conduct his own research, but when this is done it probably results in the most immediate form of application. Even when the clinician cannot actually carry out the research, the application of research findings and concepts depends on some active effort on the part of practitioners. If provision for this effort is not specifically built into the research planning, it is not likely to occur.

New knowledge is certainly not the realm of research alone. Rather, research can raise questions that will alert the practitioner to look, in his practice experience, for data from which new concepts and theories may be developed. It is our hope that the material presented in this volume will stimulate such endeavors.

NOTE TO EPILOGUE

1. For a discussion of this point and a report on the early phases of the research, see Leichter, Hope J., and Judith Lieb, "Implications of a Research Experience with Caseworkers and Clients," *Journal of Jewish Communal Service,* vol. 36, Spring, 1960, pp. 313–321.

Research Methods

A fuller discussion of the methods used in this study will be presented in separate papers. At present we will consider the highlights of the methods employed in data collection and analysis.

Various levels of data were collected using the following procedures and instruments: questionnaires, tape-recorded open-ended interviews that were later transcribed verbatim, interviews structured by interview guides, home observations, caseworkers' reports about the client and case record information, one-way screen observations of interviews, participant observation, interview genealogies, kin contact logs, and documents. The analysis combines these various levels of data. The research demonstrated that it is feasible to employ a wide variety of procedures within an agency setting.

Data were mainly obtained from three basic sources: (1) from clients about themselves, (2) from caseworkers about clients, and (3) from caseworkers about themselves. Data were also collected from clients with specific experiences relevant to special aspects of the research.

THE CLIENT QUESTIONNAIRES

Three different procedures of questionnaire administration were successfully used during the research, with three types of questionnaires.[1]

First, questionnaires were used at an early stage of the research to obtain certain demographic data needed for research planning. Caseworkers were asked to obtain the data from the client. The caseworker filled in the questionnaire—a short, single-page form.

Second, for research, administrative, and casework reasons, a questionnaire was initiated, which is now a routine agency procedure, and given to all clients in continuing treatment. This questionnaire is filled out directly by the client and returned to the caseworker or fee clerk in the district office. The caseworker gives out the questionnaire and is thus directly involved in the procedure. The questionnaire asks for certain routine background information.

A third questionnaire, for specific research purposes of obtaining information on relationships with kin, was mailed to a random sample of clients in active treatment. This questionnaire was sent with covering letters from the agency administration and from the director of research. Caseworkers were asked to indicate if there were any casework considerations that would preclude sending questionnaires, but there were virtually no reservations. These questionnaires were mailed from the Research Department and returned by mail from the clients directly to the Department; thus the caseworker and the casework process were not involved.

For the research questionnaire, a random sample was selected from the clients of the agency with intact families, that is, where both husband and wife lived in the same household, and where at least one of the marital pair was Jewish. Because the agency provided family casework service, the families in the sample constitute the most typical portion of the agency's caseload. The sample consisted of 298 families selected from 1,226 such families who were on the agency lists at that time, November, 1960. (See Chapter 2 for the sociocultural characteristics of this sample.) Comparisons with random samples of the agency's families drawn for other purposes indicate that this research sample was similar to other samples in the background characteristics of its families.

Questionnaires were also sent to an additional group of clients from the agency's special Service to the Aged, in order to make possible comparisons with a group at a later stage of the life cycle. At the time there were only 128 cases in this Service, and of those, only 55 were intact marriages. Questionnaires were therefore sent to all of these intact families, because a further sample would have made the number of cases too small.

Each family received two questionnaires, one for the husband and one for the wife. The husband's form and the wife's form were modified versions of the same questionnaire. It was deemed feasible to send questionnaires to both husbands and wives, because the family was regarded as the client for agency purposes. The differences between the forms for husbands and wives were designed to avoid duplication of data where possible. These modifications will be discussed further below.

The questionnaires were returned by one or both individuals in 210 families. In 25 cases the wives returned the forms but the husbands did not; the total number of individuals returning the questionnaires was therefore 395.

In the Service to the Aged, questionnaires were returned by both individuals in 28 families, that is, by 56 individuals. The total returns from both the regular clients and the Service to the Aged were 238 client families, or 451 individuals. Therefore, 67 per cent of the families to whom questionnaires were sent returned them.

A special survey of reactions to these questionnaires was carried out by a member of the research staff through interviews with caseworkers about the clients in this sample. In general, the proportion of returns was reasonably high, comparing favorably with results under other circumstances. Findings indicated that those who returned the questionnaires tended to have characteristics that would indicate somewhat more positive reactions toward, and more involvement with, the agency than those who did not return them. Thus positive experience in treatment may be an important motivation in research participation. This conclusion was also confirmed through research contact with clients in the course of follow-up letters and telephone calls to those who did not return the questionnaires at first; in a few cases clients indicated that they had not returned the questionnaires because of negative reactions to their agency contact.

It is conceivable that the less positive attitudes of those clients who did not return the questionnaires stem in part from cultural differences between themselves and their caseworkers. If this is true and if differences in kin relationships exist between those who did and those who did not return the questionnaires, these could well be in the direction of even greater kin involvement on the part of those who did not return the questionnaires. There do not seem to be equally compelling reasons for presuming that those who did not return the questionnaires would be less kin-oriented than those who did. Thus it does not seem likely that the picture of kin involvement of clients has been overstated as a result of biases introduced through questionnaire returns.

Items for the questionnaires were developed initially from material collected in open-ended interviews with nine client families. These families were selected through discussion with caseworkers. The items were then pretested on 13 families who were administered the questionnaires in interviews. These families were selected on the basis of data obtained in interviews with caseworkers.

The questionnaires provided two levels of data: responses to close-ended and to open-ended questions. Not all clients answered all items completely or clearly, so that the number of responses for some items may be fewer than the number of questionnaires returned. However, the number of "no answers" did not vary from one item to another in ways that would suggest systematic bias.

CLIENT INTERVIEWS

Data on the kin relationships of client families were also collected through intensive interviews with 22 families during pilot and later interviews. A total of 174 interviews, all of one hour or longer, were conducted with these families. The interviews were conducted by members of the research staff.

Explanations about the request for research participation were initially given to these families by their caseworkers, who emphasized that they would be making a contribution to the agency and its understanding of the family by their participation. The research interviews were clearly distinguished from therapeutic interviews by both the caseworkers who introduced the researchers and by the researchers themselves in their explanations to the families. It proved feasible to maintain this distinction of research and treatment roles with the family.

Families were interviewed and observed in their homes. These interviews were tape-recorded and transcribed verbatim and the transcript distributed to the caseworker treating the family, to members of the research staff, and to agency executives. In this way the caseworker thus could know what had occurred in the research interview. Data were obtained in each case from the caseworker when the caseworker and the researcher compared information on the family. The researcher also had access to the case record, but it generally proved more profitable to discuss the family with the caseworker than to read the record.

Caseworkers often had information relevant to the research that was not recorded in the case record.

In addition, a total of 18 psychiatric interviews were conducted with 10 of these interview families. With the client's permission the psychiatric interviews were observed by the research staff through a one-way screen, making it possible to compare the data obtained by interviews with varying approaches. Interviews were also conducted with families having the special experience of being in business with kin or being members of family circles and cousins clubs. Twenty-one families were interviewed about family-kin businesses. Data from interviews and observations were obtained on 25 family circles and cousins clubs.

These interviews provided extensive data on several levels: (1) tape-recorded statements of clients about their kin interaction, (2) observations of clients in their home and in some cases with kin present in the home, (3) clients' written records of their kin contacts recorded in the kin contact logs, and (4) genealogies.

Families were selected for the first pilot interviews in terms of suggestions made by caseworkers about the cases that would be suitable for research interviews. These families tended to have been in treatment somewhat longer than average. At a later point, after it had been demonstrated that research interviews did not interfere with treatment relationships, families were selected for interviews primarily in terms of research criteria. The families chosen for interviews were selected so as to obtain as many varied examples as possible of kinds of involvement with kin. Statistical analysis was done from questionnaires, not from interviews. The interviews were used to add qualitative depth to the questionnaire findings, and initially to formulate items for the questionnaires so that sampling questions were not critical for the interviews.

ANALYSIS OF DATA ON KIN RELATIONSHIPS

The analysis is primarily descriptive and is based on both interview and questionnaire data since different issues arose in various portions of the analysis. Questions about specific areas of data are considered here in the order presented in the text to enable easy reference. Comparisons between groups and tests of statistical significance were employed only at special points in the analysis.

Kinship Values

Data on kinship values were derived from interviews and from a set
of mainly normative statements in the questionnaires called: "Opinions
About Family Life." Clients were asked to respond to these statements
in one of five ways: "strongly agree," "agree," "no opinion," "disagree,"
"strongly disagree." For convenience of analysis, answers of "strongly
agree" and "agree" were combined, as were "strongly disagree" and
"disagree," leaving three categories.

Analysis of the values items in the questionnaires was based on the
frequency of the various categories of response taken in conjunction
with explanations of the meaning of responses to these items given in
interviews, and client reports in interviews of how kin acted in various
situations. No inter-item correlations were made on the consistency of
response within the values items. Rather the analysis was based on the
face meaning of the item in terms of certain theoretically defined groupings, for example, marriage systems, obligations to interact with kin. As
will be discussed below, client responses to the values items were compared with those of caseworkers. No attempts were made to correlate
the values responses of particular clients with their behavior in the area
to which the values items referred because the behavioral data were not
always exactly comparable to the values items.

Interpretation of the significance of values responses is complex because of the multiplicity of levels of values. Clues are needed about the
reasoning that goes into agreement or disagreement, as well as the level
of verbalization or action implied in the responses. A particular response may be given, for example, because the client believes this is the
way things should be and lives in accordance with this belief, or because opposite experience has strengthened the belief that things should
be different. The availability of extensive interview data on the values
items, however, helped to clarify the probable significance of responses
in questionnaires.

The Extensiveness of Kin Ties

Data used to examine the extensiveness of kin ties were collected
through standard anthropological genealogical techniques in interviews
and also through the questionnaires. Some genealogy was collected
from all of the 22 families interviewed. One such genealogy was included in the presentation to indicate the amount of knowledge of kin

that is possible. However, it became evident during interviews that once a basic genealogy had been mapped out, further probing, for example, by questioning about the kin present at specific events, would almost always add kin not initially included in the genealogy. The significance of this flexibility of the boundaries of the kin network has been considered in Chapter 4. From the standpoint of methods, this flexibility meant that any estimate based on even a fairly full initial genealogy was likely to be incomplete. This pattern became apparent only after many of the first series of interviews had been completed. Thus in counting the number of kin, data were used only from those genealogies in which some attempt had been made to "probe for limits," primarily in the second series of interviews.

The collection of genealogical data in interviews, even when no attempt was made to probe for limits, proved so time-consuming that it was decided to collect certain genealogical data from the questionnaires. Although the collection of genealogies in interviews is standard anthropological technique, collecting genealogical data through questionnaires constituted an innovation and therefore it was necessary to devise special procedures. The categories of kin present vary enormously from one family to another, depending, for example, on the number of siblings of parents and whether there have been divorces and remarriages. Thus it is impossible to include all theoretically possible categories of kin in a questionnaire. The questionnaire results represent what may be considered a skeleton genealogy and inevitably underestimate the number of kin in a family. However, the inclusion of the same categories for each family made it possible to estimate network size in a way that is consistent from one family to the next with more families than could be interviewed, thus extending the conclusions from interviews to a larger number of families.

Proximity and Communication

To obtain data on geographic proximity of kin required drawing boundaries of the household and of geographic areas that are meaningful for social interaction. The boundaries were difficult to draw for several reasons: physical boundaries of an apartment or house may not correspond to the boundaries that define the social unit of many household activities such as cooking and shopping; the perception of what is within walking distance differs from person to person, depending, for example, on age; the definition of the New York City area may not correspond to its actual geographic or political boundaries. In fact, it appears that one of the most meaningful definitions of New York City boundaries is the area of local telephone calls. Definitions of boundaries were thus left to be interpreted by the respondent in open-ended questions.

The problems of coding write-in information on kin proved great here as elsewhere in the questionnaires, particularly because nonspecific categories such as "my brother's family" or "my cousins" were often given, resulting in what is unquestionably an underestimation of the number of kin in geographic proximity.

To avoid duplication, data on the kin living in proximity were obtained only from the wife, but on the basis of interview findings, it does not seem likely that the husband would have reported these particular data differently.

Most of the client families had a high proportion of their kin living in the New York City area, so that only limited data were obtained on communication by mail because other forms were more important, especially telephoning and visiting.

A number of interview families were asked to keep Kin Contact Logs or records of who telephoned or visited whom in a one-week period. (See example in Chapter 4.) These data provided a detailed, ongoing record of certain kinds of kin contact. A record of this sort gives data that come closer to those obtainable in first-hand observations over a period of time than those that can be obtained in after-the-fact interview reports, thus offering an additional level of data on kin contacts.

Assistance and Reciprocity

Interviews often provided the opportunity to observe the importance of kin assistance and reciprocity, for example, when kin dropped in during an interview to bring something to the family, or when they telephoned for information or advice, or to make arrangements connected with giving assistance. Data from the questionnaires provided information on the frequency with which specific kinds of assistance were given to or received from kin. Some items included checklists to indicate the relative frequency with which clients received assistance from kin, friends, and institutional sources such as hired help, employment agencies, banks, social workers.

Kin Groups and Assemblages

In the analysis of ad hoc kin assemblages, family-kin businesses, and family circles and cousins clubs, the unit of analysis was not the nuclear family but the kin group. Here the focus was on the composition and function of the group or organization itself. Thus although certain data were obtained from clients, they refer to organizations that are not made up entirely of client families. Their existence and the kin relationships that they structure are not determined alone by client families and thus cannot be seen merely as reflecting the problems of a client group. In this portion of the analysis, therefore, the data from the regular case-load were combined with those from the Aged.

Data on kin gatherings were obtained in interviews where they were brought up by clients as important kin events, for example, weddings and bar mitzvahs. Data from the questionnaires on ad hoc kin assemblages were obtained for only one such gathering, the previous Thanksgiving. These data were obtained from the wife. Religious holidays, such as Passover, were not selected because it was felt that their celebration or noncelebration might depend more on religious orientations than on relationships with kin. A gathering presumed to be relatively small was selected to avoid burdening clients with writing a long list of kin in questionnaires that were already long.

For purposes of this study, family-kin businesses were defined as those where kin are partners and those where one kin is employed by another. On the basis of data from the interviews and the research questionnaire a number of families having family-kin businesses were identified. Eleven of these families were then selected to be interviewed specifically on their family-kin business. They were interviewed about a variety of types of business experience from which to formulate hypotheses about family-kin businesses and kin relationships, in particular, the ways in which joint business activity influences kin ties and the influence of family-kin business upon the nuclear family, as well as the effects of kinship on the functioning of the business. Data from the questionnaires on family-kin businesses were obtained only from husbands although interview data were obtained from both spouses wherever possible.

Data about the existence of family circles and cousins clubs in the family's kin network and whether the family participated in such groups were obtained in the questionnaires.

Detailed data on 25 of these kin groups, including genealogies and documents such as constitutions, minutes of meetings, family histories, and financial records were obtained from a series of special interviews and observations.

Kin Conflicts and Kinship Structure

Data on kinship bonds were derived from responses of the sample families to the questionnaires. Several questions of sampling arose in analyzing these data. In a few instances data were derived from check-lists of kin categories, but most of the data were derived from lists of kin provided by the respondents. Thus the selection of kin was not biased by a prior choice of categories, except where choices among kin who had at some time been in the same nuclear family were analyzed; and here the theoretical basis for looking at choices within these categories is clear.

The issue of sampling of activities is more crucial. The areas included in the questionnaires were based on preliminary interviews. It is possible, however, that kinship bonds might be different if other areas of activity had been analyzed. If a bias does exist, it can be taken into account by future researchers because the activities are specified.

Two open-ended questions on conflicts with and about kin were included in the questionnaires. These two questions were analyzed as one. The unit of analysis was the conflict situation as described by the clients. The kin categories mentioned in these descriptions of conflict situations were analyzed. As indicated by the quoted material in the text, the answers to these open-ended questions were often quite full. The analysis was enlightened by interviews where conflicts were often described in considerable detail.

CASEWORK INTERVENTION IN RELATIONSHIPS WITH KIN

Data on the ways in which relations with kin come up and are dealt with in casework treatment were obtained from two sets of interviews conducted with various agency personnel. All supervisors and heads of district offices, a total of 19 individuals, were asked to give their impressions of the types of relationships with kin, and particularly the problems in these relationships, that are typical of the client population.

They were asked how these problems come up in casework treatment and how they are dealt with. Their hypotheses were used to formulate questions for caseworkers.

Caseworkers were asked about specific cases, not the agency caseload generally. After giving some background information on the family, the caseworker was asked to discuss the kinship relations of that family, its problems in relations with kin, and the solutions that the caseworker had either attempted to bring about or saw as goals. An interview guide was used for the caseworker interviews.

A random sample of 200 cases from the four district offices was selected from those cases in the agency statistical files. Later, 33 cases from the Special Service to the Aged, the entire population of clients in this Service at the time, were added.

A total of 79 caseworkers were interviewed, each discussing from one to six cases, depending on the number of cases that fell into the caseworker's caseload. From the regular sample of 200, it was possible to obtain information on 178. Information on the remaining 22 cases could not be obtained for a variety of reasons related mainly to turnover of either clients or staff. Some information was obtained on all the cases in the Service to the Aged on the records at the time.

Some data on intervention were also collected from responses to the research questionnaire items on agency contacts and from other interviews with clients, although these data were not specifically sought in interviews with clients.

CASEWORKER-CLIENT COMPARISONS

Data for the comparisons of the kinship values and experience of caseworkers and clients were obtained from a modified version of the client questionnaires sent to caseworkers. The modifications were designed to take into account the single status of many caseworkers. Some specific items on professional training and experience were added to the caseworkers' form, and certain questions on their agency contacts were omitted as appropriate only to clients. In other respects, the basic questions were the same for caseworkers and clients.

These questionnaires, which were confidential, were also administered to members of the agency professional staff. It was considered important that the questionnaire not be taken as an administrative inquiry into their personal lives, and that it not be connected with the administrative or supervisory process. This was ensured by having the questionnaire returned by the caseworker directly to the research department; 123 individuals, or 99 per cent returned it. This high return can be taken as an indication that confidentiality was successfully ensured, as well as of willingness to devote time to the research participation. Interest in the research was also indicated by members of the agency board who volunteered to participate through filling out a comparable questionnaire.

Tests of statistical difference were used in analyzing the comparisons between the values responses of caseworkers and clients because the forms of the answers were comparable. Chi square (X^2) was used to test the statistical significance of the differences between caseworkers and clients. Differences, among the clients in the Service to the Aged, the regular clients, and the caseworkers were not tested for statistical significance because there were too few cases in the Service to the Aged to make such tests appropriate. Analysis of the Aged data rests on the consistency of difference from one area to another, rather than on the statistical significance of any one difference.[2] No specific tests of the reliability of the Values Form were made because the analysis rests on data from interviews, as well as from questionnaires.

Caseworkers had a higher proportion of no opinions than clients on 19 items, but on 15 items the clients had a higher proportion of no opinions than the caseworkers; on one item they were equal. Out of the 35 items 26 differences were significant at the 0.001 level, four items were significant at the 0.01 level, two at the 0.05 level; and three were not significant. Therefore, the Values Form had tapped values where caseworkers and clients were to a considerable degree different. The analysis was based on comparisons of specific items. No intercorrelation of items was done. Instead, the items were arranged and analyzed in terms of their face value, and the logical relation of the content to specific dimensions of the kinship system. Five items were omitted from this portion of the analysis on the ground of face content, mainly because the content did not, upon reflection, fit into the specific questions about kinship with which the analysis dealt. Some of these items deal with relationships within the nuclear family, related to kinship, but not directly at issue, for example, "A *father should be the strongest authority in the home.*" The omission from the analysis was because of logical content, not statistical significance; on all of the five omitted items, the differences between caseworkers and clients were significant at the 0.001 level. The value differences between caseworkers and clients transcend the specific topics of kin relationships that are the present concern.

In most items where significant differences between caseworkers and clients were found the Aged also differed from the caseworkers, even more than the other clients. As already indicated, tests of significance were not employed for the data from the Aged because of the small size of the sample. The significance tests refer throughout to the differences between caseworkers and clients. But the direction of the differences among caseworkers, clients, and Aged is consistent for a high proportion of the items. Conclusions based on comparisons with the Aged therefore rest on consistency of differences rather than their statistical significance.

At other points in comparing experiences with kin such statistical comparisons could not be made because the data were not always comparable, particularly for comparisons between single caseworkers and married clients. An attempt was made to determine whether differences between caseworkers and clients derived from factors in the caseworkers' sociocultural background, such as age, sex, marital status, or position within the agency. Although no consistent differences appeared among the caseworkers on any of these dimensions, the size of the sample and the small number of individuals in certain positions made it impractical to pursue this analysis in detail.

Value differences between caseworkers and clients did not appear to derive entirely from the greater youth of caseworkers or from their more frequent single status. The analysis does assume, however, that although it may not be possible to determine the source of these differences in detail, whatever their source, they have consequences for the therapeutic relationship.

NOTES TO APPENDIX

1. Copies of the questionnaires may be obtained by writing to the Jewish Family Service, 33 West 60th Street, New York, N.Y. 10023. No detailed discussion of its contents is given here.

2. For a discussion of the chi square formula employed, as well as a general discussion of the use of the chi square, see McNemar, Quinn, *Psychological Statistics*, John Wiley and Sons, New York, 1949, pp. 212–242.

Selected Bibliography

This bibliography is intended as a guide for the reader interested in learning more about the specific topics discussed in the book and about the general background of current interests in social work research. The first section includes works on the relationships between the social sciences and social work, a subject central to the theme of this book. The second section includes works that give more background on the culture and traditions of the American Jews than was possible to describe in the text. The third section lists studies of the effects of urbanization and industrialization on kinship patterns, including both comparative works and works on specific cultures. Publications that have developed from the work of the personnel of the Jewish Family Service in the field of family diagnosis and treatment are listed in the fourth section. The final section includes publications and papers resulting from the authors' and their associates' work on the project.

Except in the last section, no attempt has been made to include all the relevant material, for each section has a sizable literature in its own right. In cases where a work might be relevant to more than one section, it has been included only in the most appropriate section. Further works may be found in bibliographies in some of the books cited, and the interested reader is urged to follow the current periodical literature for more material on these subjects.

A. SOCIAL SCIENCE AND SOCIAL WORK

ANGELL, ROBERT C., "A Research Basis for Welfare Practice," *Social Work Journal*, vol. 35, 1954, pp. 145–148, 169–171.

BOEHM, WERNER W., "Social Work and the Social Sciences," *Journal of Psychiatric Social Work,* vol. 21, 1951, pp. 4–8.

BOEHM, WERNER W., "Social Work and the Social Sciences," *Mississippi Quarterly,* vol. 9, 1956, pp. 43–55.

BOEHM, WERNER W., AND OTHERS, *Objectives of the Social Work Curriculum of the Future,* vol. 1 of the Social Work Curriculum Study, and *The Social Casework Method in Social Work Education,* vol. 10 of the Social Work Curriculum Study. Council on Social Work Education, New York, 1959.

BUTLER, RUTH M., *An Orientation to Knowledge of Human Growth and Behavior in Social Work Education,* vol. 6 of the Social Work Curriculum Study. Council on Social Work Education, New York, 1959.

COTTRELL, LEONARD S., JR., "The Analysis of Situational Fields in Social Psychology," *American Sociological Review,* vol. 7, 1942, pp. 370–382.

COUNCIL ON SOCIAL WORK EDUCATION, *Sociocultural Elements in Casework: A Case Book of Seven Ethnic Studies.* The Council, New York, 1953.

COYLE, GRACE L., "New Insights Available to the Social Worker from the Social Sciences," *Social Science Review,* vol. 26, 1952, pp. 289–304.

  Social Science in the Professional Education of Social Workers. Council on Social Work Education, New York, 1958.

  "Concepts Relevant to Helping the Family as a Group," *Social Casework,* vol. 43, 1962, pp. 347–354.

DAVIES, STANLEY P., "The Relation of Social Science to Social Welfare," *Social Work Journal,* vol. 31, 1950, pp. 20–26, 32.

EATON, JOSEPH W., "Whence and Whither Social Work? A Sociological Analysis," *Social Work,* vol. 1, 1956, pp. 11–26.

FOSTER, ALICE O., "The Use of Social Science Concepts in the Diagnostic Process," *Social Casework,* vol. 44, 1963, pp. 385–388.

FRENCH, DAVID G., "The Utilization of the Social Sciences in Solving Welfare Problems" in *Proceedings of Symposium—Social Work Practice in the Field of Tuberculosis,* edited by Eleanor E. Cockerill. University of Pittsburgh School of Social Work, Pittsburgh, 1954, pp. 15–30.

GREENWOOD, ERNEST, *Toward a Sociology of Social Work.* Welfare Council of Metropolitan Los Angeles, Los Angeles, 1953.

  "Social Science and Social Work: A Theory of Their Relationship," *Social Service Review,* vol. 29, 1955, pp. 20–33.

"Social Work Research: A Decade of Reappraisal," *Social Service Review,* vol. 31, 1957, pp. 311–320.

HERZOG, ELIZABETH C., "What Social Casework Wants of Social Science Research," *American Sociological Review,* vol. 16, 1951, pp. 68–73.

HILLMAN, ARTHUR, *Sociology and Social Work.* Public Affairs Press, Washington, 1956.

HOFFMAN, ISAAC L., "Research, Social Work and Scholarship," *Social Service Review,* vol. 30, 1956, pp. 20–32.

HOLLIS, FLORENCE, "The Implications of the Curriculum Study for Social Casework," *Journal of Jewish Communal Service,* vol. 37, 1960, pp. 135–142.

KADUSHIN, ALFRED, "The Knowledge Base of Social Work" in *Issues in American Social Work,* edited by Alfred J. Kahn. Columbia University Press, New York, 1959, pp. 39–79.

KAHN, ALFRED J., "The Nature of Social Work Knowledge" in *New Directions in Social Work,* edited by Cora Kasius. Harper and Bros., New York, 1954, pp. 194–214.

"The Function of Social Work in the Modern World" in *Issues in American Social Work,* edited by Alfred J. Kahn. Columbia University Press, New York, 1959, pp. 3–38.

"Social Science and the Conceptual Framework for Community Organization Research" in *Social Science Theory and Social Work Research,* edited by Leonard S. Kogan. National Association of Social Workers, New York, 1960, pp. 64–79.

KLEIN, PHILIP, "Mary Richmond's Formulation of a New Science" in *Methods in Social Science: A Case Book,* edited by Stuart A. Rice. University of Chicago Press, Chicago, 1931, pp. 95–106.

KOGAN, LEONARD S., "Discussion: The Relationships Among Social Work Practice, Social Work Research, and the Social Sciences" in *Social Science Theory and Social Work Research,* edited by Leonard S. Kogan. National Association of Social Workers, New York, 1960, pp. 135–139.

LIPPITT, RONALD, "Applying New Knowledge About Group Behavior" in *Selected Papers in Group Work and Community Organization.* Presented at the 78th Annual Meeting of the National Conference of Social Work. Health Publications Institute, Raleigh, N.C., 1951, pp. 7–17.

MAAS, HENRY S., "Collaboration Between Social Work and the Social Sciences," *Social Work Journal,* vol. 31, 1950, pp. 104–109.

"Use of Behavioral Sciences in Social Work Education," *Social Work*, vol. 3, 1958, pp. 62–69.

MACDONALD, MARY E., "Social Work Research: A Perspective" in *Social Work Research*, edited by Norman A. Polansky. University of Chicago Press, Chicago, 1960, pp. 1–23.

MAYER, JOHN E., AND AARON ROSENBLATT, "The Client's Social Context: Its Effect on Continuance in Treatment," *Social Casework*, vol. 45, 1964, pp. 511–518.

MEYER, CAROL H., "Quest for a Broader Base for Family Diagnosis," *Social Casework*, vol. 40, 1959, pp. 370–376.

MEYER, HENRY J., JR., *Sociology and the Field of Social Work*. Russell Sage Foundation, New York, in preparation.

OLDS, VICTORIA, "Role Theory and Casework: A Review of the Literature," *Social Casework*, vol. 43, 1962, pp. 3–8.

PERLMAN, HELEN H., *Social Casework: A Problem-Solving Process*. University of Chicago Press, Chicago, 1957.

A review of *The Social Casework Method in Social Work Education* by Werner W. Boehm in "Goals of Social Work Education: Reviews of the Social Work Curriculum Study," *Social Service Review*, vol. 33, 1959, pp. 423–428.

"Intake and Some Role Considerations," *Social Casework*, vol. 41, 1960, pp. 171–177.

POLLAK, OTTO, *Integrating Sociological and Psychoanalytic Concepts*. Russell Sage Foundation, New York, 1956.

POLLAK, OTTO, AND ASSOCIATES, *Social Science and Psychotherapy for Children*. Russell Sage Foundation, New York, 1952.

RICHMOND, MARY E., *Social Diagnosis*. Russell Sage Foundation, New York, 1917. Paperback ed., The Free Press, New York, 1965.

ROSENBLATT, AARON, "The Application of Role Concepts to the Intake Process," *Social Casework*, vol. 43, 1962, pp. 8–14.

SCHROEDER, DOROTHY, "Integrating Social Science Theory Through Case Discussion," *Social Casework*, vol. 44, 1963, pp. 379–384.

SHERMAN, SANFORD N., "The Influence of Social Science on Casework Practice," *Journal of Jewish Communal Service*, vol. 41, 1964, pp. 55–59.

SIPORIN, MAX, "The Concept of Social Types in Casework Theory and Practice," *Social Casework*, vol. 41, 1960, pp. 234–242.

STEIN, HERMAN D., "Social Science in Social Work Practice and Education," *Social Casework*, vol. 36, 1955, pp. 147–155.

STEIN, HERMAN D., AND RICHARD A. CLOWARD, *Social Perspectives on Behavior*. The Free Press, Glencoe, Ill., 1958.

TEICHER, MORTON I., "The Concept of Culture," *Social Casework*, vol. 39, 1958, pp. 450–454.

TOWLE, CHARLOTTE, *Some Reflections on Social Work Education*. Family Welfare Association, London, England, 1956.

TREUDLY, MARY B., "The Concept of Role in Social Work," *American Sociological Review*, vol. 9, 1944, pp. 665–670.

UNESCO, *The Contribution of Social Sciences in Social Work Training*. United Nations, Paris, 1961.

WEISS, VIOLA W., "An Application of Social Science Concepts in Family Diagnosis," *Social Casework*, vol. 40, 1959, pp. 377–380.

WELFARE COUNCIL OF METROPOLITAN LOS ANGELES, RESEARCH DEPARTMENT, *Social Sciences and Social Work*, Special Report Number 28. The Council, Los Angeles, 1951.

Toward a Sociology of Social Work, Special Report Number 37. The Council, Los Angeles, 1953.

Building Social Work Theory with Social Science Tools, Special Report Number 41. The Council, Los Angeles, 1954.

WERBLE, BEATRICE, "The Implications of Role Theory for Casework Research" in *Social Science Theory and Social Work Research*, edited by Leonard S. Kogan. National Association of Social Workers, New York, 1960, pp. 28–31.

WILSON, GERTRUDE, AND GLADYS RYLAND, "Social Classes: Implications for Social Group Work" in *Social Welfare Forum*. Columbia University Press, New York, 1954, pp. 168–186.

YOUNG, DONALD, "Sociology and the Practicing Professions," *American Sociological Review*, vol. 20, 1955, pp. 641–648.

YOUNG, KIMBALL, "Social Psychology and Social Casework," *American Sociological Review*, vol. 16, 1951, pp. 54–61.

B. SOCIAL PATTERNS OF AMERICAN JEWS

ARONSON, SIDNEY H., "Conspicuous Success: The Failure of the Traditional Jewish Family in America," *Adult Jewish Leadership*, vol. 6, 1960, pp. 3–9.

BARON, SALO, *A Social and Religious History of the Jews*. Columbia University Press, New York, vols. 1–8, 1952–1965.

BRESSLER, MARVIN, "Selected Family Patterns in W. I. Thomas' Unfinished Study of the *Bintl Brief*," *American Sociological Review*, vol. 17, 1952, pp. 563–571.

FINKELSTEIN, LOUIS, editor, *The Jews: Their History, Culture, and Religion.* Jewish Publication Society of America, Philadelphia, 1949.

GANS, HERBERT J., "Progress of a Suburban Jewish Community," *Commentary,* vol. 23, 1957, pp. 113–122.

GLAZER, NATHAN, "What Sociology Knows About American Jews," *Commentary,* vol. 9, 1950, pp. 275–284.

GORDON, ALBERT I., *Jews in Transition.* University of Minnesota Press, Minneapolis, 1949.

HANDLIN, OSCAR, *Adventure in Freedom: Three Hundred Years of Jewish Life in America.* McGraw-Hill Book Co., New York, 1954.

HURVITZ, NATHAN, "Sources of Middle-Class Values of American Jews," *Social Forces,* vol. 37, 1958, pp. 117–123.

JOFFE, NATALIE F., "Non-Reciprocity Among East European Jews" in *The Study of Culture at a Distance,* edited by Margaret Mead and Rhoda Métraux. University of Chicago Press, Chicago, 1953, pp. 386–389.

The American Jewish Family: A Study. National Council of Jewish Women, New York, 1954.

KAPLAN, BENJAMIN, *The Eternal Stranger: A Study of Jewish Life in the Small Community.* Bookman Associates, New York, 1957.

KAPLAN, MILTON, "Private Enterprise in the Bronx" in *Commentary on the American Scene: Portraits of Jewish Life in America,* edited by Elliot E. Cohen. Alfred A. Knopf, Inc., New York, 1953, pp. 243–254.

KRAMER, JUDITH E., AND SEYMOUR LEVENTMAN, *Children of the Gilded Ghetto.* Yale University Press, New Haven, 1961.

LANDES, RUTH, AND MARK ZBOROWSKI, "Hypotheses Concerning the Eastern European Jewish Family," *Psychiatry,* vol. 13, 1950, pp. 447–464.

MANDELBAUM, D. G., *Change and Continuity in Jewish Life.* Oscar Hillel Plotkin Library, Glencoe, Ill., 1955.

MAYER, JOHN E., *Jewish-Gentile Courtships.* The Free Press of Glencoe, New York, 1961.

POLL, SOLOMON, *The Hasidic Community of Williamsburg.* The Free Press of Glencoe, New York, 1962.

SANUA, VICTOR D., "Differences in Personality Adjustment Among Different Generations of American Jews and Non-Jews" in *Culture and Mental Health,* edited by Marvin K. Opler. Macmillan Co., New York, 1959, pp. 443–466.

SKLARE, MARSHALL, editor, *The Jews: Social Patterns of an American*

Group. The Free Press, Glencoe, Ill., 1958.

SNYDER, CHARLES R., *Alcohol and the Jews.* The Free Press, Glencoe, Ill., 1958.

"Culture and Jewish Sobriety: The Ingroup-Outgroup Factors" in *Society, Culture and Drinking Patterns,* edited by David J. Pittman and Charles R. Snyder. John Wiley and Sons, New York, 1962, pp. 188–225.

SOMBART, WERNER, *The Jews and Modern Capitalism.* The Free Press, Glencoe, Ill., 1951.

WAGLEY, CHARLES, AND MARVIN HARRIS, *Minorities in the New World.* Columbia University Press, New York, 1958.

WARNER, W. LLOYD, AND LEO SROLE, *The Social Systems of American Ethnic Groups.* Yale University Press, New Haven, 1945.

WIRTH, LOUIS, *The Ghetto.* University of Chicago Press, Chicago, 1928.

WOLFENSTEIN, MARTHA, "Two Types of Jewish Mothers" in *Childhood in Contemporary Cultures,* edited by Margaret Mead and Martha Wolfenstein. University of Chicago Press, Chicago, 1955, pp. 424–440.

ZBOROWSKI, MARK, "The Children of the Covenant," *Social Forces,* vol. 29, 1951, pp. 351–364.

"Cultural Components in Responses to Pain," *Journal of Social Issues,* vol. 8, 1952, pp. 16–30.

"The Place of Book-Learning in Traditional Jewish Culture" in *Childhood in Contemporary Cultures,* edited by Margaret Mead and Martha Wolfenstein. University of Chicago Press, Chicago, 1955, pp. 118–141.

ZBOROWSKI, MARK, AND ELIZABETH HERZOG, *Life is With People: The Jewish Littletown of Eastern Europe.* International Universities Press, New York, 1952.

C. KINSHIP AND URBAN INDUSTRIAL SOCIETIES

AXELROD, MORRIS, "Urban Structure and Social Participation," *American Sociological Review,* vol. 21, 1956, pp. 13–19.

BARBER, BERNARD, "Family Status, Local Community Status, and Social Stratification: Three Types of Social Ranking," *Pacific Sociological Review,* vol. 4, 1961, pp. 3–10.

BARNETT, MILTON L., "Kinship as a Factor Affecting Cantonese Economic Adaptation in the United States," *Human Organization*, vol. 19, 1960, pp. 40–46.

BELL, NORMAN, "Extended Family Relations of Disturbed and Well Families," *Family Process*, vol. 1, 1962, pp. 175–193.

BELL, WENDELL, AND M. D. BOAT, "Urban Neighborhoods and Informal Social Relations," *American Journal of Sociology*, vol. 62, 1957, pp. 391–398.

BELLIN, SEYMOUR S., *Family and Kinship in Later Years*. Mental Health Research Unit Publication, New York State Department of Mental Hygiene, New York, 1960.

BENNETT, JOHN W., AND LEO A. DESPRES, "Kinship and Instrumental Activities: A Theoretical Inquiry," *American Anthropologist*, vol. 62, 1960, pp. 254–267.

BLOOD, ROBERT O., JR., "The Extended Family Network" in *Marriage*. The Free Press of Glencoe, New York, 1962.

BOTT, ELIZABETH, *Family and Social Network*. Tavistock Publications, Ltd., London, England, 1957.

CODERE, HELEN, "A Genealogical Study of Kinship in the United States," *Psychiatry*, vol. 18, 1955, pp. 65–79.

CUMMING, ELAINE, AND DAVID M. SCHNEIDER, "Sibling Solidarity: A Property of American Kinship," *American Anthropologist*, vol. 63, 1961, pp. 498–507.

DESPRES, LEO A., "A Function of Bilateral Kinship Patterns in a New England Industry," *Human Organization*, vol. 17, 1958, pp. 15–22.

DORE, R. P., *City Life in Japan: A Study of a Tokyo Ward*. University of California Press, Berkeley and Los Angeles, 1958.

FARIS, R. E. L., "Interactions of Generations and Family Stability," *American Sociological Review*, vol. 12, 1947, pp. 159–164.

FIRTH, RAYMOND, *Family and Kinship in Industrial Society*. Reprinted from *The Sociological Review*, Monograph No. 8, *The Development of Industrial Societies*, edited by Paul Halmos. University of Keele, Keele, England, October, 1964, pp. 65–87.

FIRTH, RAYMOND, editor, *Two Studies of Kinship in London*. London School of Economics, Monographs on Social Anthropology 15. The Athlone Press, London, England, 1956.

FRAZIER, FRANKLIN E., "The Impact of Urban Civilization upon Negro Family Life" in *Cities and Society: The Revised Reader in Urban Sociology*, edited by Paul K. Hatt and Albert J. Reiss, Jr. The Free Press, Glencoe, Ill., 1957, pp. 490–499.

GANS, HERBERT J., *The Urban Villagers: Group and Class Life of Italian-Americans.* The Free Press of Glencoe, New York, 1962.

GOODE, WILLIAM J., *World Revolution and Family Patterns.* The Free Press of Glencoe, New York, 1963.

GREER, SCOTT, "Urbanism Reconsidered: A Comparative Study of Local Areas in a Metropolis," *American Sociological Review,* vol. 21, 1956, pp. 19–25.

ISHWARAN, K., *Family Life in the Netherlands.* Uitgeverij van Keulen, N.V., The Hague, 1959.

KOMAROVSKY, MIRRA, "The Voluntary Associations of Urban Dwellers," *American Sociological Review,* vol. 11, 1946, pp. 686–698.

KOSA, JOHN, LEO D. RACHIELE, AND CYRIL O. SCHOMMER, S.J., "Sharing the Home with Relatives," *Marriage and Family Living,* vol. 22, 1960, pp. 129–131.

KUPER, HILDA, *Indian People in Natal.* University of Natal Press, Pietermaritzburg, South Africa, 1960.

LANCASTER, LORRAINE, "Some Conceptual Problems in the Study of Family and Kin Ties in the British Isles," *The British Journal of Sociology,* vol. 12, 1961, pp. 317–333.

LEVY, MARION J., JR., *The Family Revolution in Modern China.* Harvard University Press, Cambridge, Mass, 1949.

LEWIS, OSCAR, *Five Families.* Basic Books, New York, 1959.

LITTLE, KENNETH L., *West African Urbanization.* Cambridge University Press, London, 1965.

LITWAK, EUGENE, "The Use of Extended Family Groups in the Achievement of Social Goals: Some Policy Implications," *Social Problems,* vol. 7, 1959–1960, pp. 177–187.

"Geographic Mobility and Extended Family Cohesion," *American Sociological Review,* vol. 25, 1960, pp. 385–394.

"Occupational Mobility and Extended Family Cohesion," *American Sociological Review,* vol. 25, 1960, pp. 9–21.

Extended Kin Relations in an Industrial Democratic Society. Reprinted from *Social Structure and the Family: Generational Relations,* edited by Ethel Shanas and G. F. Streib. Prentice-Hall, Inc., Englewood Cliffs, N.J., 1965.

LOUDON, J. B., "Kinship and Crisis in South Wales," *The British Journal of Sociology,* vol. 12, 1961, pp. 333–350.

MARRIS, PETER, *Family and Social Change in an African City: A Study of Rehousing in Lagos.* Routledge and Kegan Paul, London, England, 1961.

MILLS, C. WRIGHT, CLARENCE SENIOR, AND ROSE K. GOLDSEN, *The Puerto Rican Journey.* Harper and Bros., New York, 1950.

MINER, HORACE M., *St. Denis: A French-Canadian Parish.* University of Chicago Press, Chicago, 1939.

MOGEY, JOHN M., *Family and Neighborhood: Two Studies in Oxford.* Oxford University Press, London, England, 1956.

ORENSTEIN, HENRY, "The Recent History of the Extended Family in India," *Social Problems,* vol. 8, 1961, pp. 341–350.

PADILLA, ELENA, *Up From Puerto Rico.* Columbia University Press, New York, 1958.

PARSONS, TALCOTT, "The Kinship System of the Contemporary United States," *American Anthropologist,* vol. 45, 1943, pp. 22–38.

"The Social Structure of the Family" in *The Family: Its Function and Destiny,* edited by Ruth N. Anshen. Harper and Bros., New York, 1949, pp. 173–201.

"A Revised Analytical Approach to the Theory of Social Stratification" in *Class, Status and Power: A Reader in Social Stratification,* edited by Reinhard Bendix and Seymour M. Lipset. The Free Press, Glencoe, Ill., 1953, pp. 92–128.

"The American Family: Its Relations to Personality and to the Social Structure" in *Family, Socialization and Interaction Process,* edited by Talcott Parsons and Robert F. Bales. The Free Press, Glencoe, Ill., 1955, pp. 3–33.

SCHNEIDER, DAVID M., AND KATHLEEN GOUGH, editors, *Matrilineal Kinship.* University of California Press, Berkeley and Los Angeles, 1961.

SCHORR, ALVIN L., *Filial Responsibility in a Modern American Family.* U.S. Social Security Administration, Division of Program Research, Government Printing Office, Washington, 1960.

SHANAS, ETHEL, AND G. F. STREIB, editors, *Social Structure and the Family: Generational Relations.* Prentice-Hall, Inc., Englewood Cliffs, N.J., 1965.

SHARP, HARRY, AND MORRIS AXELROD, "Mutual Aid Among Relatives in an Urban Population" in *Principles of Sociology,* edited by Ronald Freedman and associates. Rev. ed. Holt, Rinehart and Winston, New York, 1956, pp. 433–439.

SJOBERG, GIDEON, "Familial Organization in the Preindustrial City," *Marriage and Family Living,* vol. 18, 1956, pp. 30–36.

SUSSMAN, MARVIN B., "The Help Pattern in the Middle Class Family," *American Sociological Review,* vol. 18, 1953, pp. 22–28.

"Parental Participation in Mate Selection and Its Effect upon Family

Continuity," *Social Forces,* vol. 32, 1953, pp. 76–81.

"Family Continuity: Selective Factors Which Affect Relationships Between Families at Generational Levels," *Marriage and Family Living,* vol. 16, 1954, pp. 112–120.

"The Isolated Nuclear Family: Fact or Fiction," *Social Problems,* vol. 6, 1959, pp. 333–340.

"Intergenerational Family Relationships and Social Role Changes in Middle Age," *Journal of Gerontology,* vol. 15, 1960, pp. 71–75.

SUSSMAN, MARVIN B., AND LEE BURCHINAL, "Kin Family Network: Unheralded Structure in Current Conceptualizations of Family Functioning," *Marriage and Family Living,* vol. 24, 1962, pp. 231–240.

"Parental Aid to Married Children: Implications for Family Functioning," *Marriage and Family Living,* vol. 24, 1962, pp. 320–332.

SUSSMAN, MARVIN B., AND R. CLYDE WHITE, *Hough: A Study of Social Life and Change.* Western Reserve University Press, Cleveland, Ohio, 1959.

TOWNSEND, PETER, *The Family Life of Old People: An Inquiry in East London.* The Free Press, Glencoe, Ill., 1957.

WILENSKY, HAROLD, AND HAROLD L. LEBEAUX, *Industrial Society and Social Welfare.* Russell Sage Foundation, New York, 1958.

WILKINSON, THOMAS O., "Family Structure and Industrialization in Japan," *American Sociological Review,* vol. 27, 1962, pp. 678–682.

WILLIAMS, ROBIN M., JR., "Kinship and the Family in the United States" in *American Society: A Sociological Interpretation.* Alfred A. Knopf, Inc., New York, 1951, pp. 36–77.

WINCH, ROBERT F., *The Modern Family.* Henry Holt and Co., New York, 1952.

WIRTH, LOUIS, "Urbanism as a Way of Life," *American Journal of Sociology,* vol. 44, 1938, pp. 1–24.

WUARANTELLI, ENRICO L., "A Note on the Protective Function of the Family in Disasters," *Marriage and Family Living,* vol. 22, 1960, pp. 263–264.

YANG, C. K., *The Chinese Family in the Communist Revolution.* Massachusetts Institute of Technology Publication, Harvard University Press, Cambridge, Mass., 1959.

YOUNG, MICHAEL, "The Role of the Extended Family in a Disaster," *Human Relations,* vol. 7, 1954, pp. 383–391.

YOUNG, MICHAEL, AND HILDRED GEERTZ, "Old Age in London and San Francisco: Some Families Compared," *The British Journal of Sociology,* vol. 12, 1961, pp. 124–141.

YOUNG, MICHAEL, AND PETER WILMOTT, *Family and Kinship in East*

London. The Free Press, Glencoe, Ill., 1957.

ZELDITCH, MORRIS, JR., "Family, Kinship and Marriage" in *Handbook of Modern Sociology*, edited by Robert E. L. Farris. Rand McNally and Co., Chicago, 1964, pp. 680–733.

D. THE AGENCY'S WORK ON FAMILY DIAGNOSIS AND TREATMENT

ACKERMAN, NATHAN W., *The Psychodynamics of Family Life*. Basic Books, New York, 1958.

ACKERMAN, NATHAN W., FRANCES L. BEATMAN, AND SANFORD N. SHERMAN, editors, *Exploring the Base for Family Therapy*. Family Service Association of America, New York, 1961.

BEATMAN, FRANCES L., "Family Interaction: Its Significance for Diagnosis and Treatment," *Social Casework*, vol. 38, 1957, pp. 111–118.

GOMBERG, M. ROBERT, "The Specific Nature of Family Case Work" in *A Functional Approach to Family Case Work*, edited by Jessie Taft. University of Pennsylvania Press, Philadelphia, 1944, pp. 111–147.

"Family Diagnosis: Trends in Theory and Practice," *Social Casework*, vol. 39, 1958, pp. 73–83.

LEADER, ARTHUR L., "The Role of Intervention in Family-Group Treatment," *Social Casework*, vol. 45, 1964, pp. 327–332.

LEICHTER, ELSA, AND GERDA L. SCHULMAN, "The Family Interview as an Integrative Device in Group Therapy with Families," *The International Journal of Group Psychotherapy*, vol. 13, 1963, pp. 335–345.

MARCUS, ESTHER S., AND GILCHRIST, MARILYN M., "A Pilot Study in the Selection of Psychiatric-Hospital Patients for Treatment in a Family Agency," *Social Casework*, vol. 40, 1959, pp. 551–558.

MITCHELL, CELIA BRODY, "Family Interviewing in Family Diagnosis," *Social Casework*, vol. 40, 1959, pp. 381–384.

"Integrative Therapy of the Family Unit," *Social Casework*, vol. 46, 1965, pp. 63–69.

SHERMAN, SANFORD N., "Joint Interviews in Casework Practice," *Social Work*, vol. 4, 1959, pp. 20–28.

"The Sociopsychological Character of Family-Group Treatment," *Social Casework*, vol. 45, 1964, pp. 195–201.

SHERMAN, SANFORD N., FRANCES L. BEATMAN, AND NATHAN W. ACKERMAN, "Concepts of Family Striving and Family Distress: The Contribution of M. Robert Gomberg," *Social Casework*, vol. 39, 1958, pp. 383–391.

E. PAPERS RESULTING
FROM WORK ON THE PROJECT

LEICHTER, HOPE J., "Life Cycle Changes and Temporal Sequence in a Bilateral Kinship System." Paper read at the Annual Meeting of the American Anthropological Association, Washington, November, 1958.

"Kinship and Casework." Paper read at the Groves Conference, Chapel Hill, N.C., April, 1959.

"Normative Intervention in an Urban Bilateral Kinship System." Paper read at the Annual Meeting of the American Anthropological Association, Mexico City, December, 1959.

"Boundaries of the Family as an Empirical and Theoretical Unit" in *Exploring the Base for Family Therapy*, edited by Nathan W. Ackerman, Frances L. Beatman, and Sanford N. Sherman. Family Service Association of America, New York, 1961, pp. 140–145.

"Kinship Values and Casework Intervention" in *Casework Papers— 1961*. Family Service Association of America, New York, 1961, pp. 58–78.

"The Role of the Sociologist: The Sociologist as Staff Member in Welfare and Community Service." Paper read at the Annual Meeting of the American Sociological Association, Washington, 1962.

"The Relationship of Organization and Structure to the Development of Research in Private Welfare Agencies." Paper read at the National Conference on Social Welfare, Minneapolis, 1963.

"Technological Implementation of Kinship Ties." Paper read at joint session of the Society for the Study of Social Problems and the American Sociological Association, Los Angeles, August, 1963.

"Nature and Varieties of Family Changes in Response to Social Changes." Paper read at the Annual Meeting of the American Orthopsychiatric Association, San Francisco, April 13–16, 1966.

LEICHTER, HOPE J., AND JUDITH LIEB, "Implications of a Research Experience with Caseworkers and Clients," *Journal of Jewish Communal Service*, vol. 36, 1960, pp. 313–321.

LEICHTER, HOPE J., AND WILLIAM E. MITCHELL, "Feuds and Fissions Within the Conjugal Kindred." Paper read at the Annual Meeting of the American Anthropological Association, Minneapolis, November, 1960.

MITCHELL, WILLIAM E., "Descent Groups Among New York City Jews," *Jewish Journal of Sociology*, vol. 3, 1961, pp. 121–128.

"Lineality and Laterality in Urban Jewish Ambilineages." Paper read at the Annual Meeting of the American Anthropological Association, Philadelphia, November, 1961.

"The American-Jewish Thanksgiving Day Dinner: A Structural Study of Kin Assemblages." Paper read at the Annual Meeting of the American Anthropological Association, Chicago, November, 1962.

"Theoretical Problems in the Concept of Kindred," *American Anthropologist,* vol. 65, 1963, pp. 343–354.

"The Kindred and Baby Bathing in Academe," *American Anthropologist,* vol. 67, 1965, pp. 977–985.

"Proximity Patterns of the Urban Jewish Kindred," *Man,* vol. 65, 1965, pp. 137–140.

MITCHELL, WILLIAM E., AND HOPE J. LEICHTER, "Urban Ambilineages and Social Mobility." Paper read at the Annual Meeting of the Eastern Sociological Society, New York, April, 1961.

"Technology and Kinship: The Telephone." Paper read at the Annual Meeting of the American Anthropological Association, Denver, November, 1965.

ROGERS, CANDACE, AND HOPE J. LEICHTER, "In-laws and Marital Conflict Among Jewish Families" in *Readings on the Family and Society,* edited by William J. Goode. Prentice-Hall, Inc., Englewood Cliffs, N.J., 1964, pp. 213–218.

Index

Index

tionships, 34; linking, 151; omni-
presence of, 96–114; positive impact
of, 160–162; reciprocity and
assistance among, 114–125. *See also*
Casework intervention; Kinship
Kin assemblages: caseworkers and
clients compared, 242–245; defined,
128; functions of, 128, 133–134; and
genealogical data, 132; large, 132–
134; and psychological support, 134;
research methods, 315–316;
Thanksgiving gatherings, 129–132,
244–245; types of, 128. *See also*
Family circles; Kinship
Kin assistance and reciprocity, 114–125;
ceremonial gift giving, 123; and
emotional dependency, 124–125;
financial, 119–120; illness, 117–118;
reciprocity, 120–125; research
methods, 314; sources of assistance,
114–120. *See also* Kinship
Kin conflicts: caseworkers and clients
compared, 245–254; casework
intervention, 185–208 *passim*, 264–
267; compared with English, 176;
content of, 177–180; distinctions
among, 174; distribution of, 174;
effect on marital relationship, 173,
175, 249–250; language of conflict,
245–249; levels of, 162–166, 172–
173; perspectives on, 165–166; regularities in, 172–181; and regularities
in kin relations, 166–172; research
methods, 316; and role strain, 163–
164; the structuring of, 249–254.
See also Family-kin businesses;
Kinship
Kin contact logs, 104–107
Kin groups. *See* Descent groups; Family
circles; Family-kin businesses; Kin
assemblages
Kin networks, 89–126, 242; assistance
and reciprocity, 114–125, 238–242;
boundaries, 18; communication with
kin, 103–114; conflicts in, 172–181;
defined, 18; defining boundaries of,
94–96; extensiveness, 89–96; face-to-
face visits, 110–111; features of, 18;
interaction boundaries of, 92–93;
knowledge boundaries of, 90–92;
proximity of kin, 96–103, 234–236;
regularities in, 166–172; use of telephone, 103–110, 236–237. *See also*
Kinship
Kin relationships. *See* Kin networks
Kindred. *See* Kin networks
Kinship: and assistance, 23, 76–77;
authority and control, 29–30; casework intervention and, 162, 194–208,

275–290; categories of, 166–172; and
economic relations, 30, 76–78; and
economic systems, 22–23; and emotions, 33–35; and functions for social
organization, 22–24; and generation,
171–172; implications of therapeutic
change for, 264–292; as an involuntary relationship, 13; and laterality,
168; life-cycle changes in, 280–282;
and Oedipus complex, 31; and
personality, 28–35; and religious
activity, 24; research focus on, 6–7;
and sex, 170–171; and sleeping
arrangements, 31–32; and social
control, 23; and social mobility, 24,
73–76; and social status, 23; and
socialization, 30–33; and society,
22–28, 279–282; in urban industrial
society, 25–28, 275–279. *See also*
Client families; Family; Family
circles; Family-kin businesses; Kin;
Kin assemblages; Kin assistance and
reciprocity; Kin conflicts; Kin networks; Kinship bonds; Kinship
systems; Kinship values
Kinship bonds, 19–20, 34–35, 67, 173,
222; and concept of role, 19; and
cross-sibling relationships, 47; defined, 19; and gift giving, 124;
husband-wife versus parent-child,
34, 35, 79–80, 66, 69, 187, 222–224;
and kinship statuses, 20. *See also*
Kinship; Kinship values
Kinship roles. *See* Kinship; Kinship
bonds; Roles
Kinship systems, 66; concepts, 13–35;
conflict and strain in, 21, 27, 193;
and primary bonds, 173, 222; questions about, 35; relationships among
features of, 20–22, 66–67; and
societal conditions, 24–28; some
features of, 14–20. *See also* Kinship
Kinship terminology, 20
Kinship values: business relations with
kin, 76–78; caseworkers and clients,
209–233; changes in, 87–88; clients
and the aged, 85–88; content of,
68–85; differentiation of nuclear
family from kin, 80–83, 224–228;
husband-wife versus parent-child
bonds, 79–80, 222–225; husbands
and wives, 85; kin and nonkin institutions, 76–79, 220–222; kin interaction, 72–73, 216; kin versus
friends, 78–79; and kinship position,
85–88; marriage, 69–70, 212–214;
obligations to parents, 83–85, 228–
230; parental sacrifices for children,
84–85; research methods, 312; resi-